Acclaim for Gerald J. Prokopowicz's

Did Lincoln Own Slaves?

"Full of surprises, and splendidly imaginative in concept and format, Gerald Prokopowicz's *Did Lincoln Own Slaves?* is also learned, entertaining, fair-minded, witty, up-to-date, readable, and truly informative. A bargain of a book, it must surely capture the wide audience it deserves." —Richard Carwardine, author of *Lincoln: A Life of Purpose and Power*

"While Gerald Prokopowicz's book may be another in the long line of Lincoln tomes, it is not just another. Far from it. In the expanding universe of Lincoln literature . . . this volume of questions and answers deserves placement well up the list, for initiate and faux expert alike. . . . This is history for regular folks, not just historians, but it doesn't talk down, condescend or offer up easy shortcuts or over-simplifications. . . . This book proceeds both thematically and chronologically, giving it, if not quite the immediacy and connection of biography, then beyond that a rich and entertaining multiplicity of perspectives between Lincoln and the dialectic of the public and the historian. . . . [T]hink of these question-and-answer series almost as Socratic dialogues."

—*The Herald-Sun* (Durham, NC)

"*Did Lincoln Own Slaves?* is a wonderful book, as witty as it is wise. Addressing every question that conceivably can be raised about Abraham Lincoln, Gerald Prokopowicz provides answers that are short, accurate, and in many instances highly amusing. Every Lincoln student must own this book." —David Herbert Donald, author of *Lincoln*

"Although this won't be the last book written on Lincoln, it'll certainly be one of the most entertaining for readers. The surprises found on almost every page should delight anyone even remotely interested in our national history." —Larry Cox, *King Features*

"From his birth to his death (not to mention the century and a half since), here is everything one ever wanted to know about Abraham Lincoln—told authoritatively and entertainingly by a fine scholar and gifted writer. Facts are reported, myths punctured, and controversies analyzed in a text that proves both an essential reference and a page-turning good read." —Harold Holzer, cochairman, U.S. Abraham Lincoln Bicentennial Commission

"Gerald Prokopowicz's fresh and informative guidebook to navigate the land of Lincolnistas makes this a wonderful addition to any American history lover's library. *Did Lincoln Own Slaves?* answers the perennial question, 'Is there anything new to say about Lincoln,' by convincing us 'Yes'—and that we really do need this compact, yet compelling, appraisal." —Catherine Clinton, Queen's University-Belfast, author of *The Plantation Mistress*

"Of the thousands of books about Lincoln (you can get the exact number, and many other facts from this book) very few bring to the reader as much of the information the reader really wants about the sixteenth president, and none is more pleasantly amusing. The device of answering the questions the public keeps asking really works. If you have any interest in Lincoln, and start reading this book, you will have a hard time stopping." —William Lee Miller, author of *Lincoln's Virtues: An Ethical Biography* and *President Lincoln: The Duty of a Statesman*

"Witty, intelligent and informative, *Did Lincoln Own Slaves?* is just what the world needs as we begin our celebration of the bicentennial of Lincoln's birth. This is a book that every level of Lincoln student—from grade school to scholar—will find useful. Prokopowicz has provided accurate answers to the essential questions about our sixteenth president; no more digging around in the Lincoln library is required."

—Jean H. Baker, author of *Mary Todd Lincoln*

"From first to last, the author is not a sage-on-a-stage but a guide-by-the-side. A clear writing style and a concise delivery of the facts presents the reader with an enjoyable experience. A foundation of facts with citations offers the reader a thoughtful and scholarly return on the time invested." —Rea Andrew Webb, *Civil War Librarian*

GERALD J. PROKOPOWICZ

Did Lincoln Own Slaves?

Gerald J. Prokopowicz served for nine years as the Lincoln Scholar at the Lincoln Museum in Fort Wayne, Indiana. He is the author of the critically acclaimed *All for the Regiment: The Army of the Ohio, 1861–1862* and was the editor of *Lincoln Lore*, the quarterly journal of the Lincoln Museum. He is a frequent public speaker on Lincoln-related topics and a member of the Abraham Lincoln Bicentennial Commission Board of Advisors. He is currently chair of the history department at East Carolina University in Greenville, North Carolina.

Did Lincoln Own Slaves?

Did Lincoln Own Slaves?

AND OTHER FREQUENTLY ASKED QUESTIONS ABOUT ABRAHAM LINCOLN

GERALD J. PROKOPOWICZ

VINTAGE CIVIL WAR LIBRARY
Vintage Books
A Division of Random House, Inc.
New York

FIRST VINTAGE CIVIL WAR LIBRARY EDITION, JANUARY 2009

The Library of Congress has cataloged the Pantheon edition as follows:
Prokopowicz, Gerald J.
Did Lincoln own slaves? : and other frequently asked questions about Abraham Lincoln /
Gerald J. Prokopowicz.
p. cm.
Includes bibliographical references and index.
1. Lincoln, Abraham, 1809–1865—Miscellanea. 2. Presidents—United States—
Biography—Miscellanea. I. Title.
E457.909.P76 2008
973.7092—dc22
[B] 2007020889

Vintage ISBN: 978-0-307-27929-3

Author photograph © Emily Prokopowicz
Book design by Robert C. Olsson

www.vintagebooks.com

Printed in the United States of America

To my mother and father

CONTENTS

CHAPTER FIVE: **SPEAKER**

CHAPTER SIX: **PRESIDENT**

CHAPTER EIGHT: GETTYSBURG

CHAPTER TEN: LINCOLN THE MAN

CHAPTER ELEVEN: MARTYR

ILLUSTRATIONS

ACKNOWLEDGMENTS

For the questions in this book, I am indebted to the many people who asked them: to visitors at the Lincoln Museum in Fort Wayne, Indiana; to students at IPFW in Fort Wayne and East Carolina University in Greenville, North Carolina; to members of various Civil War Round Tables throughout the Midwest and Upper South, the Harvard Alumni Association, the Rotarians, the Optimists, and other audiences I have had the pleasure of addressing; and to friends, relatives, and casual acquaintances at parties who wanted to know if it was really true that Lincoln once said this or did that. Specific thanks for some of the more thought-provoking questions are due to the listeners of Civil War Talk Radio (especially John Matthew IV) and the online contributors to Consimworld (especially Brian Stouder).

For answering my question, "What are people asking you about Lincoln these days?" and for sharing with me their years of research and writing that have answered so many Lincoln questions, I am happy to express my thanks to Jean Baker, Kim Bauer, Lerone Bennett, Gabor Boritt, Michael Burlingame, Catherine Clinton, Hank Cox, Cullom Davis, Jack Davis, Rodney Davis, David Herbert Donald, Daniel Mark Epstein, Jennifer Fleischner, Doris Kearns Goodwin, Allen Guelzo, Harold Holzer, Charles Hubbard, Michael Kauffman, Elizabeth Leonard, David Long, John Marszalek, James McPherson, Edna Greene Medford, William Lee Miller, Lucas Morel, Mark E. Neely, Jr., Phillip Paludan, James Percoco, Steven Rogstad, Thomas Schwartz, John Sellers, Joshua Shenk, John Y. Simon, Daniel Stowell, Craig Symonds, Tim Townsend, Paul Verduin, Michael Vorenberg, Daniel Weinberg, Frank Williams, and Douglas Wilson.

I have received help in the form of useful bits of Lincoln information, invitations to talk about Lincoln, ideas for interesting sites to visit, and places to stay when visiting those sites, all from more people than I can remember, and in thanking these few I mean to thank you all: Christopher Beck, Steve Carson, Brooks Davis, Kim and Bill Fenoglio, Angela Gilmer, Judy and Bruce Jones, Brian Melton, the late Mrs. R. Gerald McMurtry, Lucien and Peggy Nedzi, Dr. Gregory Prokopowicz, Pete and Bonnie Prokopowicz, Jonathan Reid, Brian Riley, Art Ross, Chad Ross, Jack Smith, Teej Smith, Don Tracy, Annette Westerby, and Eric and Johanna Zorn.

For illustrations, I am exceptionally grateful to Cindy VanHorn of the Lincoln Museum for going beyond the call of duty. Thanks also to others for permission to use their images, specifically to Peter Norvig for his Gettysburg Powerpoint slide; to the Library of Congress; to Jaak Jarve for the *Classics Illustrated* cover; and to *MAD* magazine both for wasting many hours of my youth and for the Nixon illustration, which requires this notice on this page: "From MAD 161 © 1973 E.C. Publications, Inc. All Rights Reserved. Used With Permission."

From 1993 to 1995, the staff of the Lincoln Museum collaborated with Formations, Inc. of Portland, Oregon, on a major Lincoln exhibit. Hoping it is not too late, I would like to thank Alice Parman and Craig Kerger of Formations for my first and still most memorable lesson in bringing history to the public. Among my former colleagues at the Lincoln Museum, I owe thanks to Jan Shupert-Arick and Carolyn Texley for teaching me about their respective fields; my experience there also taught me a lot about the importance of competent leadership. To my present colleagues at East Carolina University, thank you for a supportive and stimulating environment, and particular thanks to Michael Palmer for giving me the time and encouragement needed to finish this book.

Several people generously spent their time to read and offer detailed critiques of the manuscript. The most indefatigable Lincoln researcher of our generation, Michael Burlingame, and the most prolific Lincoln writer, Harold Holzer, each offered many valuable corrections. Scott Bushnell, a gifted communicator (who brought me to the Lincoln Museum in 1993), did the same. Emily Prokopowicz found mistakes that everyone else missed. The text was greatly improved by all of their efforts, and while I would like to say that the errors and omissions that remain are also their fault, of course they are entirely mine.

Acknowledgments

The manuscript would never have become a book without the efforts of a few talented people whom I am honored to thank: Charles Calhoun, for the example of his scholarship and for inspiring me to approach Alfred A. Knopf; my editor, Keith Goldsmith, for his patient support of this project; Walter Havighurst, for his thoughtful copyediting; and Victoria Pearson, for her production editorial work.

From my mother, Aulga Prokopowicz, I received not only the unconditional love and support that has been indispensable to anything I have ever accomplished but also a careful reading and correction of the manuscript such as can be done only by a retired high school teacher with an affinity for crossword puzzles.

As always, my greatest debt is to my wife, Emily, and our daughters, Caroline and Maria.

INTRODUCTION

Historians are like deaf people who go on answering questions no one has asked them.

—attributed to Leo Tolstoy

When I was in graduate school, I had the Tolstoy quote above posted on the bulletin board of the office I shared with my classmate Thomas Sugrue. One day Tom (who went on to become a prize-winning historian) said to me that Tolstoy might be correct, but only because people weren't asking the right questions. His comment stuck with me, because it seemed at once to embody the best and worst of the historical profession. Yes, those of us who have received professional training in the practice of history do have a duty to ask bold, innovative questions that others have not yet asked about the past. But who are we to say that whatever questions the public may already be asking about history are not the "right" ones?*

The purpose of this book is to answer questions about Abraham Lincoln asked by the public, not the professors. I worked as a historian at the Lincoln Museum in Fort Wayne, Indiana, for nine years, and had the opportunity to talk to thousands of people about Abraham Lincoln. They asked lots of questions. Some were stimulating, provocative, or

*In the 1970s, questions weren't professionally "right" unless they were based on an economic (preferably Marxian) interpretation of the past. By the 1990s, questions of race, class, or gender had become "privileged," to use the jargon of the era, with bonus points if two of the three categories could be woven into the same topic. In the postmillennial decade, the prefix "post-" has been the secret handshake of the profession: postmodern, poststructural, postcolonial, etc. It is surprising how many historians behave as if they are unaware of the historical dimension of their own craft, treating each historiographical trend when it comes along as though it were timeless wisdom instead of a reflection of the moment, due to be replaced in its turn by the next generation's view.

perceptive. Some were funny or weird. Some were based on legends, myths, or half-remembered history lessons. Many were asked out of a desire to learn, while others revealed the speaker's prejudice or ignorance. Some were closely related to the topics that professional scholars were addressing in books and journal articles; others were not professionally "right," but no less important to the questioner for that.

This book will tell you something about the life and times of Abraham Lincoln, but it's not meant to substitute for a full-length scholarly biography. If you've already read one, perhaps that of David Donald or Stephen Oates, you already know the better part of what is in this book. If you are a professional historian, or a history buff who has read half a dozen books on Lincoln, the odds are pretty slim that you will find anything new to you here. And if you are one of my friends and colleagues who makes a living studying Abraham Lincoln, then you certainly know far more about the subject than is contained in this volume, which I urge you to drop at once (after checking the index to be sure that your name is spelled correctly), so that you can return to the archives and continue making the important documentary discoveries that make books like this one possible.

What this book is meant to do is to help reconnect the public and professional approaches to the study of Abraham Lincoln. This is not so great a problem with Lincoln as it is in other areas of history, where professionals employ impenetrable jargon while writing on obscure topics while the public tunes in to the History Channel, but even with Lincoln there has been to some degree what Mark E. Neely, Jr., called an "abdication of scholarship [that] led to the triumph of irresponsibly cynical and iconoclastic popular theories."[1] This book alone can't turn back the march of cynical and iconoclastic popular theories, but it can try to provide a synthesis of the best of academic Lincoln scholarship, supported by references, presented in an accessible fashion, so that you can confidently deal with those theories yourself the next time someone starts to tell you what they think they know about Abraham Lincoln. If it answers your questions or, better still, prompts you to read another book for a fuller answer, it will have done its job.

A note on reference notes. Authors use them for various purposes. In a dissertation, notes are the culmination of a seven-year hazing ritual, intended primarily to impress readers (and secure a job for the author) by demonstrating a deep knowledge of the sources and a willingness to perform tedious archival research. In books by (and for) professional historians, notes document the research behind the text, so that interested readers can verify the author's conclusions and future scholars can build on the work that has already been done. In books for everyone else, notes are a convenient place to mention interesting tidbits that don't quite fit into the main text.

In this book, the notes do a little of each. Their volume and breadth have been carefully calculated to impress the casual reader. If you actually read the notes, they should give you some confidence that my answers are based on the words of Lincoln or his contemporaries, and are not just my personal take on the many legends and myths surrounding Abraham Lincoln. Some notes identify additional material that might be of interest, but is too specialized to warrant inclusion in the "For Further Reading" sections, while others are digressions from the text. In all cases, I have deviated from traditional citation style by giving only the information necessary in the Internet era to find the books cited (author, title, year), omitting the publisher and city.

Did Lincoln Own Slaves?

{ CHAPTER ONE }

The Boy Lincoln

It is a great piece of folly to attempt to make anything out of my early life.

—Lincoln's reply to journalist John L. Scripps, 1860, when asked to provide information for a campaign biography

When and where was Lincoln born?

February 12, 1809, in a log cabin on the south fork of Nolin Creek, near Hodgenville, Kentucky.

Is the cabin still there?

Sort of.

The site is marked today by a curious memorial on the grounds of the original Lincoln farmstead. There, at the top of a wooded hill, stands what appears to be an old-fashioned bank building incongruously looming over an otherwise bucolic setting. A grand flight of fifty-six stone steps, one for each year of Lincoln's life, leads the visitor to a pair of imposing bronze doors, hidden behind six massive Doric columns. Within this Greek temple on a Kentucky hillside, resting on the granite floor in the center of the room, is the cabin where Abe Lincoln was born.

Unfortunately, it's not really Lincoln's cabin. The National Park Service, which maintains the memorial, describes the crude wooden structure as the "traditional" Lincoln birthplace cabin, inventively using the word "traditional" in place of a more accurate adjective, such as "fake."*

*Perhaps this definition will one day enter common usage, as in "The wily coach called for a traditional field goal," or "Dear, for our anniversary I've bought you this traditional

The real cabin almost certainly fell down at some point in the decades after the Lincoln family moved away, there being no reason at the time to preserve it. A speculator named A. W. Dennett purchased the farm in 1894, hoping it would become a tourist attraction. He found a two-story cabin nearby that might have been standing when Lincoln was a boy, took it apart, transported it to the birthplace farm, and reassembled it into a smaller one-story cabin. When he found few customers willing to make the pilgrimage to his remote corner of central Kentucky, Dennett took the building apart again with the idea of moving it to places more frequented by potential viewers. For good measure, he bought and disassembled another cabin that supposedly was the birthplace of Jefferson Davis. The two cabins appeared side by side at fairs in Nashville, Buffalo, and other cities.

Eventually Dennett went bankrupt, and both cabins were taken apart (again) and put in storage. In 1906, the Lincoln Farm Association, a group formed to build a Lincoln birthplace memorial, found the pieces in a basement in New York. By that time the logs that formed the two already dubious cabins were hopelessly intermingled. The association sorted out the components and used some of them to make a one-story structure that resembled descriptions of the original Lincoln cabin. The LFA also constructed the present memorial building to house their prize, but when it was completed in 1911, it turned out that the reassembled cabin was too large to fit inside easily. To make room for visitors to walk around it, they sawed off about a quarter of its length, creating the "traditional" birthplace cabin that you can see today. It's possible (if unlikely) that some tiny fraction of the wood really did once form part of a building that was associated with Lincoln; but it's also possible that the exhibit now on display has as much to do with Jefferson Davis as it does with Lincoln.[2]

Haven't I seen the cabin somewhere else?

You probably have.

There are several versions around the country, most of them replicas of the Park Service "birthplace cabin." One is in Milton, Massachusetts,

---

diamond." For the Park Service use of the term "traditional birthplace cabin" see, e.g., Robert W. Blythe, Maureen Carroll, and Steven Moffson, *Abraham Lincoln Birthplace Historic Resource Study,* revised by Brian F. Coffey (2001), ch. 3, fig. 51 caption.

commissioned in 1923 by Mary Bowditch Forbes.* There's another in Fort Wayne, Indiana, built by the Lincoln National Life Insurance Company in 1916, that at one time was carefully furnished with antiques to give a sense of what Lincoln's childhood home might have looked like. Now, however, it sits neglected in a wooded corner of a public park, used by the maintenance staff as a storage shed for snowblowers.

Replica of a replica of Lincoln's birthplace in Ft. Wayne, Indiana.
(Courtesy of The Lincoln Museum, Fort Wayne, IN, TLM 625)

About the original birthplace cabin—is it true that Lincoln helped his father build it with his own hands?

Next question, please.

Who were Lincoln's parents?

Thomas Lincoln (1778?–1851) and Nancy Hanks Lincoln (1784?–1818).

His father married Lincoln's stepmother, Sarah Bush Johnston Lincoln (1788–1869), in 1819.

*Of the Boston Forbeses (distantly related to Massachusetts senator John Forbes Kerry), not the magazine Forbeses. The cabin is part of the Mary Bowditch Forbes Lincoln Collection, at the Captain Forbes House Museum in Milton.

Were Thomas and Nancy married to each other when Abraham was born? I heard that he was born out of wedlock.

Yes, they were married, and no, he was not illegitimate.

Thomas Lincoln and Nancy Hanks were married on June 12, 1806. Their first child, Sarah, was born the following year. Abraham was born in 1809. There is no reasonable doubt that Lincoln was conceived by and born to a lawfully wedded couple, but the question still pops up persistently, probably due to confusion between the matter of Lincoln's legitimacy and that of his mother, which is indeed doubtful.

His mother was born out of wedlock?

Probably . . .

. . . but you can no longer get into a bar fight over the issue. The question today is forgotten by everyone but a handful of antiquarians who are determined to puzzle out the Lincoln-Hanks genealogy.

In the 1920s, however, this issue bitterly divided the field of Lincoln scholars. Museum director Louis Warren passionately defended the honor of Lincoln's grandmother Lucey Hanks, while author William Barton and most others just as avidly insisted that her daughter Nancy was a child of sin. Barton's eventually became the accepted view of the matter, in part because Lincoln himself had apparently shared it. He believed that his mother was born out of wedlock and that his real grandfather was a Virginia aristocrat who took advantage of a "poor and credulous" girl, if the recollections of Lincoln's law partner William Herndon are accurate.[3]

Today, the very terms of the debate give off a musty odor of obsolescence. Defending her honor? Child of sin? Born out of wedlock? These phrases are rarely heard in connection with single parenting in the twenty-first century. But in the 1920s, unwed motherhood still carried much of the deep social stigma that it had in Lincoln's day. Further, the 1920s were a decade of upheaval in social and sexual mores, as teenagers took advantage of the invention of the automobile to abandon traditional front-parlor courtship rituals in favor of the modern concept of dating. Contraception became a divisive topic, with Margaret Sanger and others fighting to legalize it, opposed by social conservatives who were horrified at the very idea of discussing the subject publicly. Like the issue of gay marriage eighty years later, the birth control debate exposed deep cultural fault lines.

In Indiana, where Louis Warren lived, many older people were upset by challenges to the society they had known. They were shocked by new ideas about sex and disturbed by the influx of immigrants from Europe speaking strange languages, as well as the growing number of dark-skinned domestic migrants from the Deep South. It is no coincidence that when the Ku Klux Klan was reborn around 1915, it soon had more members in Indiana than in any other state, including (at one point) the governor. It was in this reactionary climate that Warren, a preacher by trade, founded a "Lincoln Shrine and Museum" in Fort Wayne, Indiana, in 1928. To Warren, the idea that his hero's mother might herself be a product of the same immorality and sexual promiscuity that seemed to be the hallmark of the modern age must have been anathema, and he spent years arguing that it could not be so.

The argument over Nancy Hanks's birth was also fueled by public interest in the emerging science of eugenics. The idea that personality traits were inherited persuaded thirty-three states (starting with Indiana in 1907) to pass laws authorizing the sterilization of the feebleminded, insane, criminalistic, epileptic, inebriate, diseased, blind, deaf, deformed, and dependent, hoping to remove undesirable elements from the gene pool.[4] This line of thinking was eventually discredited by the monstrous eugenic experiments of the Nazi regime in the 1930s, but in the 1920s, when the Nancy Hanks paternity debate raged, it was still socially and scientifically acceptable to talk in terms of "purity of bloodline," and to assume that Lincoln's noble character meant that he could only have sprung from noble ancestors. There was no room for a tramp in the Lincoln family tree.

So was Lucey Hanks married when she gave birth to little Nancy? By the end of the twentieth century the consensus was clearly no, based in part on the extensive research of Paul Verduin. Nancy was born in 1783 or 1784, when her mother was still a teenager living in Virginia with her father, Joseph Hanks. The identity of the baby's father (Abraham's maternal grandfather) remains unknown, but he could have been any one of several wealthy young men of the neighborhood, including one who was a relation of the famous Lee family. Lucey later moved to Kentucky and married Henry Sparrow, but he refused to admit his bride's illegitimate daughter to his household, and Nancy was raised by other relatives.[5]

Lincoln's suspicions that he had a Virginia aristocrat among his ancestors, and that his grandfather never married his grandmother, were likely true. If so, Lucey was hardly alone in conceiving a child before marriage; based on marriage and birth records from the colonial era, some historians estimate that more than a quarter of all brides were already pregnant on their wedding day.[6]

Was Abraham's last name really Lincoln?

Some relatives pronounced the name "Linkhorn" instead of "Link-un," but it was still spelled the same way.[7]

No, I mean, was Thomas Lincoln really his father?

Yes, despite claims to the contrary on behalf of numerous others, including:

- Samuel Emory Davis (1755/58–1824), the father of Jefferson Davis, president of the so-called Confederate States of America*
- Senator John C. Calhoun of South Carolina (1782–1850)
- a wandering Virginia aristocrat who took a shine to Nancy Hanks Lincoln
- local farmer Abraham Enlow (or Enloe or Inlow), late of North Carolina (or Virginia)

As historian J. G. de Roulhac Hamilton observed, "Any male person in the United States who was, in 1808, within striking distance of puberty was likely to be saddled with the paternity of Abraham Lincoln."[8] Of those listed, the last is the only one with even a shadow of an authentic claim. When Lincoln was a boy, rumors floated around the neighborhood that the mumps or some other misfortune had rendered Thomas

*Lincoln never recognized the Confederacy as a nation, or indeed as anything more than an illegal rebellion. Using the adjective "so-called" for the Confederate States of America is apparently much more effective than challenging the paternity of Nancy Hanks if you are interested in starting an angry history-related confrontation, especially when addressing a Sons of Confederate Veterans meeting. For this information I am indebted to my colleague Charles Calhoun at East Carolina University.

incapable of fathering children, leading in turn to all kinds of improbable suggestions as to the identity of Abe's real father. William Herndon collected a story from John B. Helm, according to which Enlow claimed Abraham as his son and challenged Thomas Lincoln to a fight, in which he lost both a piece of his nose and his claim to the boy. The Helm story is weakened by its implication that Nancy Hanks was pregnant with Abraham when she married Thomas Lincoln, which cannot be true since the marriage took place in 1806 and Abraham was not born until 1809.[9]

The real significance of the many rumors of Lincoln's true paternity is that they show the power of genetic misconceptions in the public mind. To those who believe that biology is destiny, it's inconceivable that someone as great as Lincoln could be the product of the humble genes of his pioneer parents.

So Lincoln's greatness was due to his environment, not his genes?

His environment certainly shaped him, but it shaped a lot of people . . .

. . . and they didn't all turn out like Lincoln. There was another fellow who was born in a log cabin, grew up on the frontier, moved west as a boy, lost a parent at an early age, lost a sibling, traveled to New Orleans, went off to war but didn't see action, started life on his own in a small town, and got a minor government job while he looked for his way in life. All just like Lincoln, but his name was Nathan Bedford Forrest. He became a wealthy slave trader, then a Confederate cavalry general whose men massacred black Union soldiers after they surrendered at Fort Pillow in 1864, and finally the first leader of the Ku Klux Klan in Tennessee.[10] So perhaps it was neither genes nor environment alone that was responsible for Lincoln's character.

Where did Lincoln's ancestors come from?

On his father's side, his great-great-great-great-grandfather Samuel migrated from Hingham, England, to Hingham, Massachusetts, in 1637.

From there, each succeeding generation of Lincolns moved west or south (or both), deeper into the country, migrating to Pennsylvania and then Virginia. Lincoln's grandfather, also named Abraham, moved to Kentucky around 1781 with his three sons and was killed by Indians.

Was Lincoln's father a good-for-nothing bum?

No . . .

. . . but neither was he the model for Lincoln's restless ambition. There is a traditional belief that Thomas Lincoln was poor and shiftless, the better to exalt his son's achievement in rising to greatness. Thomas's stoutest defender, historian Louis Warren, overcompensated by portraying him as a successful farmer who possessed most of the virtues of the Victorian middle class. Perhaps the best pieces of evidence in favor of Thomas are the beautiful cabinets he crafted, which show more skill and aesthetic sensibility than one would expect from a drunken loser.

Thomas Lincoln was persistent but not particularly lucky in his pursuit of the agrarian version of the American dream. In Kentucky, he bought several farms in succession, but three times his ownership came into question due to legal issues involving property titles. This was not unusual, as Kentucky at the time used the "metes-and-bounds" system of recording land titles, in which a property line might be described as running along a particular creek to a certain boulder, and thence to a specific tree. Unfortunately, trees fall down, boulders can be moved, and streams change their courses. With thousands of settlers entering the state and squatting on whatever land seemed available, questions of who owned which patch of Kentucky were bound to arise, and not just for Thomas Lincoln. In the suit over title to the farm on Knob Creek, which he purchased (or thought he did) when Abraham was two years old, Thomas was one of ten farmers who were named as defendants. Eventually he would move his family north to Indiana and then west to Illinois, still pursuing the ideal of a secure, comfortable, self-sufficient agricultural life.

Why did Thomas and Nancy choose the name "Abraham"?

To honor Thomas's father, who was also named Abraham Lincoln.

Although Lincoln never knew his grandfather Abraham, he certainly knew the dramatic story of his grandfather's death, which he once described as "the legend more strongly than all others imprinted upon my mind and memory."[11] The first Abraham Lincoln had been an officer in the Kentucky militia that battled the native inhabitants of the "Dark and Bloody Ground" in the late eighteenth century. One day in 1784, as he was tending to his fields, Captain Lincoln was ambushed and killed by an Indian, who then seized the captain's little son Thomas. As he was about to return to the woods with the captive boy, a shot rang out from the doorway of the Lincolns' cabin, and the attacker fell. Thomas's older brother Mordecai had grabbed a musket and fired it just in time to save the life of the future president's father.

While the battle line between Indians and settlers had moved west of Kentucky by the time young Abraham was born, accounts like these kept the memory of conflict fresh. The loss of an ancestor in the Indian wars was hardly unusual among the residents of the frontier, but it was remarkable that Lincoln did not seem to inherit any of the animosity of those days, and that in his own encounters with Indians he would display malice toward none.

What was Lincoln's middle name?

He didn't have one.

Did he have any brothers or sisters?

One of each.

He had an older sister, Sarah (born in 1807), and a younger brother, Thomas. He also had a stepbrother, John D. Johnston, and two stepsisters, Elizabeth and Matilda Johnston.

Not much is known of Sarah Lincoln. She was two years older than Abraham, married Aaron Grigsby in 1826, and died in childbirth in 1828. Abraham was apparently quite close to his sister and held a grudge against Grigsby for her death. Even less is known of Lincoln's little brother, Thomas, who was born after the family moved to a farm near Knob Creek, in 1810 or 1811. He died "in infancy," according to Lincoln, but his age at death remains unknown. Dennis Hanks (Nancy Hanks's cousin) later said that the baby "did not live 3 days." Baby Thomas's grave, not far from the Knob Creek cabin site, remained undiscovered until 1933.[12]

Lincoln once said, "All I am, or hope to be, I owe to my angel mother." Did he mean his natural mother or his stepmother?

Probably Nancy, his natural mother . . .

. . . but he had good reason to say the same about his stepmother. After Nancy Lincoln died in 1818, Thomas married the widow Sarah Bush

Johnston the next year. She treated Abe as one of her own and developed a loving relationship with the boy.

Many years later, Lincoln said to William Herndon, "God bless my mother; all that I am or ever hope to be I owe to her." Early biographers like Josiah Holland and George Alfred Townsend inserted the adjective "angel" and made it appear that Lincoln was referring to Sarah.[13] More likely, whenever Lincoln used the phrase "angel mother," it was to identify the late Nancy, as opposed to the living Sarah. More significant, in the conversation that Herndon remembered, is that Lincoln was speaking of his belief that he was descended from a Virginia aristocrat, on his mother's side. If so, Lincoln was really taking a backhand slap at his father, implying that he owed none of his inherited virtues to Thomas Lincoln's side of the family.

Of course, it is certainly possible that he was not criticizing his father but simply praising his stepmother. Abraham and Sarah became very close and remained so. Almost every mother will say, "He was such a nice boy" of her son, even after he grows up to be a serial killer or divorce attorney, but the second Mrs. Lincoln was specific in what was special about her stepson: "I can say what scarcely one woman—a mother—can say in a thousand and it is this—Abe never gave me a cross word or look and never refused in fact, or Even in appearance, to do any thing I requested him . . ."[14]

Lincoln returned the affection. Although he did not attend his father's funeral, he made a point of visiting his stepmother as almost his last act before leaving Illinois to go to Washington as president-elect in 1861. His gratitude for all that she had done for him would certainly have justified his calling her his "angel mother."

Lincoln didn't go to his own father's funeral?

True.

Relations between Thomas and Abraham were never particularly warm. Unlike his father, Abraham preferred reading to plowing, and he resented the laws that required him to turn over all his earnings to his father until he was "emancipated" at the age of twenty-one. He had no interest in making his living from the land by the sweat of his brow as his father did, choosing instead a life of intellectual labor as a lawyer and politician. Once Lincoln left home in 1831, he had little more to do with his father. His parents did not attend his wedding to Mary Todd (which was admittedly a spur-of-the-moment ceremony), nor did they ever meet his wife or see any of their grandchildren. In 1851, when Lincoln received word that his father was dying, he wrote back that he could not spare the time to see him, because he was too busy with his law practice and did not want to leave Mary's side after the recent birth of their son Willie. More to the point, he added that "if we could meet now, it is doubtful whether it would not be more painful than pleasant."[15]

On the other hand, it is hardly necessary to follow those scholars who have exaggerated the distance between son and father into an oedipal conflict that Lincoln could only resolve by ritually "slaying" the Founding Fathers and recasting the Union as his own creation. If Lincoln rejected Thomas's deathbed call in 1851, it was at least in part because he had dropped everything in 1849 to answer a similar letter that turned out to be a false alarm. He later paid for a marker for his father's grave, and in 1853 he and Mary named their fourth son Thomas.[16]

Did Lincoln have a happy childhood?

More or less.

Many of the early memories that Lincoln shared in later life were relatively pleasant. "My childhood-home I see again / And gladden with the view" was the beginning of a poem he wrote when he was thirty-four years old.[17] If he maintained a sanguine view of his youth, however, it may have been more due to the psychological phenomenon that most people are "about as happy as they make up their minds to be" (an observation often attributed to Lincoln, although there is no reliable record of him actually saying it) rather than to the circumstances in which he grew up.

Lincoln remembered nothing of his first home, the farm at Sinking Spring marked today by the marble memorial with the faux cabin. When he was two, his family moved a few miles to Knob Creek, where he lived until he was seven. He "was raised to farm work," helping his father as soon as he was old enough to do so.[18] One of his first memories was of dropping pumpkin seeds in a newly planted cornfield, "two seeds every other hole and every other row," and then watching the next day as a flood washed away the topsoil, "corn, pumpkin seeds and all," wiping out all of his labor.[19] The futility of the experience may have been in Lincoln's mind in 1860 when he insisted to a would-be campaign publicist that there was little worth recalling from his youth: "It can all be condensed into a single sentence, and that sentence you will find in Gray's *Elegy*, 'The short and simple annals of the poor.' That's my life, and that's all that you or any one else can make of it."[20]

If Lincoln was born in Kentucky, why do Illinois license plates say "Land of Lincoln"?

He moved there later. But the state that really gets shortchanged in the Lincoln story is Indiana . . .

. . . where he lived for fourteen years. The Lincolns moved there in 1816, when Abraham was seven.

Did they really spend their first winter in Indiana living outdoors?

No, the stories of the "half-faced camp" are greatly exaggerated.

When the family left Kentucky, Thomas Lincoln went ahead of the party, scouting out the land. He found the place he had chosen for settlement and built for himself a three-sided temporary shelter, known as a half-faced camp. Somehow in legend this became the home of the entire family when they arrived in Indiana, as described by Carl Sandburg and others.[21] The idea of the Lincolns huddling in an open shelter for weeks at a time, shivering and pale, while Thomas idly looks at the massive trees all around that could provide a fourth wall in a matter of hours, is ludicrous. That such a story could take hold shows in what low regard many writers once held Thomas Lincoln.

Why did the Lincolns move to Indiana?

"Partly on account of slavery; but chiefly on account of the difficulty of land titles in Ky." . . .

. . . according to Lincoln himself.[22] It is not surprising that Thomas Lincoln tired of the uncertainties of Kentucky land ownership and decided to head for Indiana, which was then part of the Northwest Territory. There the land was organized into orderly square lots by federal surveyors, and secure title could be purchased directly from the government. Even today, travelers flying over the middle of the country can see the sharp contrast where the Ohio River separates the curving, organic shapes of Kentucky's roads and property lines from the precise right angles of farm boundaries in southern Ohio, Indiana, and Illinois.

What did slavery have to do with their move?

Thomas Lincoln was opposed to slavery . . .

. . . and Kentucky was a slave state. The road that passed by the Lincoln farm on Knob Creek was sometimes used by slave traders convoying their human cargo to the Deep South. Thomas Lincoln was a member of a Baptist church that opposed slavery, and as a small farmer he found himself in economic competition with the owners of large, slave-worked plantations. In Indiana, which was free territory under the Northwest Ordinance of 1787 and became a free state in 1816, he could distance himself from the threat, both moral and commercial, that slavery posed.

What did Abe do in Indiana?

Mostly work.

By then he was old enough to have an "axe put into his hands."[23] He continued to experience the joys and tragedies of a frontier boyhood, including the hardest blow of all: the death of his mother in 1818.

How did his mother die?

Nancy Hanks Lincoln was a victim of milk sickness.

In the wilderness of southern Indiana, pioneers like the Lincolns found in the dark forests a plant unknown in Europe or the eastern United States. It grew several feet tall and was covered with white blossoms, in season. Cattle avoided eating it if they could find anything better, but in hard times they would browse on its leaves.

The plant was white snakeroot, and it contained the toxin tremetol. Animals that ate too much of it died from "the trembles," and lactating cows that ate it passed the poison along in their milk. The settlers soon made the connection between the consumption of cow's milk and the onset of an often fatal disease marked by nausea, paralysis, and coma, but they did not know the source of this "milk sickness." In 1818, it took the lives of Thomas Sparrow and Elizabeth Hanks Lincoln, Nancy's aunt and uncle, who had settled not far from the Lincolns. The next to fall ill was Abraham's mother. After several days of suffering, she died on October 5, 1818.

Can people still get milk sickness?

Yes . . .

. . . but only if they drink milk from their own cows. It is not unknown for cows today to eat white snakeroot, but commercial farms blend the milk of many cows, diluting to a harmless level the poison that any one of them might have absorbed.

Did Abraham show any signs of future greatness when he was a boy?

Well, he was different from other children.

Most boys loved to hunt, for example. Lincoln learned how to shoot, but after he killed a wild turkey when he was eight years old, he "never since pulled a trigger on any larger game."[24]

Did he did hunt smaller animals?

Yes . . .

. . . he had no problem with squirrel hunting, and was apparently quite a good shot. Then as now, squirrels fell below the threshold of compassion for the average American man, who will swerve his car dangerously to avoid hitting a dead dog by the side of the road but cruise right over a flattened squirrel carcass without much more than a disgusted glance in the rearview mirror.

How else was Abe different from other children?

For fun, his playmates liked to torture animals. He didn't.

One game was to put hot coals on the backs of turtles to see them scurry about in pain. When Lincoln saw this, he made the other boys stop. As they grew older, most young men on the frontier took to drinking, smoking, chewing, swearing, and voting Democratic. Lincoln didn't adopt any of these ways.

Yet, as author William Lee Miller has pointed out, he had the rare ability to set himself apart from his peers without alienating them. He could be moral without being moralistic. He was popular with other children, in part because he could tell funny stories, mimic adults, and as he grew larger, defend himself physically.[25]

Is it true that Lincoln was nearly killed when he was a boy?

Yes, at least twice.

When he was nine years old, he was kicked in the head by a horse and knocked unconscious.[26] The blow inflicted permanent nerve damage, the evidence of which appears in almost every photograph of Lincoln. Cover one side of his face with your hand, and he appears to be smiling; cover the other side and a more serious expression emerges. The drooping eyelid and curled corner of the mouth almost certainly are the results of his brush with death in 1819.

He also nearly drowned several times, if his childhood companions are to be believed. He was hanging out with his playmate Austin Gollaher (whose tombstone one day would read "Lincoln's Playmate") when they got the idea to try to slither across Knob Creek on a log. Lincoln fell in, and Gollaher pulled him out. Lincoln's loquacious cousin (once removed) Dennis Hanks claimed credit for rescuing Lincoln from a watery grave on another occasion, as did a local girl named Mary Berry.

Did this really happen three times?

No, probably just once.

If near-drownings were such a regular occurrence for the boy Lincoln, you'd think he would eventually have taught himself a rudimentary dog paddle, but we have no evidence that he ever learned to swim. In his study of Lincoln's childhood, Louis Warren (who was not ordinarily given to humorous observations about his hero) expressed his skepticism by writing, "Evidently, Lincoln must have been in deep water most of the time, even in childhood."[27]

Like almost everything else we know of Lincoln's childhood, the rescue incidents come to us from recollections of the participants, written down many years after the fact. Miss Berry's version survives only in a

1967 newspaper clipping of a family tale.[28] Dennis Hanks, by his own telling, was present at every memorable moment in Lincoln's childhood. Austin Gollaher, who told his version to a friend in 1866, is the most plausible witness of the three. The story fits in with his account of other adventures at the ol' swimmin' hole with Lincoln, like the time Lincoln climbed a tree and dropped a paw paw into a hat.

What's a paw paw?

The paw paw is a fruit . . .

. . . that, when ripe, is soft and extremely pungent, and thus perfectly appropriate for dropping into your friend's hat, if you are a seven-year-old boy sitting on a tree branch. Seeing that Austin was taking a nap at the foot of the tree, with his upturned hat at his side, Lincoln for a joke took aim and released a paw paw. Gollaher, however, was not really asleep and anticipated the prank. While Abe had his back turned, Gollaher switched his hat for Lincoln's, so the headgear that the future president targeted was his own.

That, at least, is how Carl Sandburg and other writers have told the story, sanitizing it for sensitive audiences and imposing another filter between what we know of Lincoln's youth and what really happened. In the original version, as Lincoln told it, there were no paw paws involved, and the reason his back was turned during the hat switch was this: "I noticed his hat sat straight with the reverse side up [and] I thought I would shit in his hat . . . [but] when I let the load drop he swaped [*sic*] hats and my hat caught the whole Charge." Lincoln laughed "heartily" after telling a White House visitor this story. Since I first read it, I have never been able to look at his trademark stovepipe hat in quite the same way.[29]

How much schooling did he have?

About one year's worth.

Lincoln wrote that he went to school "by littles," meaning a little here and a little there, whenever the farm chores were not too pressing and there happened to be a schoolmaster in the area. He received the equivalent of a sixth-grade education, judging by the content of the lessons he completed. When filling out a biographical form for the *Dictionary of*

Congress in 1858, he summed up his scholastic record in two words: "Education defective."[30]

While it is certainly remarkable that he was able to advance as far as he did from such a limited educational beginning, it is worthwhile to remember that his education was about average for an American of his generation living anywhere west of the long-established New England states.

Did he write his school lessons on the back of a shovel, using a piece of charcoal?

Not usually.

According to one account, young Abraham used a flat wooden shovel when paper was not available, covering it with writing and then shaving off the surface with his knife and starting over. His stepmother recalled that he wrote on boards "when he had no paper," but there are enough surviving scraps of Lincoln's school work, written on paper, to suggest that wooden shovels and boards were occasional expedients, not his primary medium.[31]

The myth: Lincoln writing on the back of a shovel. (Courtesy of The Lincoln Museum, Fort Wayne IN, TLM 318)

The reality: Lincoln's homework, on paper. (Courtesy of The Lincoln Museum, Fort Wayne, IN, TLM 505)

Who taught him?

Nobody you've heard of.

In an era when it didn't take much to be a schoolteacher, Lincoln's early teachers were not extraordinary. Lincoln later wrote that "No qualification was ever required of a teacher, beyond '*readin, writin, and cipherin*'," and if a wandering schoolmaster revealed that he had command of a little Latin, "he was looked upon as a wizzard." Andrew Crawford, James Swaney (pronounced "Sweeney," if Lincoln's memory was correct some forty years later), and Azel Dorsey were the three men who led Lincoln through "blab school."[32]

What's a "blab school"?

A school where every student talks at once, or else gets rapped on the knuckles with a stick.

The schools Lincoln attended were held in small rooms filled with children of various ages, each of whom read his or her own lessons aloud at the same time. The resulting din of "blabbing" students gave the schoolmaster proof that everyone was hard at work.

Did Lincoln ever go to college?

No.

Once he became famous, however, he did receive honorary doctor of law degrees from Knox College in 1860, Columbia College (now Columbia University) in 1861, and the College of New Jersey (now Princeton University) in 1864.

Although his political supporters were happy to play up Lincoln's image as a self-taught son of the prairie, he always remained a little self-conscious about his lack of schooling. While in Galesburg, Illinois, to debate Stephen Douglas in 1858, he walked through the main classroom building of Knox College to reach the speaker's platform, which gave him the opportunity to joke awkwardly, "At last I can say I've gone through college." In 1860, the same year that he was awarded an honorary degree from Knox, he wrote that he regretted his "want of an education."[33]

If his education was so limited, how did he get so smart?

Reading . . .

. . . was the most important factor. Nancy Lincoln could not write her own name, but she apparently could read enough to teach her son his ABCs. Her cousin Dennis Hanks, who accompanied the Lincolns when they moved to Indiana, recalled that in Kentucky Abe accompanied his sister Sarah to school for a few months, where "a man by the name of [Caleb] Hazel hellped to teach Abraham his letters." Hanks also claimed part of the credit for teaching Abraham to write, but many who knew Dennis Hanks considered him a hopeless liar; one former neighbor said in 1865, "the idea that he taught Lincoln to read and write is to me preposterous."[34] The question of exactly who taught Lincoln to read is almost certainly beyond a definitive answer, like so many other details of his childhood.

However he got his start, he soon became a voracious reader. There were few books in the house, but he studied these over and over, including the Bible, King James Version. As he gained access to other books, such as *Pilgrim's Progress,* Aesop's *Fables, Robinson Crusoe,* and various histories, he devoured them as well. Neighbors remarked on his habit of reading while plowing and thought him lazy for it. He borrowed every book he could. He read Parson Weems's imaginative *Life of Washington,* with its invented episodes of the chopped cherry tree and the dollar thrown across the Potomac, and was so deeply impressed by Weems's description of the Revolution that he talked about it in 1861, on the eve of the Civil War: "I recollect thinking then, boy even though I was, that there must have been something more than common that those men struggled for."[35]

Did he once accidentally ruin a book that he borrowed?

Yes. This is a Lincoln story everyone has heard that happens to be true.

There are several versions, all of which agree that Lincoln once borrowed a book from a neighbor and left it overnight in a crack between two logs in the wall of his cabin. An unexpected rain soaked the book through. Lincoln offered to pay for the damage by working for the neighbor, who rewarded him by giving him the book, one of the first he ever owned.

FOR FURTHER READING

Easily the single most important published source of information on Lincoln's early life is *Herndon's Informants* (1998), edited by Douglas L. Wilson and Rodney O. Davis. Almost immediately after Lincoln's death, William Herndon began collecting information for a biography of his famous former law partner. He sent written inquiries to and conducted interviews of dozens of people who had known Lincoln. Most of the notes he compiled survived only on microfilm that languished in the Library of Congress until Wilson and Davis took up the challenge of deciphering Herndon's atrocious handwriting. The resulting volume contains the bulk of the firsthand evidence we have regarding Lincoln in Kentucky, Indiana, and New Salem, Illinois. Since it consists of the recollections of people telling stories about a man they had known thirty or forty years earlier, much of it is contradictory and inconsistent, but it remains the best place to start learning about the young Lincoln. The early chapters of *Herndon's Lincoln* (1889), a biography ghostwritten for Herndon by Jesse Weik, are based on the same material, as explained in the extremely thorough annotations in the 2006 edition of the work, also edited by Wilson and Davis.

On Lincoln's family, Louis Warren, *Lincoln's Parentage and Childhood* (1926), is the first and still the most thorough treatment of the subject, but it suffers from Warren's intense admiration for Lincoln's parents. Early treatments of the question of Lincoln's paternity include William E. Barton, *The Paternity of Abraham Lincoln: Was He the Son of Thomas Lincoln?* (1920) and *Lineage of Lincoln* (1929), but the leading modern authority on the subject, Paul Verduin, describes Barton's research as "superficial at best," at least regarding the legitimacy of Lincoln's mother. You can find Verduin's version of the Hanks genealogy in an appendix to *Herndon's Informants.*

On Lincoln's childhood, William Lee Miller, *Lincoln's Virtues: An Ethical Biography* (2002), is by far the most entertaining and thought-provoking exploration of how the boy Lincoln developed the traits that would lead him to the White House.

{ CHAPTER TWO }

Rail-splitter

A piece of floating driftwood . . .

—Lincoln's description of himself as a young man in New Salem, Illinois[1]

What's a rail-splitter?

Someone who makes logs into fence rails.

You take a log and carefully drive a wedge into it at one end, then use a maul or sledgehammer to pound on the wedge until a crack appears. Go to the end of the crack, usually about three feet or so down the log, and insert another wedge. Pound, crack, insert, and pound again until eventually the crack reaches the other end of the log, which then splits in two lengthwise. Now set the pieces flat side down, repeat the process for each one, and you end up with four rails, ready to be stacked in zigzag fashion for a worm fence, or piled on top of one another between pairs of stakes to make a split rail fence.

Abraham Lincoln was never a full-time rail-splitter, but he performed the chore often enough on his father's farm or to help out a neighbor. There was plenty of demand for the skill, since it took an acre of timber to provide the trees to fence in ten acres of land, and most frontier farms were far larger than ten acres. On one occasion Lincoln agreed to split rails in exchange for cloth to make a pair of pants, at a rate of four hundred rails per yard of material. To make such a bargain, Lincoln must have been a fast and efficient rail-splitter.

When Lincoln was seeking the nomination of the Republican Party for president in 1860, one of the critical moments of the campaign took place at the Illinois state nominating convention, held in Decatur on May 9 and 10. John Hanks (a cousin of Lincoln's mother) and another man entered the convention hall and paraded around with a pair of rails bearing a sign reading, "Abraham Lincoln, the Rail Candidate for President in 1860. Two rails from a lot of three thousand made in 1830 by John Hanks and Abe Lincoln." The cheering that followed lasted for fifteen minutes, and Lincoln was unanimously chosen to be the favorite son of Illinois at the upcoming national convention.[2]

Lincoln's handlers understood the value of playing up a candidate's rustic "man of the people" image. They remembered how William Henry Harrison had won the presidency in 1840 with his "Log Cabin and Hard Cider" campaign, despite the fact that Harrison had actually been born in a mansion. Lincoln might not have ever been a professional rail-splitter, but he had split plenty of rails in his youth, and his claim to humble beginnings was considerably stronger than Harrison's. The rail-splitter image stuck. Lincoln didn't care for it at first, as he had spent his life to that point trying to move beyond the manual labor of his frontier upbringing, but he came to accept its political value. It would remain with him for the rest of his life and even extended to the next generation when newspaper reporters during Lincoln's presidency referred to his oldest son, Robert, as "The Prince of Rails."

Technically, of course, a person who splits logs to make rails should be called a log-splitter, but that does not make nearly as euphonious a nickname as "The Railsplitter."

So Lincoln didn't really split rails for a living. What did he do, before he became a lawyer and politician?

Almost anything he could find . . .

. . . that would keep him from following in his father's footsteps as a frontier farmer. At the age of eighteen he constructed a small flatboat, with the idea of floating goods down the Ohio River to the Mississippi. One day a pair of travelers hired him to row them and their trunks out to a passing steamboat. The passengers paid him half a dollar each for the chore, which was more money than he had ever earned at one time before. Fifty cents was a full day's pay for unskilled labor (if cash was available, which was seldom on the frontier), so this was a substantial windfall.[3] "The world seemed wider and fairer before me," he later recalled, now that he saw the possibility of making a living in the market economy, instead of scratching one out of the earth.[4] From this day forward, Lincoln consistently sought ways to work for cash. In an era when

Lincoln is frequently pictured splitting rails with an axe instead of a maul, which would explain why he looks so tired. (Courtesy of The Lincoln Museum, Fort Wayne, IN, TLM 4635)

many Americans, from Thomas Lincoln to Thomas Jefferson, believed that the ideal life was that of the self-sufficient landowner, Lincoln could not wait to get off the land.

He took his first steps toward economic independence the next year, in 1828. By then he was regularly ferrying passengers to steamboats, and knew something of the ways of the Ohio River. A neighbor named James Gentry hired him to build a flatboat and carry a load of produce down to New Orleans. Lincoln, with Gentry's son Allen, made the voyage successfully, though not without at least one life-threatening incident. One night in Louisiana, a gang of slaves tried to rob the boat but were driven off by Lincoln and Gentry. Lincoln earned a few dollars for the trip, but as a minor he was obligated to give it all to his father, which was perhaps a further spur to his desire to seek economic independence.

Was this the trip when Lincoln saw slave markets in New Orleans and decided he would dedicate himself to ending slavery?

"If I ever get the chance to hit that thing, I'll hit it hard" . . .

. . . was what Allen Gentry claimed Lincoln said. It's certainly possible that Lincoln was affected by the sight of human beings bought and sold like cattle in New Orleans. The slaves of the Crescent City were not the first he had seen, having grown up in Kentucky, but such large slave markets were new to him. Although the importation of slaves from Africa had been banned in the United States since 1808, the domestic trade flourished, and a slave ship from Virginia, ironically named the *United States*, was docked in New Orleans with a cargo of people to sell at the time that Lincoln and Gentry were there.

Whether the details of Lincoln's alleged statement are accurate is another question. A very similar story was told about Lincoln's second flatboat trip to New Orleans, in 1831, which could not have been true. Lincoln undertook the second trip (when he was a twenty-two-year-old adult, entitled to keep his earnings) at the behest of big-talking merchant Denton Offut, accompanied by John Hanks and his stepbrother John Johnston. Hanks later related Lincoln's righteous indignation at the sight of human beings paraded about like cattle for potential buyers, but Hanks, as Lincoln took pains to note in an 1860 campaign autobiography, was some seven hundred miles away when the flatboat reached New Orleans, having gotten off when it was docked in St. Louis. Whatever Lincoln's powers of oratory, he could not have said anything in New Orleans that Hanks could have heard in 1831, so the story is at best a thirdhand tale passed from Johnston to Hanks to us. Perhaps the 1828 story is more accurate, but more likely both are inventions to fit Lincoln's image as the Great Emancipator.[5]

Lincoln's biographers have magnified the significance of some incidents on his two river trips and neglected others. Certainly the slave markets must have made an impression on Lincoln, but so did his encounter with the Louisiana slaves who tried to rob him. Could it be that the latter incident helps to explain why Lincoln, unlike some other antislavery figures, neither patronized nor romanticized African Americans? Having been physically assaulted by victims of the "peculiar institution," he had evidence that not every slave was a noble repository of natural virtue like Uncle Tom (the Christlike character in Stowe's novel, not the self-hating caricature that most people associate with the name). He also had reason to disbelieve the stereotypes that enslaved people were childlike or lazy and need not be taken seriously; the ones who tried to seize his boat and kill him certainly required his serious attention.

The first river trip may have affected him in another way, in that he had to work hard for several months, only to see his wages paid not to him but to his father. This was not slavery, of course, but the experience may well have sharpened his sense of the injustice that any men should claim the right of "wringing their bread from the sweat of other men's faces," as he would put it in his Second Inaugural Address.[6]

What about his other jobs? Wasn't he a storekeeper?

Yes, for a while.

When he returned from his second trip to New Orleans, he set up on his own in the tiny village of New Salem, Illinois, where his first job was clerking in a store owned by Denton Offut, the man who had hired him to make that trip. Offut was always full of plans and was considered by his neighbors the kind of man who "talked too much with his mouth."[7]

Did he really once walk two miles to return change to a customer?

Probably

. . . but we don't know for sure. In fact, we know very little for certain about Lincoln's early life, including his few years in New Salem, because nobody at the time was taking notes. Only after Lincoln became famous did the incidents of his youth begin to assume mythic proportions. Fortunately, in the years after Lincoln's death, his faithful law partner William Herndon made a heroic effort to gather as much evidence as he could of those days, by interviewing or corresponding with Lincoln's former neighbors. Although New Salem itself had vanished by then, a failed frontier boomtown, Herndon was able to find many of the people who had once lived there, and he used the information he gathered as a basis for his biography, which became known as *Herndon's Lincoln.*

What we know about Lincoln in New Salem, then, is mostly based on reminiscences of varying reliability, written down many years after the fact. This is true of the "short change story," which appeared in many early Lincoln biographies, but without attribution to a specific source. In 1936, a resident of Petersburg, Illinois, set out to verify the story, and concluded that the customer in question was Clarissa Hornbuckle, the amount she overpaid was 6¼ cents, and the distance to her cabin from the store was three miles. His source for the story was Mary Hornbuckle, who had heard it from her mother-in-law, Clarissa, and had told it in turn to several people before her death in 1927.[8] It's not the most reliable evidence, but it is consistent with Lincoln's scrupulous honesty.

What else did he do for a living?

He eventually bought a share of the store with borrowed money . . .

. . . but his partner William Berry drank up a substantial part of the inventory and died. The enterprise soon "winked out," as Lincoln put it, leaving him deeply in debt. He taught himself surveying, and got himself appointed postmaster, as ways to keep himself solvent, but the hole he was in was too deep, and the sheriff foreclosed on his surveying tools. It was a sign of the impression he had already made on his community that at the sheriff's auction, one of his neighbors bought the surveying gear and promptly gave it back to Lincoln so he could continue to earn a living.

If his partner drank up the store's stock, are you saying that Lincoln kept a saloon?

No . . .

. . . although later he was accused of doing so by his political opponents, like Stephen A. Douglas. The Lincoln and Berry store was a "grocery," meaning that it had a license to sell liquor in bulk but not by the glass.

When he got a job as a postmaster, did he really carry letters around in his hat?

Yes, he did.

There was no home delivery of mail in the 1830s, so Lincoln's job as postmaster was a sinecure that allowed him to sit around the post office and read other people's newspapers before they picked them up, which helped him expand his knowledge of national affairs. Although it was not his job to deliver the mail, he made it a point to do so (taking the letters in his hat) if he happened to be traveling to some distant part of Sangamon County, saving someone a long walk to town.

While Lincoln was not responsible for carrying the mail, as the postal service is today, he also did not have the modern luxury of Sundays off. In 1810, Congress passed a law requiring post offices to be open for mail pickup at least one hour every day, including Sundays. For the next two decades a political controversy raged over whether the government should recognize the Christian Sabbath by prohibiting Sunday mail. Curiously, it was evangelical Baptists who led the opposition to the Sabbatarian movement. A massive religious revival known as the Second Great Awakening, beginning around 1800, had catapulted the Baptists and Methodists to numerical supremacy among American Protestants, overtaking more traditional sects like the Congregationalists and Episcopalians, but the older groups still held political power. In Connecticut, for example, Congregationalism remained the official state religion until 1818. Such lingering connections between traditional churches and the state made members of the newer evangelical denominations deeply suspicious of any government action involving religion, even something as apparently innocuous as banning Sunday mail.

What did Lincoln think about this? What was his religion?

In his New Salem days, Lincoln didn't leave many clues about his views on Sabbatarianism, or on religion in general.

His father had been a member of the Little Pigeon Creek Baptist church, and Lincoln must have been exposed to doctrines like predestination at an early age, but he never joined the Baptist church. New Salem had many believers but no churches, so Lincoln's failure to belong was not obvious. We know that it was at this time in his life that Lincoln read Thomas Paine's *Age of Reason,* and probably the works of Voltaire and other Enlightenment skeptics. By the time he moved to Springfield in 1837, he had begun to develop his unique worldview, a mixture of skepticism and providential fatalism that would continue to mature and evolve throughout his life.

Wasn't he secretly baptized when he was older?

No, nor was he planning to convert to (fill in the church of your choice) on Easter Sunday, 1865, only to be tragically murdered on the preceding Good Friday.

The answers to questions about Lincoln's church membership are not the ones that most people are hoping to hear. He was never a member of the church you attend, or any church. His religious beliefs were dynamic, complex, and powerful, but not conventional. He wasn't a Baptist, despite being raised in a Baptist tradition. He wasn't a Presbyterian, although he attended Presbyterian services much of his adult life. He was not a Catholic, contrary to rumors started by the ravings of Reverend Charles Chiniquy, who published a bizarre diatribe called *Fifty Years in the Church of Rome* (1886), which accused Catholics of claiming that Lincoln had been born into their church.[9] According to Mary Todd Lincoln, who ought to have known, he was not even a Christian. Many stories have circulated about Lincoln being secretly baptized, or planning to be, but they are all unsubstantiated.[10]

And yet Abraham Lincoln was in many ways the most deeply spiritual person ever to occupy the White House. In the same 1866 interview with William Herndon where Mary said that her husband "was not a technical Christian," whatever that might mean, she also said that "he was a religious man always" who "had a Kind of Poetry in his Nature."[11] Certainly no one who reads the Second Inaugural Address, Lincoln's profound meditation on God's role in earthly events and the proper response thereto, can doubt this.

For most of the twentieth century, historians tended to respond with dismayed contempt to the public's desire for a conventionally religious Lincoln. They argued that Lincoln's real faith was his almost mystical devotion to the Union and harked back to one of Lincoln's earliest speeches, in which he called for Americans to make a "civil religion" out of "obedience to the laws."[12] Lincoln's many biblical references in his speeches and writings were treated as metaphor or rhetorical embellishment. Not until the late 1990s, particularly after the publication of Allen Guelzo's *Abraham Lincoln: Redeemer President* in 1999, did it become fashionable for historians to treat Lincoln's religious and philosophical views with the same serious attention they had long devoted to his politics.

If Lincoln wasn't a Christian, why are his speeches full of talk about God?

Because he believed in God . . .

. . . or Providence, or some kind of supernatural power beyond this earth that controlled the fates of people and nations. He sometimes quoted Shakespeare's line, "There's a divinity that shapes our ends, / Rough-hew them how we will," which must have appealed to the former axman in him.[13] As a child, he absorbed a stern Calvinism from Baptist preachers who emphasized the power of an omnipotent God, the kind of deity who notes the fall of every sparrow. As an adult, he must have spoken of his religious beliefs to his law partner William Herndon often enough to pique Herndon's curiosity but not fully enough to satisfy it, as evidenced by Herndon's inclusion of questions about religion in almost all of his interviews with Lincoln's New Salem acquaintances.

Lincoln's ideas, whatever they were, were not easy to grasp. While he accepted the notion of Providence, and referred to it often, he rarely spoke publicly of Jesus Christ. In New Salem, Lincoln associated with freethinkers who doubted the divinity of Jesus, and he wrote an essay mocking the idea that Jesus was the son of God. Lincoln's friends, anxious to protect his budding political career, threw the manuscript into the fire.[14]

As he matured, Lincoln learned to be more careful about expressing his views on religion. He must have said enough, however, to develop a reputation as an infidel. In 1846, when he ran for Congress against a well-known Methodist preacher named Peter Cartwright, he found himself on the defensive against Cartwright's charges that he was not a believer. Lincoln responded with a public statement that would remain the longest explanation of his religious beliefs he would ever write.

"I have never spoken with intentional disrespect of religion in general, or of any denomination of Christians in particular," Lincoln wrote, in carefully measured words that reflect the tone of more recent political denials. Although strictly true, Lincoln left open the possibility that he had spoken with unintentional disrespect.* In the next paragraph he

*Lincoln's technique of saying less than the whole truth, without explicitly lying, differed from that of his successor Bill Clinton, whose most famous less-than-fully-true statements (such as "I did not have sexual relations with that woman," January 26, 1998) depended on definitional

agreed with his readers that it would be wrong for any candidate to scoff openly at religion and stated that he himself would not vote for such a person, because "I still do not think any man has the right thus to insult the feelings, and injure the morals, of the community in which he may live." Lincoln again managed to have it both ways: he seemed to share his audience's disapproval of all "infidels" but in fact only criticized those infidels who scoffed "openly" and thereby insulted the majority's feelings. He didn't say that he belonged to the majority, and tacitly reserved the possibility that he too scoffed at religion, just not openly.[15]

Over time, Lincoln's interest in religion grew. The death of his son Eddie in 1850 gave him cause to ponder the brevity and meaning of life on earth, and of course the casualties of the Civil War forced him to confront the issue every day. By the time he came to write the Second Inaugural Address in 1865, with its mature theological contemplation of the inscrutability and justice of the Almighty, he had gone far beyond the easy skepticism of his youth.

This religious conversion he went through—didn't this happen at Gettysburg?

No, it wasn't a "conversion," and it didn't happen in any one place.

There is no evidence that he ever underwent a conversion experience, but the historical record does give us glimpses of Lincoln gradually developing a more personal relationship with God. For example, in the late summer of 1862, Lincoln was ready to issue the Emancipation Proclamation but was waiting for the military situation to improve before doing so. When he met with his cabinet on September 22, a few days after Lee's first invasion of the North was halted at the battle of Antietam, Lincoln told his advisers that the time was right, not just in strategic terms but as a matter of keeping a divine covenant. He had made a promise "to his Maker," he explained, that he would issue the proclamation if the rebel army were driven out of Maryland, and now he was keep-

---

hairsplitting rather than the omission of relevant possibilities. In the right hands, Lincoln's style of denial allows the practitioner to avoid telling the whole truth without significant repercussions. In contrast, the absolute and unambiguous declarative style of non-truth-telling (e.g., Richard Nixon's "I am not a crook," November 18, 1973) may buy some time for the liar but tends to increase his or her humiliation when exposed.

ing his promise. He acknowledged that "It might be thought strange" to make the decision on this basis, but "God had decided this question in favor of the slaves."[16]

Two years later, Lincoln's old friend Joshua Speed paid a visit to Washington. In a lecture he gave after the war, Speed claimed that he came upon Lincoln reading the Bible and gently mocked him for it, asking if Lincoln had recovered from his youthful skepticism. Lincoln, according to Speed, said that he had and urged Speed to do the same. Indicating the Bible, Lincoln told Speed that he should "take all of this Book upon reason that you can, and the balance on faith, and you will live and die a happier man."[17]

These two stories reveal Lincoln's greater willingness to accept some of the ideas and sources of traditional Christianity, but they fall far short of implying any kind of conversion experience. In the former, Lincoln referred to his "Maker," not to Jesus Christ personally, much as he did in all of his religious writings. Lincoln's God was his Maker, the Old Testament God, the Almighty, a single all-powerful Providence, rather than the triune Christian God who offers salvation specifically through the medium of a personal relationship with His only Son. When Lincoln recommended the Bible to Speed (assuming the story is accurate), he did not say that he believed everything in it, nor that he considered belief necessary for salvation. His endorsement instead conveys the impression that he regarded it as a sort of self-help book that might be in part beyond the bounds of reason but ought to be taken on faith anyway in order to "live and die a happier man." The utility of Lincoln's Bible ends with death; it's not a ticket to the afterlife. In this, as in most of his religious and philosophical thought, Lincoln showed no evidence of undergoing a conversion to conventional Christianity.

What did Lincoln do for fun as a young man? Did he play sports?

Yes.

Could he dunk a basketball?

He probably could have . . .

. . . but he never tried, since it was not until 1891 that James Naismith nailed the first peach baskets to the gym balcony in the Springfield,

Massachusetts, YMCA. We can only speculate whether the Great Emancipator would also have been a great rebounder. Physically, he had the tools.* At about six feet four, he was certainly tall enough. (Spud Webb of the Atlanta Hawks once won the NBA slam dunk contest, and he was only five-seven.) He was strong enough too, with arms and shoulders that were powerfully developed by years of chopping trees in the forests of Indiana. One day late in the Civil War, after visiting soldiers at a military hospital, Lincoln amused onlookers by picking up a heavy ax, swinging it a few times at a nearby log, and then holding it by the end of the handle parallel to the ground with his arm outstretched. After he set the ax down and walked away, several young soldiers tried to imitate him and found that none could hold the ax steady in that position.[18] (You can try doing this yourself but be sure that nobody is standing too close, because unless you have Lincoln's arm strength you're going to be dropping a sharp tool in just a few seconds.) Even as he lay on his deathbed, where his body labored through the night after suffering the fatal shot fired by John Wilkes Booth, the doctors attending Lincoln could not help marveling at his powerful musculature while mourning their inability to save him.

So, what sports did he play?

Mostly those that didn't require specialized equipment, like running and wrestling.

Wrestling was a particularly significant element of frontier culture in Lincoln's youth. In 1831, when he first arrived in New Salem, he was immediately challenged to prove his courage by wrestling the bully of the town, Jack Armstrong. It's not clear who won; they may have fought to a draw, or Armstrong may have beaten Lincoln with an illegal leg whip. In

*An apocryphal Lincoln story has him at age fourteen jumping up to grab a buck's horn nailed to a wall and hanging there until it breaks, like a school yard show-off hanging on a basketball rim until it pulls free from the backboard. The point of the story is supposed to be that Lincoln confessed to the crime in Washingtonian cherry tree fashion, but the real crime is how authors manufactured stories about Lincoln's youth, complete with pages of fabricated dialogue. In later versions, the buck's horn becomes an entire buck's head. See William M. Thayer, *The Pioneer Boy, and How He Became President* (1863), 61–62, and Wayne Whipple, *The Story-Life of Lincoln* (1908), 45.

either case, Lincoln performed well enough to win the friendship and respect of Armstrong and his gang, the "Clary's Grove Boys."[19] While Lincoln recognized the importance of getting on the good side of the local thugs, he was only willing to go so far to do it. He risked his own health in wrestling with their leader, but he took no part in some of their

Lincoln wrestles Jack Armstrong on the cover of Classics Illustrated, *142, 1958.* (©2007 First Classics Inc. All Rights Reserved. By permission of Jack Lake Productions Inc.)

more sadistic practices, like stuffing someone in a barrel and rolling him down a hill, or cooking a live pig to hear it squeal.[20]

Lincoln continued to engage in sports the rest of his life. He played "fives," a variation of handball, to pass the time on May 18, 1860, while waiting for telegraph messages from the Republican convention in Chicago that would let him know if he had won the party's nomination for president. According to one account he also played billiards that day; he knew enough about the game to make analogies to it in conversation. Baseball was just starting to grow in popularity in Lincoln's lifetime (with no particular help from future Civil War general Abner Doubleday, contrary to legend), and he occasionally played town ball, an early form of the game with bases laid out in a square instead of a diamond.[21]

The presidential election of 1860 as a baseball game. Lincoln carries a split rail for a bat. Baseball was already popular before the Civil War, contrary to the Abner Doubleday legend. (Courtesy of The Lincoln Museum, Fort Wayne IN, TLM 3498)

What else did he do for fun? Did he drink a lot when he was young?

No.

Stephen Douglas said Lincoln "could ruin more liquor than all the boys of the town together" during their famous debates in 1858, but this was merely political rhetoric.[22] In an era when per capita consumption of alcohol in the United States was roughly three times higher than in the year 2000, Abraham Lincoln was unusual in choosing not to indulge. He tried whiskey and found that it made him feel "flabby and undone."[23] For someone as devoted to reason and as careful with his emotions as Lincoln, the idea of deliberately weakening his self-control with alcohol had no appeal.

Lincoln did not impose his views on others. Alcoholism was a serious social problem in the 1830s and 1840s, leading to calls for government action. Lincoln did not support prohibition, but he endorsed the views of the Washingtonian movement in an 1842 speech to the Springfield Washington Temperance Society. The Washingtonians were a sort of nineteenth-century Alcoholics Anonymous, in that they treated alcoholism as a disease rather than a sin and sought to reduce excessive drinking through moral suasion instead of legal coercion. This suited Lincoln, who argued that persuasion would be more effective than condemnation or force in limiting the evil effects of alcoholism, essentially prefiguring the stance he would take against slavery in the 1850s. When he was president, he did not require that his guests share his temperate views (as "Lemonade Lucy" Hayes and other White House hostesses would later do) but allowed wine to be served at some White House functions, occasionally touching a glass to his lips.

Did he smoke or chew tobacco?

No.

Although cigar makers later used his image on their products, Edward W. Mills had it right about Abe and tobacco when he composed the immortal 1944 poem "Lincoln Never Smoked a Cigarette."*

*Of course cigarettes were not widely popular until a machine for mass-producing them was invented in the 1880s, some fifteen years after Lincoln's death.

Did he gamble?

No.

"He did not know one card from another, therefore could not play," claimed his friend Joshua Speed.[24] Given that he could tell one chess piece from another enough to play that game, Lincoln probably could have played cards well, had he wanted to, but gambling was antithetical to his nature.

Did he swear or tell dirty jokes?

You be the judge.

Here's a story Lincoln is supposed to have told: A boy runs to his father and breathlessly shouts, "Paw, come quick. The hired man and Sis are up in the haymow, and he's a-pullin' down his pants and she's a-liftin' up her skirts. Paw, they're gettin' ready to pee all over our hay!" To which the father replies, "Son, you've got your facts absolutely right, but you've drawn a completely wrong conclusion."[25] Perhaps not a knee-slapper, but Lincoln told it to a jury during a lunch break, and later that day after the opposing attorney had finished a lengthy summation, Lincoln won the case simply by telling the jurors, "My learned opponents have their facts absolutely right, but they have drawn completely wrong conclusions." Sometimes timing is everything.

More to the point, does this qualify as a dirty joke? Lincoln told stories involving bodily functions that today would be rated PG-13 at worst but which were considered highly improper by many in the mid-nineteenth century. When a contemporary tells us that Lincoln had "an insane love in telling dirty and Smutty Stories," it's hard to judge what he means, because the people most offended by Lincoln's stories were the ones least able to bring themselves to write down just what it was that he said.[26] This was, after all, an era when the weak-bladdered Edward Everett, before giving the two-and-a-half-hour oration at Gettysburg that preceded Lincoln's address, nearly exhausted his store of euphemisms in trying to communicate to the other dignitaries in his backstage tent that he needed them to leave so he could urinate.[27] Occasionally a four-letter word in a Lincoln story makes it through the filter of memory and propriety to the present (for example in the one about

Ethan Allan),* but more often all we have are bowdlerized versions that leave us wondering what the fuss was about.

Was he lazy?

As a teenager in Indiana, he was considered "lazy—a very lazy man" . . .

. . . according to Dennis Hanks, because "He was always reading—scribbling—writing—Ciphering—writing Poetry &&."[28] I'd be a happier teacher if more of my students were lazy like that.

So did Lincoln have any *bad habits?*

Remarkably, no.

Even more remarkable was that he didn't flaunt his nonconformist virtue. He was the butt of his own story about the stagecoach passenger who declined the offer of a chew of tobacco from a fellow rider, then turned down a cigar, and finally refused a sip of brandy from a silver flask. When the hospitable passenger got up to leave, his last words to his abstemious companion were, "My experience has taught me that a man who has no vices has d——d few virtues. Good day."[29]

How about good manners?

OK, now we have something on him.

The young Lincoln did not know how to behave in company, which is not surprising considering his upbringing. Lincoln was not rude by nature, but he was uneducated in drawing room manners. When he moved from tiny New Salem to the metropolis of Springfield (pop. 2,000) in 1837, he had no idea how to fit in. He would remain dreadfully

*It seems that Revolutionary War hero Ethan Allan was visiting England after the war, and his hosts tried to tease him by putting up a picture of George Washington in the outhouse. Allan saw it, returned to the main house, and declared that it was a very appropriate place for the picture, because "their is Nothing that Will Make an Englishman Shit So quick as the Sight of Genl Washington." Wilson and Davis, *Herndon's Informants*, 174. Doris Kearns Goodwin, touring in support of her best-selling *Team of Rivals: The Political Genius of Abraham Lincoln* (2005), got a lot of mileage out of this story, including a recitation on *The Daily Show with Jon Stewart.*

ignorant of proper etiquette until he was eventually taken in hand by his future wife, Mary Todd.

He probably didn't need much in the way of manners for his first girlfriend, Ann Rutledge, did he?

Yes, it's safe to assume that the relationship of Abraham Lincoln and Ann Rutledge was not overly formal . . .

. . . but that's about all that it's safe to assume. The story that she was Lincoln's first love, and his only true love ever, has roiled the waters of Lincoln devotees since it was first expounded by Billy Herndon in 1866.

Here's what is known for sure: Ann Rutledge was the daughter of New Salem's tavern keeper, she was engaged to another man, and Lincoln was stricken with depression when she died in 1835 at the age of twenty-two. That's pretty much it. Her name does not appear in any of Lincoln's writings.

What made her famous was Herndon's lecture, first given in Springfield on November 16, 1866, based on his interviews with old New Salem residents. Some of them recalled that Abe and Ann had been close, and since Ann's fiancé had not been heard from for several years after he left town, maybe (some said) Ann had even agreed to marry Abe instead. When Herndon was Lincoln's law partner, he and Mary Lincoln became rivals for Abraham's time and attention, a rivalry that outlasted Lincoln's death. For his 1866 lecture, Herndon built upon a few shreds of historical evidence to popularize the story that Ann, not Mary, was Lincoln's first and only true love.

The public ate this up. In the 1920s, muckraking journalist Ida Tarbell was taken in by forged historical documents that provided fresh, if untrue, details of the Lincoln-Rutledge romance. The relationship figured prominently in two great Lincoln movies, *Young Mr. Lincoln* (1939), starring Henry Fonda, and *Abe Lincoln in Illinois* (1940), with Raymond Massey. The Rutledge romance became such a large part of the Lincoln story that it finally provoked the great James Randall of the University of Illinois to write a substantial appendix to the first volume of his magnum opus, *Lincoln the President* (1945), demolishing the whole thing. Randall (or more accurately, his wife Ruth Painter Randall, who would publish a biography of Mary and actually wrote the appendix) argued that the Rutledge romance was nothing but legend. Randall showed how the evidence cited by Herndon consisted only of the unreliable reminiscences of old New Salemites. The testimony that Herndon had collected fell into disrepute among scholars, and Ann Rutledge went into the dustbin of history.

The problem with Randall's attack is that almost everything known about Lincoln's early life is based on similar testimony. In 1990, the *Journal of the Abraham Lincoln Association* published an article by John Y. Simon calling for a "reexamination of the evidence and its treatment by biographers," and shortly afterward Michael Burlingame urged fellow historians to take a fresh look at the archive of recollections that Herndon had gathered, instead of "treating it as if it were high-level nuclear waste." The result was the rehabilitation of Ann Rutledge. Although she is no longer remembered by the public as she was in the early twentieth century, her story once again appears in most Lincoln biographies as a cloudy but real episode that had a substantial effect on Lincoln's emotional development.[30]

Did he leave New Salem because of Ann Rutledge?

Nobody knows, although that could certainly have been part of the reason.

By 1837, Lincoln had outgrown the tiny community. After he left, New Salem became a ghost town, as though raising Lincoln had been its purpose for being. That's certainly the message implied in the orientation film you can see at the New Salem visitor center, which makes good sense for a tourist attraction—when you can imagine the place as a mystical frontier Brigadoon, who wants to spend time analyzing the soulless economic forces that actually led to its rise and fall?[31] New Salem was like many other pioneer villages that rose up from nothing, flowered briefly, and disappeared. Because of its Lincoln connection, however, New Salem was reborn in the twentieth century, in the form of a reconstructed village in a state park that continues to draw large numbers of visitors.

As for Lincoln himself, having studied law and gotten himself elected to the state legislature, it made sense for him to relocate to Springfield, then (as now) the Paris of lower west central Illinois. It was by far the biggest place in which Lincoln had ever lived. He arrived in April 1837 (the precise midpoint of his life, as David Donald observed) and walked into the store of Joshua Speed to purchase the items he would need to set up housekeeping. When he realized that he could not afford everything to furnish his own apartment, Speed offered to share his room above the store. Lincoln went upstairs, dropped the saddlebags containing all his possessions on the floor, came back down, and reported, "Well, Speed, I'm moved."[32]

FOR FURTHER READING

Even more than for Lincoln's childhood, *Herndon's Informants* is the most important source of original material for the New Salem era. Most of what can be found on this subject in the standard Lincoln biographies can be traced to Herndon's research, filtered through *Herndon's Lincoln* where it first appeared in print. Beginning in 1830, we start to hear Lincoln's own voice through his writings, for which the standard source is Roy P. Basler, ed., *The Collected Works of Abraham Lincoln* (1953), published as eight volumes and two supplements. The first eight volumes are available online as a searchable archive at http://www.hti.umich.edu/l/lincoln/.

For many years the best book on Lincoln's religion was William J. Wolf, *The Almost Chosen People: A Study of the Religion of Abraham Lincoln* (1959), which remains a good place to start. The turn of the twentieth century brought a flowering of scholarship on the topic, beginning with Allen Guelzo's important *Abraham Lincoln: Redeemer President* (1999). Stewart Winger, *Lincoln, Religion, and Romantic Cultural Politics* (2003), is more complex but also very rewarding.

Returning to earth, Benjamin Thomas, *Lincoln's New Salem* (1954), is still a wonderful introduction to that legendary place. For the wrestling match with Jack Armstrong, the definitive source is chapter 1 of Douglas Wilson's *Honor's Voice: The Transformation of Abraham Lincoln* (1998). The Ann Rutledge story is told by John Evangelist Walsh in *The Shadows Rise: Abraham Lincoln and the Ann Rutledge Legend* (1993). For an imaginative treatment of Lincoln's early manhood, read Richard Slotkin's novel *Abe* (2000).

{ CHAPTER THREE }

Springfield

I have been spoken to by but one woman since I've been here, and should not have been by her, if she could have avoided it.

—Lincoln to Mary S. Owens, May 7, 1837[1]

Why did he move to Springfield?

It was, by the standards of 1837, the happening place on the Illinois frontier.

It was much bigger than New Salem, it was about to become the state capital (thanks largely to Lincoln's efforts in the state legislature), and it was a good place to meet people.

When a guy says to another guy, "It's a good place to meet people," he usually means "It's a good place to meet girls." Is that what really brought Lincoln to Springfield?

One would hope not . . .

. . . considering how things worked out. When he moved to Springfield, he was engaged, at least in his own mind, to Mary Owens, a Kentucky woman he had met back in 1833 and courted when she visited New Salem. He hadn't done a very good job of it. Once when riding with a group of couples, the party came to a stream and the other men gallantly dismounted and led their ladies' horses across the water; Abe blithely rode on alone, assuming that his date was "plenty smart to take care of [herself]." He was, as she later put it, "deficient in those little links which make up the great chain of womans happiness." Owens returned to Kentucky, but after the death of Ann Rutledge, Lincoln made a sort of informal promise to Owens's sister that if she were to bring Mary back to Illinois, he would marry her.[2]

When Miss Owens returned, late in 1836, he found that she didn't look quite as he remembered. "I knew she was over-size, but she now appeared a fair match for Falstaff," as he later wrote to a friend. He was dismayed by "her want of teeth, weather-beaten appearance in general, and from a kind of notion that ran in my head, that *nothing* could have commenced at the size of infancy, and reached her present bulk in less than thirty-five or forty years."[3] He nonetheless felt honor-bound to her, and wrote letters to her that are painful in their awkwardness, including history's least enthusiastic marriage proposal. "What you have said to me may have been in jest, or I may have misunderstood it. If so, then let it be forgotten; if otherwise, I much wish you would think seriously before you decide," followed by the romantic advice "My opinion is that you had better not do it." He was at least as relieved as he was astonished when she turned him down.[4]

Lincoln was never much of a ladies' man, according to many of the old folks who remembered him in Indiana and New Salem. When he was a teenager, he sat on the bank of a river one evening with Kate Roby, a girl of his age whom he had known for years. She commented on the beauty of the moon sinking in the sky, and he replied with a lecture on astronomy and the fact that the earth's rotation only made the moon appear to sink. Romantic words apparently did not come easily to his lips.[5]

Some have concluded from episodes like this that Lincoln was simply not interested in girls, but there is another possibility. After the death of his mother, Lincoln allowed himself to enter very few close personal relationships the rest of his life. There was his stepmother, his best friend Joshua Speed, and perhaps his wife, Mary, but beyond that he opened himself to no one. He could socialize with other boys, telling jokes, pulling pranks, and hunting squirrels together while keeping them at arm's length, but he found girls "too frivalous" (in Kate Roby's words) for such companionship. Spending time with them meant risking two unbearable outcomes: either they would offer him the emotional intimacy he feared, or worse, they wouldn't. Lincoln was, after all, as awkward and gangly a teenage boy as could be imagined, wearing clothes of buckskin that didn't fit his fast-growing frame. The same girl who forty years later remembered sitting with him on the riverbank watching the moon also described him as a "thin-leggy-gawky boy dried up & Shriveled."[6] Is it a wonder that he was reluctant to put his heart in her hands?

If he didn't do so well with the ladies, is it possible—I mean, I once heard a story that he used to visit, you know, working girls . . . ?

You mean did he ever visit a prostitute? The story you heard has been around since Lincoln's own time.

It goes like this. One day in Springfield, where Lincoln shared a one-bed apartment with the more worldly Josh Speed, he asked his roommate where a guy could go for some action in this town. Speed gave Lincoln the name of his favorite whore, and Abe paid her a visit. The two removed their clothes and were about to proceed with their transaction when Lincoln thought to ask how much this was going to cost. Five dollars was the answer, but he only had two. The young lady assured him that his credit was good, as his reputation for honesty had preceded him, but he was still trying to pay off his New Salem debts and did not want to owe more money to anyone if he could possibly avoid it. He got dressed and left, unfulfilled but unburdened by additional debt.

To Lincoln biographer David Herbert Donald, the story is nothing but a contemporary political joke, made up by Lincoln's opponents to poke fun at his "Honest Abe" image: imagine a politician too honest to accept credit from a hooker! To Douglas Wilson, another biographer, the story sounds true. Lincoln was certainly honest and debt-averse, but there are also suggestions that he later feared (incorrectly) that he had contracted syphilis, implying that he must have done something with somebody to inspire his hypochondria. Still another scholar, Charles B. Strozier, counters that nineteenth-century men feared contracting syphilis (which then had no cure) from incidental contact, and notes that the angst with which Lincoln approached his marriage implies that he must have been a thirty-three-year-old virgin on his wedding night. So what's the verdict? Without definitive proof to overturn Lincoln's reputation for upright behavior, it seems unjustified to take the story at face value; but you be the judge.[7]

You just mentioned that Lincoln and Speed slept in the same bed, and you don't think he visited prostitutes, and we know that he didn't have many girlfriends. Was Lincoln gay?

[Sound of bells and fireworks] Congratulations! You have just asked the number one Lincoln question of the twenty-first century.[8]

As *Was Lincoln gay?* walks up to the stage to receive the award, we see the other questions muttering to themselves. "No one even thought of asking such a thing until a few years ago, and now it's in first place," complains *Did Abe love Ann Rutledge?* "There's no evidence for this at all," hisses *Did he write the Gettysburg Address on the back of an envelope?* The crestfallen runner-up, *Was Lincoln a racist?* turns to his cousin *Did Lincoln own slaves?* and whispers, "You know they're never going to let a brother win this contest." "How does it even matter if he was gay?" huffs *Did Lincoln start the Civil War?*

Although they're a bunch of sore losers, the other questions do make some valid points. It's true, for example, that public discussion of the sexual life of Abraham Lincoln is a recent phenomenon. In the 1920s, when Warren and Barton battled over the legitimacy of Lincoln's mother, such a discussion would have been unthinkable. Not until the gay rights movement began to gain widespread attention did the idea that Lincoln might have been gay begin to come out of the closet. In the late 1970s, gays within Lincoln's own Republican Party hinted at the possibility when they adopted the name "Log Cabin Republicans" for their caucus. Charles Strozier's 1982 psychological analysis of Lincoln (revised in 2001) discussed it seriously, but ultimately rejected it. By 1990, the question was in circulation, but it did not really take off until 1999 when Larry Kramer got hold of it. Kramer, the founder of ACT-UP and the most controversial and outspoken gay activist of his generation, liked to use confrontational tactics to make his points. He seized the image of America's most famous president and tried to make him a gay icon by claiming that Lincoln and Joshua Speed were lovers.

Of course, claiming something and proving it are different things. People say far-fetched things about Lincoln all the time. The *Weekly World News* has run stories about Lincoln coming back from the dead, and an economist in Maryland has sold thousands of books based on the premise that Lincoln had a secret economic motive for starting the Civil War. What made Kramer's different from other outrageous claims was its tantalizing possibility. Historians had long recognized that Lincoln's relationship with Speed had been emotionally intimate. Who was to say that it was not homoerotic as well? There was a fair amount of circumstantial evidence, including the facts that Lincoln and Speed lived together, shared a bed, and wrote letters revealing their emotional closeness to one another. It was also well known that Lincoln never seemed entirely comfortable in the company of women, and that he took obvious pleasure in the society of other men, whether riding the circuit in Illinois or sharing a carriage with secretary of state William Seward during his presidency.

For a clincher, Kramer added that he had found the previously unknown diary of Joshua Speed, and that it left nothing to the imagination regarding the Lincoln-Speed friendship. Kramer never actually showed anyone the diary, however, leading to the widespread assumption among Lincoln students that it was an invention to generate publicity. If so, it was fantastically successful. Kramer's claim that Lincoln was gay appeared widely in the national media. The question of Lincoln's sexual orientation suddenly became the number-one question on people's minds when they thought about Lincoln.

Kramer had made no mistake in choosing his target. If all he had wanted to do was to show that America has had a gay man in the White House, he could have stood on much firmer historical ground by pointing to the administration of bachelor president James Buchanan (1857–61), but who wants that hapless loser on his team? Everybody, in contrast, wants a piece of Lincoln. In an era when traditional heroes like George Washington and Thomas Jefferson were being held up to increasing critical scrutiny for discrepancies between their words and deeds, Lincoln must have appeared to Kramer as an icon ripe for the picking. Without necessarily calling Lincoln a hypocrite, Kramer surely hoped to tap into the deep vein of cynicism and iconoclasm running through modern America by showing that Lincoln was not who he appeared to be.

Once the issue was out in the open, new evidence emerged. During the Civil War, Lincoln moved his family out of the White House each summer from 1862 to 1864 to a retreat known as the Soldiers' Home, on a hill overlooking downtown Washington. It was close enough for Lincoln to ride to work every day and return each evening. At this proto–Camp David, Lincoln became friendly with Captain David V. Derickson, an officer of the cavalry unit assigned to guard him. A rumor spread that when Mrs. Lincoln was away, Derickson slept in the same bedchamber as Lincoln, and that he was even seen wearing the president's nightshirt.[9]

In one respect, however, Kramer fell short of his goal of mobilizing the Lincoln image on behalf of his cause. Despite his use of intemperate language and even personal insult (calling distinguished historian David Herbert Donald a "dried up old heterosexual prune at Harvard"), not one professional historian took Kramer's bait and responded by indignantly denying the possibility that Lincoln might have been gay. Even when confronted with Kramer's truly exotic claim that Lincoln and John Wilkes Booth had some kind of sexual encounter that led the latter to assassinate the former, Douglas Wilson replied calmly, "That's pretty wild . . . If Lincoln and Booth had ever met, I would have thought we would have known more about it. But all ideas are welcome; you learn more when people argue."[10] Kramer's attempt to smoke out homophobia among the community of Lincoln historians fizzled.

Kramer went on to other issues, but in 2004, C. A. Tripp reignited the debate with his book *The Intimate World of Abraham Lincoln*, which appeared in print shortly after its author's death. Tripp argued again that Lincoln and Speed were lovers, and that Lincoln probably had erotic experiences with other men, including Derickson. Tripp convinced one Lincoln scholar (Mary Lincoln's biographer Jean Baker), and added to our knowledge of Lincoln with his insightful analysis of the emotional trajectory of the Lincoln-Speed friendship, as revealed in their letters, but he provided only new interpretations, not new evidence, to support his theory of physical as well as emotional intimacy. His determination to push his thesis beyond what the evidence would support was so intense that it drove his former collaborator to disavow the project altogether.[11]

So,* was *Lincoln gay?

No, because nobody was "gay" in Lincoln's time.

The word "homosexual" to describe someone who was exclusively attracted to others of the same sex was not coined until 1868, three years after Lincoln's death. The idea of identifying and defining a person primarily by the objects of his or her sexual desire was simply not part of Lincoln's world.[12]

But of course in Lincoln's era (as in any era) there were people who engaged in homoerotic relationships, even if they didn't choose to define themselves by such. Was Lincoln one of them? As far back as Carl Sandburg's 1926 reference to "a streak of lavender, and spots soft as May violets" in Lincoln's character, observers have recognized ways in which Lincoln refused to conform to sexual stereotypes.[13] His personality had a distinctive feminine side, one that allowed him to lead his nation through a bloody civil war without ever engaging in testosterone-laced "bring it on" posturing, belittling his enemies, or otherwise exhibiting the traits of traditional masculinity that have characterized other national leaders. And we know that he and Speed roomed together for four years, sleeping in the same bed. In the housing arrangements common to twenty-first-century America, two unrelated adult males sharing a bed would be presumptive evidence that they were having a sexual relationship.

Lincoln, however, lived in nineteenth-century frontier Illinois, where beds were scarce and expensive, and young men often shared them for the same reason that many young people of the same sex today share small apartments or college dorm rooms: to save money. When Lincoln rode the circuit with other lawyers, the scarcity of beds meant that he and two or three of his colleagues often had to sleep under one cover at the rustic inns where they stayed, but no one has ever suggested that this is evidence of orgies in the Eighth Judicial Circuit. The social taboos against homoerotic behavior were also considerably more severe than they are today, which means that even if Lincoln felt a physical attraction for his friend (of which there is no direct evidence), he would have had strong reasons to suppress the impulse and even stronger reasons to hide it later if he did act on it. But in 1864, when Lincoln appointed Speed's brother James to be attorney general, he casually mentioned that he knew Joshua even better than he knew James, "for I slept with Joshua for four years, and I suppose I ought to know him."[14] In the absence of any direct evidence of homoerotic behavior or desire, I cannot see any reason to conclude that Lincoln was gay; but given that no one who shared Lincoln's bed ever said what went on there, it is equally clear that we cannot say definitively that Lincoln never had a homoerotic experience.

Why does anyone care?

Very good question.

David Long, author of the leading study of Lincoln's reelection in 1864, spoke for many when he responded to *Was Lincoln gay?* on a C-SPAN call-in show in 1999 by countering, "If he were, how would it change the Emancipation Proclamation? How would it change the Second Inaugural or the Gettysburg Address?" We have parsed the evidence to the point that we know exactly when Lincoln shared a bed with another man, but as to what he did in bed, we know nothing for certain, other than that he fathered four children with Mary. Is it necessary to look further? If somehow we could know the most intimate details of Lincoln's sexual behavior, of what possible relevance could this be to his place in American history?

To many people, however, the question seems to matter very much. In 1994, after I had moved to America's heartland to join the staff of the Lincoln Museum in Fort Wayne, Indiana, I had dinner one evening with executives from the Lincoln National Corporation, which generously sponsored the museum. In the course of chatter about families and movies, I happened to share an observation that I had read about Disney's recent animated films (*The Lion King, Aladdin, The Little Mermaid*), namely that all the villains are gay. The conversation halted, followed by uncomfortable silence, dark glances in my direction, and a quick change of topic. Note to self: references to homosexuality not appropriate for dinner conversation with this crowd. Skip ahead to ten years later, when Tripp's book came out and the editor of a Fort Wayne newspaper asked me to write a commentary. The piece, headlined "Was Lincoln Gay?" generated a similar reaction on a larger scale, evidenced by angry letters to the editor. It made no difference that the article expressed my view that there was no convincing evidence that Lincoln was gay, nor that I argued that his sexuality did not define him in any case—all that mattered was that the issue had been mentioned in public. How dare anyone do so! The urgency with which some people declared that Lincoln's sexuality should not make any difference suggested that it made a very big difference to them indeed.

Most of the debate over Lincoln's sexual behavior seems to be motivated not by historical evidence but by the desire of both gay and straight people to validate their own sexual tendencies, by claiming that Lincoln must have shared them. They can do this only by imposing on Lincoln and his contemporaries a set of ideas and labels that did not exist then, in an era when people simply did not define themselves by their most private and intimate behaviors or desires. What would Lincoln have said if asked to endorse one such group or the other? He would probably have rejected them all, as groups, and accepted them all as individuals. Lincoln's political message was consistent, whether to native-born Americans who wanted to limit the civil rights of immigrants, to majority Protestants who sought restrictions on minority Catholics, or most of all to European Americans who tried to deny basic human rights to African Americans. Human rights, in Lincoln's view, belonged to people and were not the special property of any classes, groups, or races. As he told a Chicago audience in 1858,

> My friends, I have detained you about as long as I desired to do, and I have only to say, let us discard all this quibbling about this man and the other man—this race and that race and the other race being inferior, and therefore they must be placed in an inferior position—discarding our standard that we have left us. Let us discard all these things, and unite as one people throughout this land, until we shall once more stand up declaring that all men are created equal.[15]

Ah, we're back to Lincoln as a great historical figure again. What was it in his youth that made him great?

It depends whom you ask.

Historians, no matter what we may claim, really don't know. Just as any "psychic" who could really see the future would be picking winning lottery numbers for herself instead of advertising on late-night TV, any historian who really knew the secret of what made Lincoln great would probably have used it to win election to an important office, instead of continuing to teach the Wilmot Proviso to bored sophomores.

You can get some interesting answers to this question by going to the places where Lincoln lived, making what was once described as a "Lincoln pilgrimage."[16] At the Lincoln Boyhood National Memorial, you will learn that it was in southern Indiana that he "grew physically and intellectually into a man," that "the people he knew here and the things he experienced had a profound influence on his life," and that his values and virtues "were all born of this place and this time."[17] If you go to New Salem in Illinois, the film in the Visitors' Center will set you straight: their version of Lincoln arrives from Indiana as a blob of unfinished protoplasm and is shaped for greatness by the people and experiences of New Salem.* Springfield, Illinois, fairly crawls with Lincoln reminders, including the Lincoln home, the Presidential Museum and Library, the Old State Capitol, and the Lincoln-Herndon law office, collectively creating the impression that it was this place, not his obscure rural origins,

*While conducting a seminar in 2002 for a group of historically costumed volunteers at New Salem, I asked them to name the most important events in Lincoln's life. The death of Ann

that made Lincoln great. Of course, had he never gone beyond practicing law in Springfield, no one today would remember his name.

Lincoln never was much of a lawyer, was he?

Yes he was, contrary to his carefully cultivated image as an "aw shucks," laid-back country lawyer.

In the movie *The Fortune Cookie* (1966), actor Walter Matthau played a shyster lawyer who summarized the traditional view of Lincoln's legal career in four words: "Great president, lousy lawyer." In fact, Lincoln was one of the busiest and most sought-after attorneys in Illinois. The scope of his legal career was not fully recognized until the 1990s, when archivists set out to find whatever documents from Lincoln's cases might still be reposing in courthouses across Illinois. The Lincoln Legal Papers project began with the expectation of finding hundreds or perhaps thousands of records; the final published collection filled three DVDs and included images of more than 96,000 documents, representing more than five thousand cases or other legal matters. Over the twenty-five years that he practiced law, Lincoln (and his partners) handled an average of more than two hundred cases a year, an awesome workload.[18]

The main reason that Matthau's movie character (and many other people) thought so poorly of Lincoln as a lawyer was Lincoln himself. His typical courtroom strategy was to play dumb, conceding point after point, letting his opponent believe that he had him on the run, and then, after giving up what would turn out to be inessential, seizing upon the one key fact or principle that would determine the case. His friend and fellow attorney Leonard Swett observed that "any man who took Lincoln for a simple-minded man would very soon wake up with his back in a ditch."[19]

For example, in *Case v. Snow Bros* (1847), Lincoln represented a man who had sold a plow and a team of oxen to two young brothers. The boys had signed a note for two hundred dollars but refused to pay it. The

---

Rutledge was their first choice, followed by the wrestling match with Jack Armstrong. "What about election to the presidency, the Emancipation Proclamation, or the Gettysburg Address?" I asked them. They agreed that those were important, too.

defendants' lawyer claimed that since the signers were not yet twenty-one years old when they entered the contract, they were not legally responsible for the debt, even though they had received the plow and oxen in return. Lincoln admitted that this was true, that the boys were underage, and that the law clearly absolved them of any responsibility for paying. The case seemed open and shut against Lincoln, until he made his closing statement. "*Gentlemen of the jury,* are you willing to allow these boys to begin life with this shame and disgrace attached to their character? If you are, *I* am not." After quoting Shakespeare on the importance of one's reputation ("Who steals my purse steals trash . . ."), he turned on the opposing counsel. "These poor innocent boys would never have attempted this low villany had it not been for the advice of these lawyers." Then back to the jury: "And now, gentlemen, you have it in *your* power to set these boys right before the world." Without mentioning his own client's name, Lincoln had won his case in five minutes and made the defendants grateful to have lost.[20]

Where did he go to law school?

He didn't.

In the early 1830s, when Lincoln was a young man searching for his identity, there was only one law school west of the Allegheny Mountains. It was Transylvania University, in Lexington, Kentucky, which at the time was actually the largest university in America. In the anti-intellectual climate of the Jacksonian era, the state of Kentucky stopped supporting it, and Lincoln never attended it.

What the typical aspiring lawyer did in Lincoln's day was to apprentice himself to an established law firm and spend a year sweeping the office floor, lighting the coal stove, and absorbing legal knowledge as the partners went about practicing their craft. For Lincoln, a struggling, penniless store clerk with only a year of formal schooling, even a lowly apprenticeship like this was out of reach.

Instead, as Lincoln described his career in the third person, "He studied with nobody."[21] He taught himself, from some law books lent to him by John Todd Stuart, a prominent Springfield attorney he had met during his brief military service in the Black Hawk War. It was characteristic of Lincoln to educate himself, but to his New Salem neighbors it was another example of the peculiarity of the tall Hoosier living in their midst. One of them recalled seeing Lincoln sitting astride a woodpile, book in hand, and asking him what he was studying so hard. "Law," replied Abe. "Great-God-Almighty," was all the neighbor could say.[22]

Years later, when a young man asked him for "the best mode of obtaining a thorough knowledge of the law," Lincoln advised the same course that he had followed: "The mode is very simple, though laborious, and tedious. It is only to get the books, and read, and study them carefully. Begin with Blackstone's Commentaries, and after reading it carefully through, say twice, take up Chitty's Pleading, Greenleaf's Evidence, & Story's Equity &c. in succession. Work, work, work, is the main thing."[23]

How did Lincoln do on his bar exam?

He didn't take one . . .

. . . as lawyers do today. To receive a license to practice law in Illinois then, all you needed was to find members of the bar who would ask you a few questions and then vouch for your legal knowledge and "good moral character." In September 1836, Lincoln was examined in this fashion and admitted to the Illinois bar, and in March 1837 he was listed on the roll of attorneys kept by the clerk of the Illinois Supreme Court.[24]

What kind of law did he practice?

All kinds.

Contracts, torts, corporate law, failure to return rented ox, divorce, murder, seduction, runaway slaves, and so on.

Runaway slaves? I assume he was helping them to get free . . . or did Lincoln represent slaveowners?

Both.

As a lawyer, Lincoln took his clients as he found them. In the 1847 case of *Matson v. Rutherford*, Lincoln represented a slaveholder who had brought his "servants" into the free state of Illinois, where local abolitionists helped them to sue for their freedom. Lincoln argued that their stay in Illinois was only a temporary sojourn that did not invalidate the property rights of their owner, but the court ruled in favor of freedom. In another case, *Bailey v. Cromwell* (1841), Lincoln successfully defended a young woman against being sold into slavery.

What's his most famous case?

The "almanac trial" . . .

. . . although it was not particularly important at the time, except to those involved. In 1858, Lincoln defended Duff Armstrong, son of his old wrestling rival Jack Armstrong, in a murder trial. One night Duff and his buddies had been out drinking, a fight started, somebody hit somebody else on the head with something, and suddenly there's a dead body on the ground. A prosecution witness said that he saw young Armstrong strike the fatal blow, and under cross-examination from Lincoln testified that he was able to see the event in the moonlight. Lincoln then produced an almanac showing that the witness was wrong about that detail, because the moon was too low in the sky at the time of the murder to have given much light. This discredited the witness in the eyes of the jury, and Armstrong was acquitted.[25]

Overlooked in the cleverness of Lincoln's tactics is that they were used to free a man who almost surely had committed the murder in question. This was not unethical on Lincoln's part, as the duty of a lawyer is to provide zealous representation for his or her clients, not to judge their guilt or innocence; the judge and jury do that. Lincoln thus could (and did) represent slave and slaveholder, murderer and crime victim, penniless widow and giant railroad corporation, in the course of his career. As a lawyer, he was a "hired gun," not an ideologue.

This instrumentalist view of the legal profession remains common today, especially among conscience-stricken lawyers returning home after a long day of representing corporate interests at the expense of society, but it's not particularly heroic. American popular culture does not have much room for lawyers as heroes, but we sometimes see them as underdogs fighting for justice and the greater good, not just for their paying clients: Perry Mason, Atticus Finch, Erin Brockovich (if paralegals count). There have been many attempts to fit Abraham Lincoln into this mold, starting with his longtime law partner Herndon, who claimed that Lincoln was not at his best unless convinced of the justice of his client's cause.

It is clear that Lincoln did place a high value on social order (see the Lyceum speech), and there are a number of examples of Lincoln urging clients to settle rather than sue or simply refusing to take bad cases. In one case, he told a prospective client that he could win his six-hundred-dollar case for him and in the process "set a whole neighborhood at loggerheads, [and] distress a widowed mother and her six fatherless children," but "some things legally right are not morally right." The client was sent home with the advice to "try your hand at making six hundred dollars in some other way."[26] Lincoln the lawyer was clearly more than just a hired gun, but as the almanac trial suggests, he could also do a pretty good job even with a client he must have known to be guilty.

What was his most important case?

He had two cases that had a substantial effect on the way people lived . . .

. . . neither related to slavery. They both involved the "transportation revolution" of the early nineteenth century, when the combination of steamboats, trains, and canals dramatically reduced the time and cost of travel in America. By 1850, farmers in the Midwest could sell their grain profitably as far away as New York City. The Jeffersonian ideal of the self-sufficient yeoman farmer (like Thomas Lincoln) gave way to ever-growing markets that encouraged planters to raise a single staple crop (wheat in the Midwest, cotton in the South) and buy everything they needed with the proceeds.

Lincoln contributed to this development by representing the Rock Island Bridge Co. when it was sued by the owners of the steamboat *Effie Afton.* The plaintiffs' vessel had crashed into the bridge, which they claimed was an obstruction to navigation. It was also the first railroad bridge across the Mississippi River, and the case was in essence a contest to determine the respective rights of steamboats and railroads in the opening of the West. The railroads (and Lincoln) won when the judge dismissed the case after the jury failed to reach a verdict.[27] In *Illinois Central Rail Road v. McLean County,* Lincoln again represented a railroad, this time against an Illinois county that sought to tax the company's land. The railroad claimed that the state legislature had granted it a charter that exempted it from county taxes. Lincoln won again, when the state supreme court upheld the constitutionality of such a charter.[28] A defeat in either case could have dramatically slowed the expansion of rail transportation across Illinois.

The first half of the nineteenth century has traditionally been described by legal historians as the golden age of American law,[29] a time when far-seeing judges adapted the ancient rules of the English common law in new and creative ways to fit the rapid technological and social changes of the rapidly growing United States. In that sense, it was an ideal time for a lawyer like Lincoln, who was not steeped in legal theory but who applied himself vigorously to learning the facts of each case and to fashioning arguments based on logic, fairness, and common sense as much as on precedent. He expressed his philosophy of the lawyer's role in society in a lecture for law students that he prepared in the 1850s: "Discourage litigation. Persuade your neighbors to compromise whenever you can. Point out to them how the nominal winner is often the real loser—in fees, expenses, and waste of time. As a peacemaker the lawyer has a superior opportunity of being a good man. There will still be business enough."[30]

Did he make a lot of money as a lawyer?

On the *McLean County* case he did.

Lincoln asked for five thousand dollars from the Illinois Central for his efforts, at a time when the average American worker made about a dollar a day. This was the largest fee Lincoln ever received for a case, far more than the five dollars he often charged for minor matters, but still a bargain price for the railroad, which, had it lost, would have been vulnerable to property taxes levied by every county where it had tracks. The Illinois Central nevertheless balked at paying Lincoln, and he had to sue for his fee. In 1857, he took his wife with him to New York City, where he hoped to collect on his judgment. The Lincolns enjoyed their trip, stopping on the way for sightseeing at Niagara Falls, but he still didn't get his money. Further legal action finally persuaded the railroad to cough up $4,800, deducting a retainer that Lincoln had already received.[31] It was just in time, as the Panic of 1857 struck in the fall, sending the economy into a tailspin and leaving many corporations (including the Illinois Central) unable to pay their debts at all.

So he took Mary to New York. Is it true that the real reason he spent so much time at the office and "riding the circuit" was to get away from her?

The real reason that he rode the circuit so often was that that's where the cases were.

Rural Illinois was too thinly settled to have courthouses in every town, and it was logistically impractical to bring litigants and witnesses halfway across the state for every case, so twice a year the court came to the people. From 1839 to the spring of 1860 (except for two years when he served in Congress), Lincoln joined the lawyers and judges who traveled through the dozen or so counties of the Eighth Judicial Circuit every spring and fall.[32] At first they literally rode the circuit on horseback, but as better roads were built they were able to ride in buggies, carriages, and (by the mid-1850s) railroad cars. However they traveled, their coming was an event. When the court came to a town, people flocked to the tavern or other building that would serve as a temporary courthouse, the lawyers met with anyone who had legal business to transact, the judge banged his gavel, and court was in session.

This was Lincoln's element. His stories and jokes put juries at ease, and his logic and fairness won them to his side. The evenings were filled with storytelling at the local inn. At night the lawyers crowded two or three deep into whatever beds might be available (except for 300-pound Judge David Davis, who was usually allowed a bed to himself).

Most lawyers went home from the circuit on weekends if time permitted. Lincoln did too in the first years of his marriage but later stopped. Herndon, who had no use for Mrs. Lincoln, theorized that Abraham had an unhappy home life, but this was only theory, as Mrs. Lincoln (who had no use for Herndon) never once invited him into the Lincoln home. Lincoln's long absences may have been partly motivated by strains at home, but there were positive reasons for spending as much time on the circuit as possible. One was politics, as the circuit offered Lincoln an unparalleled opportunity to meet potential voters throughout the state and to find out what they were thinking. The foremost reason, however, was money. Lincoln was not greedy, but he never ceased to put economic distance between himself and the meager log cabin existence that his father led, and he was strongly motivated to try to provide Mary with the kind of comforts to which she was accustomed.

About Mary Todd Lincoln: Was she crazy?

Not when she met Abraham, certainly.

The Mary Todd who moved to Springfield in 1839 at the age of twenty was well educated, ambitious, not unattractive, sophisticated, politically aware, and a good dancer. There weren't a lot of women like her back in New Salem. As Mrs. Lincoln, she would impart to the former rail-splitter a veneer of refinement that would help him to reach the White House. Someone had to teach him not to use his own knife for the butter or how to answer the front door by coming downstairs instead of poking his head out of the second-story window and shouting to visitors below.

At the same time, she was emotionally high-strung and ill-prepared to handle the many tragedies that life had in store for her. The first of these was the death of the Lincolns' second son, Eddie, at the age of three in 1850. Perhaps she found some consolation in the birth of Willie about ten months later, but when he died in 1862, Mary was beyond consoling. She ceased entertaining at the White House for more than a year, and her mental health began to deteriorate, exacerbated by the pressures of life in the fishbowl of wartime Washington. In July 1863 she suffered a blow to the head in a carriage accident that may have affected her emotional stability. By 1865, with the end of the war clearly approaching, she seemed to be recovering gradually. On April 14, she shared a carriage ride with her husband, who spoke of brighter days ahead. "We must *both,* be more cheerful in the future," he urged her, "between the war & the loss of our darling Willie—we have both, been very miserable."[33] That night he was murdered by her side at Ford's Theatre.

Mrs. Lincoln was never the same. Her condition worsened substantially after the death of Tad at the age of seventeen in 1871. Her behavior became more irrational, and her mania for shopping (she bought shawls by the dozen, pairs of gloves by the hundred) spiraled out of control. Finally in 1875, her only surviving son, Robert, had her tried for insanity and committed to a sanitarium, which prompted her to attempt suicide. After a few months she was released and later declared "restored to reason" by a jury, but she found no peace. She went to France for four years, then returned in 1880 to Springfield, where she spent her last days in a darkened room in her sister's home. She died in 1882.[34]

How did Abe and Mary meet?

They met in Springfield, in 1839, possibly at this dance . . .

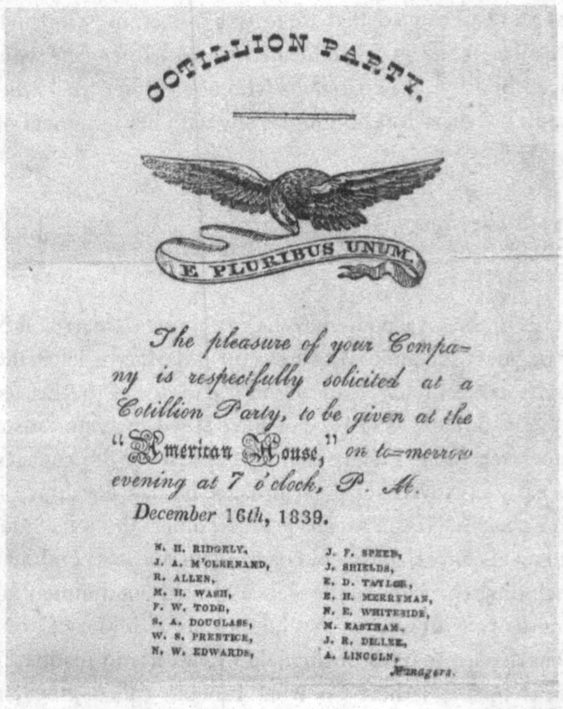

COTILLION PARTY.

E PLURIBUS UNUM.

The pleasure of your Company is respectfully solicited at a Cotillion Party, to be given at the "American House," on to-morrow evening at 7 o'clock, P. M.

December 16th, 1839.

N. H. RIDGELY,
J. A. M'CLERNAND,
R. ALLEN,
M. H. WASH,
F. W. TODD,
S. A. DOUGLASS,
W. S. PRENTICE,
N. W. EDWARDS,
J. F. SPEED,
J. SHIELDS,
E. D. TAYLOR,
E. H. MERRYMAN,
N. E. WHITESIDE,
M. EASTHAM,
J. R. DILLER,
A. LINCOLN,
Managers.

Cotillion invitation, Springfield, 1839. Everyone who was anyone was there, including the new girl in town, Mary Todd. (Courtesy of The Lincoln Museum, Fort Wayne, IN, TLM 4632)

What did she see in him?

Good question.

Her family must have wondered the same thing. She came from aristocracy (Lincoln noted that one *d* was enough for God's name, but not for the Todds), and in Springfield she lived with her sister Elizabeth, who was married to Ninian Edwards, son of the governor of the Illinois Territory. Edwards thought Lincoln was "a mighty Rough man" when he first came to Springfield, and Mrs. Edwards thought that Abraham and Mary were not suitable for each other.[35] Despite their disapproval, which increased after their engagement was broken sometime around January 1, 1841, Mary perceived that there was something worthwhile in the unsophisticated and poorly educated young lawyer. She would later be victimized by liars and charlatans who abused her trust when she was First Lady, but there was nothing wrong with her judgment of character in this case.

Who broke the engagement?

Nobody knows.

Herndon's dramatic account has the couple set to marry on New Year's Day, 1841, but Abraham never shows up and Mary is left standing at the altar (or more accurately, standing in the parlor of the Edwards house, where the wedding was to have occurred).[36] Few historians accept this story, however. Some believe that Lincoln broke the engagement, perhaps as early as November 1840, because he had developed a crush on Matilda Edwards, Ninian's teenage niece; others think that Mary broke it off; but most believe that Lincoln backed out due to a combination of factors, including the same ambivalence toward commitment and lack of self-confidence with women that he showed with Mary Owens, and the imminent departure from Springfield of best friend Joshua Speed, who closed his business there on what Lincoln called "the fatal first of Jan'y."[37]

Whatever the cause, Lincoln was emotionally devastated. He went into a deep depression and found it hard to concentrate on his work. According to Speed, his friends even made sure he didn't have any knives handy in case he felt the urge to end his life. He did not go that far, but he did apparently consider moving to South America. He wrote about his misery to John Todd Stuart, who had been his law partner but now was serving in Congress, telling him that "a change of scene might help me" and that "the matter you speak of on my account, you may attend to as you say." Six weeks later, Stuart wrote to Secretary of State Daniel Webster to recommend that Lincoln be appointed to the post of chargé d'affaires in Bogotá, Colombia (then called New Granada). That would have been a long way to go just to get away from Mary Todd.[38]

How did Abe and Mary get back together?

Mutual friends arranged it . . . and then there was the duel.

Lincoln fought a duel?

Almost.

In 1842, the year after the engagement was broken, he wrote some anonymous letters published in the *Sangamo Journal* that mocked state auditor James Shields, a prominent Democrat. Mary and her friend Julia Jayne tried their hands at writing a similar letter, also anonymously. Shields demanded to know who was insulting him. When he learned that it was Lincoln, he challenged him to a duel. Lincoln took full responsibility for all the letters and said nothing about Mary's involvement, a bit of gallantry that may have helped to bring the couple back together.

Since Shields had issued the challenge, it was up to Lincoln to choose the weapons. Had he been serious about the fight, he might have chosen pistols at ten paces, but instead he selected "cavalry broadswords of the largest size." He also specified that the duel should take place in an area ten feet wide by twelve feet deep, divided by a board that neither contestant could cross. This would make for a pretty silly fight, in which the diminutive Shields would be unable to reach Lincoln, who was much taller. Lincoln actually practiced some sword exercises and later commented, "I could have split him from the crown of his head to the end of his backbone."[39] Proposing the ridiculous spectacle of a Mutt-and-Jeff swordfight may have been Lincoln's way of trying to defuse the situation, but Shields continued to prepare for the duel, which was scheduled to take place across the Mississippi River in Missouri, where the Illinois law against dueling would not apply. Both men actually showed up and were ready to go at it, but their seconds managed to arrange a peaceable last-second settlement.

What did Lincoln write in those letters that was so bad it made Shields want to kill him?

It's not so much what Lincoln said, as how he said it.

The letters were written in dialect by "Aunt Becca of the Lost Townships." In the letter of August 27, Aunt Becca and her neighbor Jeff argue about whether Shields is a Democrat or a Whig, and Jeff points out that "Shields is a fool as well as a liar. With him truth is out of the question, and as for getting a good bright passable lie out of him, you might as well try to strike fire from a cake of tallow." Playing on Shields's well-known vanity, Jeff describes the auditor at a party fighting off a horde of women, begging them, "do, *do* remember, it is not my fault that I am *so* handsome and *so* interesting."[40]

Anonymous-attack journalism like this was common at the time, and Lincoln was good at it. He wrote dozens, perhaps hundreds, of anonymous pieces that ridiculed his political opponents.[41] Lincoln knew how to use words that hurt, and he wasn't shy about doing so, either in print or in person. In 1840, he made a scathing attack on a political opponent, mimicking his voice and gestures, until the victim was reduced to tears, in an incident recalled by Lincoln's friends thereafter as the "skinning of Thomas."[42]

Effective as it was, Lincoln felt bad about the skinning and apologized for it. The near duel with Shields two years later helped him realize that words could have enough power to kill. As time went on and Lincoln experienced more of life's triumphs and tragedies, his language mellowed. He continued to write and speak forcefully and eloquently on the issues, but he refrained from attacking his opponents personally, eventually developing a mature rhetorical style characterized more by charity than by malice.

Was Mary pregnant when she married him?

They were married on November 4, 1842. Robert Todd Lincoln was born August 1, 1843.

You do the math.

FOR FURTHER READING

The Young Eagle: The Rise of Abraham Lincoln (2001), by Kenneth J. Winkle, supplants *Here I Have Lived* (1950), by Paul Angle, as the single book to read about Lincoln's life in Springfield.

For the gay Lincoln hypothesis, C. A. Tripp lays out every scrap of evidence, and then some, in *The Intimate World of Abraham Lincoln* (2005), which also features commentary by historians Jean Baker and

Michael Burlingame. More balanced discussions of Lincoln's relationship with Joshua Speed can be found in David Herbert Donald, *"We Are Lincoln Men": Abraham Lincoln and His Friends* (2003), chapter 2; and Charles B. Strozier, *Lincoln's Quest for Union* (2001 ed.), chapter 2. *Honor's Voice: The Transformation of Abraham Lincoln* (1998), by Douglas Wilson, is indispensable for this period of Lincoln's life.

The most complete source for Lincoln's law career is without question the three-DVD set called *The Law Practice of Abraham Lincoln: Complete Documentary Edition* (2000), edited by Martha L. Benner, Cullom Davis, and a host of others. In addition to images of the actual documents from Lincoln's cases, it contains glossaries, summaries of Lincoln's law practice, sketches of historical figures, maps, illustrations, and other useful material. In terms of books, Mark Steiner, *An Honest Calling: The Law Practice of Abraham Lincoln* (2006), and Brian Dirck, *Lincoln the Lawyer* (2007), are the first on the subject to draw on the Lincoln Legal Papers. Lincoln's most famous trial is detailed in John Evangelist Walsh, *Moonlight: Abraham Lincoln and the Almanac Trial* (2000).

Mary Todd Lincoln is hard to analyze objectively. Historians divide over her on an almost visceral level. I once saw a noted Lincoln scholar privately accost another in a hallway during a conference and launch an angry red-faced attack based on their different views of Mrs. Lincoln.* The two extremes are best represented by Jean Baker's *Mary Todd Lincoln: A Biography* (1987), which gives full credit to her role in Lincoln's political rise and downplays her difficult personality, and Michael Burlingame's *The Inner World of Abraham Lincoln* (1994), which contains an unsympathetic indictment of her many faults. There is room for a new and more balanced biography between these views. Jennifer Fleischner's fascinating dual biography *Mrs. Lincoln and Mrs. Keckly: The Remarkable Story of the Friendship Between a First Lady and a Former Slave* (2003) illuminates Mary's difficult childhood relationships as a source of her later personality issues, while Stephen Berry *House of*

*From anecdotal evidence, there may be a rough correlation between how happy historians have been in their own marriages and their views on the happiness of the Lincolns, but it will take a braver historian than I am to research this point. (Note to Mrs. Prokopowicz: whatever I may have written elsewhere, you know that I believe that the Lincolns were the happiest couple ever.)

Abraham: Lincoln & the Todds, A Family Divided by War (2007), shows that Mary was not the only Todd to inherit from her family's rich store of dysfunctional behaviors. *The Insanity File* (1986), by R. Gerald McMurtry and Mark E. Neely, Jr., details the legal proceedings that Robert brought against his mother, while *Mary Todd Lincoln: Her Life and Letters* (1972), edited by Justin G. Turner and Linda Levitt Turner, allows Mary to speak in her own words. But these must both be supplemented by Jason Emerson, *The Madness of Mary Lincoln* (2007), which draws on previously unknown letters written by Mary and discovered in an attic trunk in 2005.

{ CHAPTER FOUR }

Politician

I have no other [ambition] so great as that of being truly esteemed of my fellow men.

—From Lincoln's first printed political statement, 1832[1]

It's amazing how Lincoln failed at everything he tried but kept on trying, until one day he was elected president. I read about this in "Dear Abby." How did he do it?

You might have seen the same idea on an inspirational billboard that reads . . .

. . . "Failed, failed, failed. And then . . ." with a picture of Lincoln looking presidential.

Unfortunately, the oft-quoted litany of Lincoln's failures is essentially bogus.

Here's how it appears on a poster available in various museums and bookstores:

Lost job in 1832
Defeated for state legislature in 1832
Failed in business in 1833
Elected to state legislature in 1834
Sweetheart died in 1835
Had nervous breakdown in 1836
Defeated for Speaker in 1838
Defeated for nomination for Congress in 1843
Elected to Congress in 1846
Lost renomination in 1848
Rejected for land officer in 1849
Defeated for U.S. Senate in 1854

Defeated for nomination for Vice President in 1856
Again defeated for U.S. Senate in 1858
Elected President in 1860

Now let's look at the record:

"Lost job in 1832." Not true. There's a kernel of truth inside this myth, as there is in most myths, in that Lincoln's career path was neither straight nor steady when he was a young man, but this statement gives the false impression that Lincoln was laid off or, worse still, fired. In fact, he didn't have a regular job to lose in 1832, which is one reason he joined the state militia when it was mobilized for the Black Hawk War that year.

"Defeated for state legislature in 1832." True. Since he was away on military service, he couldn't campaign for office. Even so, he did very well in his own precinct (New Salem), receiving 277 out of 300 votes. And while he did not win the election for state legislature in 1832, he did win another election that year. When the men of New Salem organized themselves into a militia company, they chose their officers by majority vote, a distinctly unmilitary procedure that would persist in American volunteer regiments until well after the outbreak of the Civil War. To his great pleasure, Lincoln was elected captain, the highest rank in the company. In 1860, after he had been nominated for president, he looked back on that first electoral victory and wrote that he "has not since had any success in life which gave him so much satisfaction."[2]

"Failed in business in 1833." True. The Lincoln and Berry store "winked out," leaving Lincoln deep in debt.

"Elected to state legislature in 1834." True, but hardly a failure.

"Sweetheart died in 1835." Whether she was his "sweetheart" is not certain, but it is true that Ann Rutledge died in 1835. Ann's death may have been a tragedy, but it was hardly a failure on Lincoln's part, as he was neither her doctor nor her bodyguard.

"Had nervous breakdown in 1836." What was once popularly called a "nervous breakdown" would today be described as a "major depressive episode," which is what Lincoln experienced shortly after Ann's death (in 1835, not 1836). Since the list of Lincoln's "failures" first began to appear in the middle of the twentieth century, medical understanding of the nature of depression has greatly increased. Today, severe depression is viewed as a treatable form of illness, not a moral or mental failing. In Lincoln's case, one author has gone so far as to argue, with some persua-

siveness, that his bouts of depression were actually a source of strength.[3] If we are going to include medical issues like Lincoln's 1835 depression on a list of his failures, we might as well add the time he was kicked by a horse in 1819, or his 1862 foot operation.

"Defeated for Speaker in 1838." This is a good example of the selective use of historical facts to prove whatever point you want. It's true that Lincoln was defeated in the election for Speaker of the House in 1838, but consider what this implies. First, that Lincoln was reelected to the state legislature in 1836 (success) and 1838 (success), and second, that he was so well regarded that his party, the Whigs, nominated him for the office of speaker (another success). Since the Whigs were the minority party in the Illinois General Assembly, Lincoln had no chance of winning on a party line vote, but this was hardly a personal defeat. A more balanced look at Lincoln's legislative career to this point would have to include his major success in engineering the passage of a bill to move the state capital from Vandalia to Springfield in 1837.

"Defeated for nomination for Congress in 1843." The list lightly skips over more of Lincoln's successes: starting his law career in 1837, reelection to the legislature in 1840, and marriage to the wealthy and sophisticated Mary Todd in 1842 (which certainly looked like a success at the time). By that year, Lincoln was ready to move up in politics, setting his sights on Congress. He thus chose not to run for the state house in 1842 and instead let it be known that he hoped to be the Whig candidate for Congress in 1844, telling one correspondent, "Now if you should hear any one say that Lincoln don't want to go to Congress, I wish you as a personal friend of mine, would tell him you have reason to believe he is mistaken. The truth is, I would like to go very much."[4]

The idea of seeking a party nomination was relatively new for Lincoln. The Founding Fathers had not anticipated the formation of political parties, deriding them as "factions" that would promote special interests rather than the common good. When the Whig Party came into being to oppose the policies of President Andrew Jackson in the early 1830s, its members initially clung to the antique notion that voters should choose the best candidate in each election, regardless of his party affiliation. Jackson's followers had meanwhile developed the concept of party discipline, which meant that they chose a single Democrat to run for each office, and then rallied behind him regardless of his personal qualifications. In the 1836 presidential election, for example, four Whig candidates split their party's votes against Democrat Martin Van Buren, who sailed into the White House with ease.*

By the 1840s, the Whigs had come to the realization that they could hope to win only by using the same tactics. In Illinois, Democrats had a comfortable majority throughout the state, with the exception of the Seventh Congressional District, which included Lincoln's own Sangamon County. From 1839 to 1843, the area was represented in Congress by a Whig, John Todd Stuart (Lincoln's first law partner and his wife's cousin), but only by a slender margin; in 1838, Stuart beat Stephen Douglas by a few dozen votes out of a total of 36,000.[5] If the Whigs were going to hold even a single Congressional seat from Illinois, it would have to be the Seventh, and they would have to organize behind a single candidate.

Unfortunately for Lincoln, two other prominent Whigs also coveted the chance to replace Stuart. One was Edward Baker, a friend after whom Lincoln would name his second son in 1846. When Sangamon County Whigs chose Baker, Lincoln as a delegate from the county found himself obliged to vote at the district nominating convention for his rival and wrote that it made him feel "like a fellow who is made groomsman to the man what has cut him out, and is marrying his own dear 'gal.' "[6] The winner of the nomination turned out to be John J. Hardin, another cousin of Mary Todd. Rather than risk losing the seat through internal conflict, the three Whigs agreed to rotate the nomination among themselves, with the next turn going to Baker, and the one after that to Lincoln. It is thus true that he did not win the nomination for Congress in 1843, but his "defeat" was consensual, and with the promise that he would receive the nomination in 1846, which he did.

"Elected to Congress in 1846." True, and of course not a failure. Although Hardin attempted to renege on the deal and run again, Lincoln got the nomination. It was in this election that his opponent played the religion card and forced Lincoln to explain his unorthodox beliefs, but he won anyway.

"Lost renomination in 1848." Lincoln chose not to seek the Whig nomination in 1848, because it was not his turn. Keeping his word was not a failure.

*The Whigs put forward three regional candidates (Daniel Webster for the Northeast, William Henry Harrison for the West, and Hugh Lawson White for the South); South Carolina voted for a Whig (Willie Mangum) of its own choosing.

Had he run again, it is true that he probably would not have won. The big issue during Lincoln's term in Congress was the war with Mexico, which had begun in 1846.* Lincoln shared the Whig Party's view that the war was an unjustified land grab engineered by President James K. Polk, largely for the purpose of expanding the institution of slavery to the west. Lincoln argued that the president had created imaginary reasons to go to war, including an incident between Mexican and American soldiers that Lincoln insisted had taken place on Mexican soil, and thus was not an act of aggression that justified retaliation by the United States. When David Wilmot of Pennsylvania offered his "Proviso" that would have prohibited slavery in any territory gained during the war, Lincoln voted for it repeatedly (more than forty times in all, he once claimed). Even though Lincoln was careful to vote in favor of bills to provide supplies to the soldiers fighting in Mexico, drawing a distinction between opposing the war and supporting the troops, it is unlikely that his prowar constituents would have sent him back for another term.

"Rejected for land officer in 1849." True. Since he was not running for reelection in 1848, Lincoln devoted himself to the Whig presidential campaign of Zachary Taylor. The Whigs had won the White House only once, with General William Henry Harrison in 1840, and in 1848 they cynically returned to the tactic of nominating a military hero, in this case one from a war they deplored. Taylor had no known political views and apparently had never even voted, but Lincoln valiantly tried to turn this into an asset, arguing that having no policies meant that Taylor could simply reflect the will of the people:

> The people say to Gen: Taylor "If you are elected, shall we have a national bank?" He answers "*Your* will, gentlemen, not *mine*" "What about the Tariff?" "Say yourselves." "Shall our rivers and harbours be improved?" "Just as you please" "If you desire a bank, an alteration of the tariff, internal improvements, any, or all, I will not hinder you; if you do not desire them, I will not attempt to force them on you."[7]

Having thus prostituted his dignity with such nonsensical arguments for the sake of his party, Lincoln hoped to be rewarded with a lucrative

*Under the peculiar rules of the time, the Thirtieth Congress (the one in which Lincoln sat) was elected in November 1846 but not seated until December 1847.

patronage job after Taylor won. He let it be known that he wanted to be commissioner of the General Land Office, but Taylor instead gave the position to Justin Butterfield, a Whig who had done little on behalf of the presidential campaign.

Lincoln was chagrined, but when he became president he, too, would follow the policy of bestowing more gifts on his enemies than on his friends, hoping to win over the former while trusting the latter to stand by him anyway. Taylor, incidentally, did not leave Lincoln entirely out in the cold. He offered him the post of governor of the remote Oregon Territory, but Mary would have none of it.[8]

"Defeated for U.S. Senate in 1854." Until 1913, most United States senators were chosen by their state legislatures, not elected by the people. Lincoln ran successfully for the Illinois state legislature in 1854, then declined the office so that he could be chosen senator by that body in 1855, when the term of Democrat James Shields (Lincoln's old dueling opponent) expired.

By 1855, Lincoln's political career was no longer simply a matter of personal ambition. One year earlier, Democratic Senator Stephen A. Douglas had thrown the country into an uproar with his Kansas-Nebraska Act, which brutally ripped the scab of compromise from the body politic to reveal the ugly wound of slavery festering within. The Kansas-Nebraska Act organized an enormous piece of Western land (including much of what would become the Dakotas, Wyoming, Montana, and Colorado, as well as Kansas and Nebraska) into two federal territories. Both territories would be open to slaveholders, with the idea that at some point in the future the settlers would decide whether to join the Union as free states or slave states. This was "popular sovereignty," Douglas's policy for solving the problem of whether the West would become slave or free.

The Kansas-Nebraska Act shocked many Americans, Abraham Lincoln included, who thought the problem of slavery in the West was already solved. The Missouri Compromise of 1820 had provided that within the territory acquired by the Louisiana Purchase, slavery was prohibited north of the 36° 30' line (the same line as the southern boundary of Missouri). All the territory covered by the Kansas-Nebraska Act was Louisiana Purchase land and had been free of slavery for thirty-four years when Douglas proposed his act, which expressly repealed the Missouri Compromise and reopened the question of slavery in the West.

"We were thunderstruck and stunned" was Lincoln's reaction to the news that slavery, which he had thought permanently confined to the South, was now to be allowed into a great portion of the West.[9] When the Illinois state senate prepared to elect a new U.S. senator in 1855, Lincoln was the choice of a coalition of former Whigs and disaffected Democrats who called themselves "Anti-Nebraska" and were determined to send an opponent of slavery's expansion to Washington. After the first ballot was counted, the results showed Lincoln leading Shields 45 to 41, with five of the six remaining votes going to Lyman Trumbull, an Anti-Nebraska Democrat.

Unfortunately, Lincoln needed a majority rather than a plurality to win, and on the ballots that followed his number fell, while the Democrats (who replaced Shields with Joel Matteson on the seventh ballot) and Trumbull both gained. At any point in the balloting, a combination of Lincoln's and Trumbull's votes would have been enough to win, but Trumbull and his followers were too true to their Democratic roots ever to vote for an old Whig like Lincoln, even if they shared the same Anti-Nebraska views. When Lincoln saw that he was not going to win, but that Trumbull still had a chance to defeat the Democrats if all the Anti-Nebraska voters united behind him, he asked his followers to do so, and Trumbull was elected. Lincoln was disappointed, and Mrs. Lincoln never again spoke to Mrs. Trumbull (the former Julia Jayne, who had been a bridesmaid at her wedding), but the U.S. Senate gained an important antislavery voice, thanks to Lincoln's sacrifice. Does this constitute a "failure"?

"Defeated for nomination for Vice President in 1856." Lincoln did not attend the Republican Party's first national convention in 1856, and was later surprised to hear that his name had been placed in nomination for the vice presidency. Rather than a failure, the nomination was a sign of his growing national reputation.

"Again defeated for U.S. Senate in 1858." This was the famous campaign in which Lincoln debated Stephen Douglas. In the fall elections for state legislators, Lincoln's Republican Party outpolled Douglas's Democrats, but not every seat was up for reelection, and the surviving Democratic majority in the state senate chose to send Douglas back to Washington. Lincoln was defeated, but the campaign brought him national attention as the obscure attorney who dared to challenge the "Little Giant" on the issue of slavery.

Lincoln's rival, the "Little Giant": Stephen A. Douglas (Courtesy of The Lincoln Museum, Fort Wayne, IN, TLM 65)

"Elected President in 1860." Success at last, according to Dear Abby, but as Lincoln allegedly said to friends after his election, "Well, boys, your troubles are over now . . . mine have just begun."[10]

There is no question that Lincoln had his share of failures, but by 1860 he was the leading lawyer in Illinois and a respected political figure whose successes far outweighed his setbacks. The "Lincoln's Failures" list retains its popularity not because it is an accurate summary of Lincoln's life, but for two other reasons. First, it's comforting to think that however much of a failure your miserable life may have been so far, the next phone call may be from the Republican National Committee asking you to run for president. Isn't that how it happened to Lincoln?[11]

Second, in its distorted way the failures list reflects a real element of Lincoln's character. He was extraordinarily determined to accomplish something memorable in his life and would not be satisfied by anything less. Before he became president, Lincoln was hardly a failure by ordinary standards, but he did not set ordinary standards for himself.

So he considered himself a failure before he became president?

Yes . . .

. . . at least in 1856, when he compared his life to that of Stephen Douglas, who had been his political rival over the past twenty-two years. They had both begun their careers as obscure state politicians, but Douglas had gone on to become the most famous political figure in the country, while "with *me,* the race of ambition has been a failure—a flat failure." Lincoln envied Douglas's prominent place and wrote, "I would rather stand on that eminence, than wear the richest crown that ever pressed a monarch's brow."[12]

Is that why he went into politics in the first place? For attention and fame?

Yes, but not just any kind of fame.

Lincoln never made any secret about his personal goal of public attention, but he was always careful to specify how he wanted to get that attention. In his first published political statement, written at the age of twenty-three in connection with his first try for office, Lincoln wrote, "Every man is said to have his peculiar ambition. Whether it be true or not, I can say for one that I have no other so great as that of being truly esteemed of my fellow men, *by rendering myself worthy of their esteem*" (italics added).[13] Celebrity alone was not the point of Lincoln's ambition, but celebrity for doing something worthwhile. After twenty-four years had passed, without apparent success, Lincoln continued to yearn for the kind of eminence that Stephen Douglas had achieved, but still he qualified his desire. He wanted fame more than "the richest crown," but only if that fame were "so reached, that the oppressed of my species, might have shared with me in the elevation." Douglas had achieved his fame in part by stepping on the backs of "the oppressed of my species," mocking African Americans as inferior and openly appealing to the racism of white voters. Lincoln's ambition was, in the words of William Herndon, a "little engine that knew no rest," but it did know its moral limits.[14]

Wasn't Mary Lincoln the real source of Lincoln's ambition? I thought that he was kind of laid-back, but she kept pushing him.

No, that was Ruth Gordon . . .

. . . the actress better known for winning an Oscar in *Rosemary's Baby* (1968) and starring in the cult film *Harold and Maude* (1971). She debuted on screen as Mary Todd Lincoln in the 1940 production of *Abe Lincoln in Illinois*, in which she played Mary as an ambitious shrew who pushed her reluctant husband into running for office. History rarely has a chance against a well-crafted Hollywood story, and today the public image of Mary Lincoln (as well as the notion that Abe had Raymond Massey's deep voice) owes a lot to this movie.

Mary was ambitious, to be sure, and at least one of Lincoln's contemporaries (John Todd Stuart, Mary's cousin and Abraham's first law partner) claimed that Mary supplied the "will and ambition" for Lincoln, who "needed driving." But Stuart was also quoted as describing Lincoln as "a kind of vegetable" who never had bowel movements, and for whom "the pores of his flesh acted as an appropriate organ for such Evacuations," so you may want to consider the source.[15]

Lincoln's early writings, predating his introduction to Mary Todd, show no lack of ambition. Take a look, for example, at his first substantial public speech, an address to the Young Men's Lyceum of Springfield in 1838. The ostensible subject of the speech was "The Perpetuation of Our Political Institutions," but Lincoln's real (if unintended) subject seems to have been himself. He identified the biggest threat to America's political institutions not as foreign invasion but as the rise of a "man possessed of the loftiest genius, coupled with ambition sufficient to push it to its utmost stretch," who would "at some time, spring up among us." Neither Lincoln nor his listeners imagined at the time that he was talking about himself; most historians believe that Lincoln was giving a partisan political speech, although they disagree over whether he expected his listeners to identify his hypothetical figure, who "thirsts and burns for distinction" as Andrew Jackson, Stephen A. Douglas, or some other evil Democrat. Perhaps because of the sheer absurdity of the idea that he himself would one day be compared to "an Alexander, a Caesar, or a Napoleon," Lincoln felt free to describe this unnamed "towering genius" in terms that would turn out to fit his own character: "Distinction will be his paramount object," not power or wealth. He would prefer to do good rather than harm, although at the last (unlike Lincoln) he would resort to any means necessary to gain the fame he craves, "whether at the expense of emancipating slaves, or enslaving freemen."[16]

What did Lincoln do in the Illinois legislature, if he was so ambitious?

Not much, actually.

He spoke of education as "the most important subject which we as a people can be engaged in," for instance, but didn't promote any significant educational legislation.[17] His biggest achievement was getting the state capital moved to Springfield. He also worked hard to pass a series of "internal improvements" bills that would have created a web of railroads and canals across Illinois, funded by bonds issued by the state bank. Unfortunately, the internal improvement scheme was wildly unrealistic. The state issued more than ten million dollars' worth of bonds, at a time when its annual revenue was not in six figures. The state bank eventually collapsed.

What Lincoln really accomplished in his years in the state legislature was to learn how things got done in a democracy. The bills he wrote were nuts-and-bolts legislation, like "An Act to Authorize Samuel Musick to Build a Toll Bridge."[18] He learned the necessity of compromise and also its limits. He became a strong advocate of party discipline and loyalty, which harnessed powerless individuals into a formidable team. He became the acknowledged leader of the Whigs in the statehouse and showed his willingness to do whatever was necessary to advance his party's program.

Didn't he once jump out of a window or a trap door or something when he was a legislator?

Yes, both, but he would thank you not to mention it.

In 1840, the Whigs' grandiose plans to build canals and railroads across Illinois were in ruins, victim of the economic downturn that historians call the Panic of 1837. The Democrats in the state legislature, who had opposed the plan, now had an opportunity to destroy one of the most important elements in the Whig plan for centralized economic development, the State Bank of Illinois. Previous legislation had specified that the state bank would be required to pay its debts in gold instead of paper money, starting with the end of the next legislative session. The bank did not have nearly enough gold on hand to meet its obligations, so the requirement to pay specie was tantamount to the ruin of the bank. The Whigs thought that they had until March 1841, when the regular legislative session normally ended, to find a solution, but the Democrats cleverly moved to adjourn the legislature in December 1840, which would trigger the bank's demise, after which they could immediately begin a new session.

There was only one way that Lincoln and his fellow Whigs could find to stop the Democratic majority from passing a motion to adjourn: don't show up. With the Whigs absent, there would be no quorum. The Democratic Speaker sent the sergeant-at-arms into the streets and saloons of Springfield to round up any nearby Whig legislators, while Lincoln and two comrades sat in the back of the room making sure that their strategy was working. Whatever satisfaction they felt at having pulled off their parliamentary trick evaporated when the Speaker recognized them as present and announced that a quorum had been met. Lincoln and his fellow Whig enforcers quickly tried to leave, and finding the chamber doors locked, resorted to climbing out of a window and dropping to the ground. Their self-defenestration was in vain, however, as the motion to adjourn passed, with the predicted consequences for the state bank.

Lincoln was afterward embarrassed by what he had done and did not speak of it.[19] He did not mind having people make fun of his appearance (and indeed he frequently told stories about it himself), but he was sensitive about having his conduct made to appear ridiculous. It was a trait that would ultimately cost him his life: cartoonists mocked the disguise he wore on the way to Washington in 1861 in response to an assassination threat, and from that point he refused to take even the most basic security precautions.

The trap door incident, as described by Herndon, was more heroic if equally undignified. In 1839, Lincoln's friend Edward Baker was speaking in a Springfield courtroom, located directly below the law office of Stuart and Lincoln, when his rhetoric provoked the crowd to the point of violence. Suddenly the trap door in the ceiling over Baker's head opened, Lincoln dropped through, and by the force of his personality (and the threat of throwing a stone pitcher that was handy) persuaded the crowd to let Baker continue his speech.[20]

Wait a minute—I've been to the Old State Capitol in Springfield, and the House chamber windows are at least twenty feet from the ground. How could he have survived that fall?

In December 1840, the Old State Capitol was not yet even the new State Capitol.

The Old State Capitol in Springfield. When Lincoln was a member, the legislature met on the second floor. (Courtesy of The Lincoln Museum, Fort Wayne, IN, TLM 613)

It was still under construction, and the legislature was meeting temporarily at the First Methodist Church, a few blocks away. There was a drop of about five feet from the meeting room's windowsills to the ground, which gave a local Democratic newspaper the chance to tease Lincoln about having legs so long that he didn't have to jump.

You keep mentioning that Lincoln was a Whig. When did he become a Republican?

In 1856.

Was he the founder of the Republican Party?

No . . .

. . . he was a loyal Whig and stayed with the party later than many after it began to implode in the mid-1850s. In 1855, Joshua Speed asked his old friend where he now stood, and Lincoln replied, "I think I am a whig; but others say there are no whigs."[21] He waited some time to see where the chips would fall before declaring himself a Republican.

What happened to the Whigs?

For the full answer, curl up with Michael Holt's *The Rise and Fall of the American Whig Party,* which in 1,248 pages will tell you all you want to know.[22]

The short answer is that in the 1850s, neither major political party was willing to take a stand expressly for or against the further expansion of slavery. The Democrats tried to have it both ways with Stephen Douglas's theory of popular sovereignty and eventually splintered into two factions in 1860. Between 1852 and 1856, the Whigs simply dissolved. Like other large political parties, then as now, the Whigs were a conglomerate of various interest groups, each of which looked to the party to promote its cause. When things were going well, these groups were willing to put aside their own interests temporarily for the good of the party, expecting that their turns would come. By 1854, however, it was clear that Northern "Conscience Whigs" who opposed slavery and Southern "Cotton Whigs" who supported it no longer had enough in common politically to sustain the process of compromise and mutual sacrifice that gave the party its cohesion. Two years later, the Whigs were in ruins, unable to put up an independent candidate for president.*

If he were alive today, what party would Lincoln belong to?

The Whigs, of course . . .

. . . assuming that if we could bring Lincoln back to life, we could also resurrect the party to which he belonged for most of his career In an 1859 campaign autobiography, Lincoln described himself as "always a whig in politics."[23]

But whenever someone asks this question, they are not looking for a smart-aleck answer about the Whigs. If you're a Democrat, you want to hear that Lincoln would be a Democrat today, based on the party's advocacy of civil rights since the 1960s; if you're a Republican, you want to hear that your party's icon would still belong to the GOP. Everyone wants Lincoln on his or her side, including historians. Allen Guelzo, a Rockefeller Republican, was sure in 2000 that Lincoln would have voted for the GOP in the previous election; Harold Holzer, a liberal, was equally certain that Lincoln's self-proclaimed "conservatism" consisted of views that would align him with the Democrats of the twenty-first century. As the longtime Illinois senator Everett Dirksen once said, everyone wants to "get right with . . . Lincoln."[24]

The problem is that since the mid-nineteenth century, America's major political parties have to a large extent exchanged philosophies, like the two brawling Irishmen who wrestled themselves into each other's overcoats in a story Lincoln once told. This is particularly the case in economics, which then as now lay at the core of most political issues. Lincoln believed strongly in free-market capitalism as the economic system that would best reward individual effort, even if it meant that not all would necessarily prosper. To a New England audience in 1860 he said, "I take it that it is best for all to leave each man free to acquire property as fast as he can. Some will get wealthy. I don't believe in a law to prevent a

*Former Whig Millard Fillmore was nominated by the Southern wing of the "Know-Nothing" American Party and received the votes of most former Whigs in the South. Most Northern ex-Whigs voted Republican.

man from getting rich; it would do more harm than good." At the heart of his vision of America was the opportunity that it provided for the individual to rise according to his talents and efforts, just as he had risen from "a hired laborer, mauling rails, at work on a flat-boat—just what might happen to any poor man's son!" to a comfortable life as a prosperous lawyer and, eventually, to the presidency of the United States.[25]

Thus far, nothing to get Abe kicked out of the Bohemian Club today. Lincoln, however, was not a laissez-faire conservative who believed that nothing more was necessary than to "leave each man free to acquire property."[26] Freedom was a necessary starting condition, but beyond that Lincoln held the orthodox Whig view that government should take an active part in the economy, for example by building canals or railroads, where private capital was not adequate to do the job. As president he put this philosophy into action on July 1, 1862, when he signed an act giving millions of tax dollars and thousands of acres of public land to railroad companies in order to encourage them to build a transcontinental railroad from the Mississippi to the Pacific. "The legitimate object of government," he once wrote, "is to do for a community of people, whatever they need to have done, but can not do, *at all,* or can not, *so well do,* for themselves—in their separate, and individual capacities."[27] Lincoln was not single-handedly responsible for the massive expansion of the federal government during his administration (the Civil War had something to do with it), but he was sympathetic to the idea of government as an agent of economic progress.

In contrast, the central tenet of the Democratic Party in the nineteenth century was a Jeffersonian fear of power, whether concentrated in government, business, or the military, because it would lead to oppression of the individual. The issue that most clearly defined the Democrats at the outset of Lincoln's political career was the fate of the Bank of the United States, a bank chartered by Congress in 1816. The bank and its branches served as a rudimentary national banking system, facilitating transactions between merchants in distant parts of the country, but Democratic president Andrew Jackson saw it as a sinister hotbed of corruption that allowed Philadelphia bankers to enrich themselves at the expense of honest farmers from the South and West. He vetoed the rechartering of the bank in 1832, leaving the country without a national currency (a role that had been filled to some extent by the bank's notes) and inspiring his opponents to form a political party (the Whigs) dedicated to his overthrow and the restoration of a national bank and high tariffs.*

When the Republican Party came into existence in the 1850s to oppose the expansion of slavery, it consisted of people who had been Whigs, Democrats, Know-Nothings, Free Soilers, and other political odds and ends, all with different views on economic issues. Before long, however, Whiggish ideas won out and the Republicans became the party of strong government action to boost the economy, including high protective tariffs and public investment in infrastructure. Former Whigs like Lincoln saw government as a tool to empower the individual. Indeed, according to Lincoln, the "leading object" of government was "to lift artificial weights from all shoulders—to clear the paths of laudable pursuit for all—to afford all, an unfettered start, and a fair chance, in the race of life." This dovetailed neatly with the Republicans' antislavery sentiment. African Americans might not necessarily be entitled to full political and social rights, Lincoln argued, but our Declaration of Independence states that every human being is entitled at least to "life, liberty, and the pursuit of happiness," with "pursuit of happiness" meaning the opportunity to improve one's economic status. Slavery was wrong because it took away not just life and liberty but the opportunity to rise in society as Lincoln had done: "I want every man to have the chance—and I believe a black man is entitled to it—in which he *can* better his condition."[28]

So today, WWLD? The evolution of political and social issues since Lincoln's day leaves both Republicans and Democrats with plenty to which they can cling. Lincoln insisted that politics required a moral basis (cheers from fundamentalist Republicans), but he rejected orthodox evangelical Protestantism as the universal source of that morality (applause from ecumenical Democrats). He believed that something morally wrong can never be made right, regardless of the will of the majority or the pronouncements of the Supreme Court (anti-abortion Republicans and anti-death penalty Democrats glare at each other). He emphasized the work ethic and individual responsibility (R), and government action to guarantee equality of opportunity (D). He wanted to

*Whigs wanted high trade barriers so that American manufacturers could flourish without bothersome competition from more technologically advanced European factories, while Democrats argued for low tariffs that would give American farmers access to cheaper manufactured goods from overseas.

create trade barriers that would keep foreign competition away from American businesses (R) and American workers (D). After weighing every issue carefully, my conclusion is to believe the same thing as most historians, namely that Lincoln today would be more comfortable ideologically in the party to which I belong. But as any honest student of Lincoln must confess, your partisan guess is as good as mine.

If Lincoln were running for office today, could he get elected?

The glib answer is no, based on his unusual appearance and high, reedy voice.

But movie star looks have never been vital to getting elected, or every political office (not just the governorship of California) would be reserved for movie stars. Lincoln turned his distinctive appearance to his advantage. As Harold Holzer has written, Lincoln made a point of getting his image in front of the people. He took time to pose for photographers, painters, and sculptors, even when he was busy running the country during the Civil War. As a result, there are dozens of photos of Lincoln as president, compared to only one wartime image of his Confederate counterpart Jefferson Davis. Lincoln made himself psychologically accessible to the voters by letting them see what he looked like, even if he was not classically handsome. He was The Rail-splitter, the master of political symbolism and imagery, and the most brilliant wordsmith in the history of the republic. If he could not get elected today, then (to quote Lincoln) "I should prefer emigrating to some country where they make no pretence of loving liberty—to Russia, for instance . . ."[29]

FOR FURTHER READING

All Lincoln biographies discuss his political career at length. For an account of Lincoln's years in the Illinois legislature, written by another Illinois legislator of note, read Paul Simon, *Lincoln's Preparation for Greatness: The Illinois Legislative Years* (1965). To understand Lincoln's economic views and their impact on his politics, the most original and important book is Gabor Boritt's *Abraham Lincoln and the Economics of the American Dream* (1978).

CHAPTER FIVE

Speaker

Billy, don't shoot too high—aim lower, and the common people will understand you.

—Lincoln's advice to William Herndon[1]

Are there any recordings of Lincoln's voice?

No, there was no practical technology for recording or amplifying sound in Lincoln's day.

Thomas Edison didn't invent a method for recording and playing sounds until 1877, more than a decade after Lincoln's death.* All we know about Lincoln's voice comes from descriptions by those who heard him speak, and they generally say that he had a reedy tenor voice that never fully lost the Kentucky twang of his youth. Robert Wilson, a fellow state legislator, said that Lincoln had a "clear Shrill monotone Style of Speaking" that could be heard by everyone in the audience, however large it was.[2]

By 1930, very few people who had actually heard Lincoln were still alive. The image of Lincoln in the public mind, shaped by the dignified statue in the Lincoln Memorial and the enormous head on Mt. Rushmore, as well as the impact of his words, seemed to require an epic voice to match. When Henry Fonda played the lead role in the 1939 movie *Young Mr. Lincoln,* he adopted a nasal quality that fit reasonably closely with written descriptions of how Lincoln sounded, but his performance did not make nearly the same impression as that of Raymond Massey in *Abe Lincoln in Illinois* (1940), who spoke with a deep, resonant voice that most people still associate with Lincoln.

*Edouard-Leon Scott de Martinville invented a "phonautograph" in 1857 that made a visual record of sounds as lines on a cylinder, but these lines could not be played back. There is no evidence for the wishful rumor that Lincoln spoke into a phonautograph in 1863

If they didn't have sound equipment, like microphones, how were big audiences able to hear Lincoln's speeches?

I'm sorry you asked that.

Lincoln and other pre-microphone orators learned to project their voices. To make themselves heard by people in the back of the crowd, they inadvertently conferred an unpleasant side effect upon the people in the front of the crowd, as described by a boy who stood in the front row when Lincoln spoke at Toulon, Illinois, on October 8, 1858. "Standing near Mr. Lincoln as I did, hatless, with upturned face, I was conscious now and then of falling mist upon my brow. This, we know, any speaker will emit addressing an outdoor audience with intent to be heard by the farthest listener. I had to keep my red bandanna handkerchief in hand for use whenever he leaned directly toward me . . ."[3]

Was Lincoln a good public speaker?

Yes . . .

. . . it was Lincoln's command of language, both spoken and written, that distinguished him from other politicians of his generation, and indeed of any generation. In his first years as a politician and lawyer in the backwoods of Illinois, Lincoln mastered the art of rough-and-tumble verbal wrestling, until he could take his opponent down with ridicule, sarcasm, humor, logic, pity, or any number of other rhetorical weapons. For example, in 1836, a prominent local citizen named George Forquer deserted the Whig Party after a Democrat appointed him register of the land office. Forquer, who had recently built the first house in Springfield to feature a lightning rod, spoke against Lincoln, who responded with a blistering talk that concluded:

> The gentleman commenced his speech by saying that this young man would have to be taken down, alluding to me; I am not so young in years as I am in the tricks and trades of a politician; but live long, or die young, I would rather die now, than, like the gentleman change my politics, and simultaneous with the change, receive an office worth three thousand dollars per year, and then have to erect a lightning rod over my house, to protect a guilty conscience from an offended God.[4]

How did he learn to speak so well?

From practice, from his reading, from his native ability, and partly from the good fortune . . .

. . . of practicing politics in an era when rhetorical styles were changing. The formal, classical rhetoric of the Founding Fathers' generation seemed out of place in the Age of Jackson, when participation in politics was no longer confined to the wealthy and the well educated. Some politicians continued to speak in the traditional style, but Lincoln recognized that this was not the way to gain votes. As he advised his young law partner, Lincoln developed a way of communicating with his audiences that did not aim too high, but did not speak down to them either. He used clear, concrete images, like the "house divided," and compressed his thoughts into brief, memorable prose poems; his most famous speeches, the Gettysburg Address and the Second Inaugural, would be among his shortest.

Did he write his own speeches?

Yes. Drafts of some of them, in his handwriting, exist to prove it.

When he became president he had a personal secretary, John Hay, who sometimes drafted correspondence or speeches for him, but his most famous works, like the Gettysburg Address, were entirely his own.

This is not to say that he didn't borrow from other writers at times. Lincoln knew that his listeners would recognize the image of the "house divided" as coming from the Bible.[5] The conclusion of the Gettysburg Address owed much to abolitionist Theodore Parker, who wrote in 1855 that "Democracy is direct self-government, over all the people, for all the people, by all the people."[6] He might have come across a phrase written by John Quincy Adams: "In charity to all mankind, bearing no malice or ill will to any human being, and even compassionating those who hold in bondage their fellow men, not knowing what they do," which is echoed in the conclusion of the Second Inaugural Address.[7] The entire last paragraph of the First Inaugural Address was drafted by Secretary of State William Seward, but Lincoln edited it to make it his own, adding phrases like "We must not be enemies" and references to "the better angels of our nature" to create a masterpiece.[8]

Didn't Lincoln once make a speech that was so good nobody wrote it down?

Yes. Lincoln's "lost speech" . . .

. . . was delivered at Bloomington, Illinois, on May 29, 1856. Apparently it was so mesmerizing that most of the reporters simply stopped taking notes and stared. In 1930, the speech became less lost when it was discovered that the Alton *Courier* of June 5, 1856, had published a brief account.[9]

In which speech did he say, "You can fool some of the people all of the time, and you can fool all of the people some of the time, but you can't fool all of the people all the time"?

Nobody knows.

Although it's one of the most famous things Lincoln ever said, it's not certain that he actually said it. The words are carved on the base of a statue of Lincoln in Clinton, Illinois, with the allegation that he said them there on July 27, 1858, but they do not appear in any written account of that speech, or anywhere else in Lincoln's writings. There is some oral testimony that Lincoln said it, but none of it is contemporary with the event, and all of it is second- or thirdhand. For example, a 1905 Washington newspaper article says that a government official named James T. Smith had been told by a local judge that he (the judge) had heard Lincoln use the words when speaking to a delegation from Ohio early in the Civil War.[10] In 1905, Ainsworth Rand Spofford, the chief assistant librarian of Congress, tried and failed to find its origins and decided it must have been said by P. T. Barnum, which seems unlikely considering Barnum's well-placed confidence in his own universal and permanent people-fooling ability.[11] In 1909, the centennial of Lincoln's birth, several people suddenly recollected that they had been present at Lincoln's "Lost Speech" and heard him use the phrase there, but this is a little too convenient to be taken seriously. The editors of Lincoln's writings associate the phrase with a different semi-lost speech at Clinton on September 8, 1858, but acknowledge that there is no actual evidence that Lincoln ever said it.[12] More recently, databases of nineteenth-century publications have shown that the phrase did not appear in American magazines or newspapers until 1887, after which it quickly entered general circulation, usually attributed to Lincoln.[13]

This fact alone does not mean that Lincoln never said it. His speech at Gettysburg was rarely quoted until the 1880s, when it began its rise to immortality. But given the absence of any contemporary references to Lincoln saying something so memorable, it seems probable that the words originated elsewhere and became associated with Lincoln posthumously. If so, the saying is ironically contradicted by its own popularity. As Lincoln scholar William E. Barton (who believed that Lincoln did say it) noted, "if Lincoln never spoke this clever apothegm, then it would almost seem possible to fool all the people all the time; for all the people, virtually, believe these words to have been Lincoln's."[14]

Are there other famous things that Lincoln didn't really say?

Yes, tons of them. Try an Internet search for "Lincoln quotes" . . .

. . . and perhaps half of what you'll get are sayings that are persistently attributed to Lincoln despite the absence of any evidence that he ever said them. For example, while it's hard to prove a negative, we know that

Whether or not he said it, Lincoln's famous phrase has resonated throughout American history. (From MAD 161 © 1973 E. C. Publications, Inc. All rights reserved. Used with permission.)

Lincoln rarely spoke in abstract aphorisms and was not given to platitudes, which makes it highly unlikely that he ever said anything as vapid as "The best thing about the future is that it comes one day at a time" or "Most people are as happy as they make up their minds to be." Likewise, he almost certainly didn't say, "Good things come to those who wait, but only those left by those who hustle," considering that the word "hustle" was used rarely in Lincoln's lifetime, and then primarily as a transitive verb meaning to push or crowd, as in "the police hustled him along," not an intransitive verb meaning "hurry" or "try hard." Further, the sentence conflicts directly with something that Lincoln did say in praise of the virtue of patience: "A man watches his pear-tree day after day, impatient for the ripening of the fruit. Let him attempt to *force* the process, and he may spoil both fruit and tree. But let him patiently *wait,* and the ripe pear at length falls into his lap."[15]

Sometimes, however, we can definitely say that Lincoln never said that. For instance, he did not write a letter to W. L. Elkin in 1864, in which he predicted that the Civil War would be followed by an even more dangerous crisis: "As a result of the war, corporations have been enthroned, and an era of corruption in high places will follow, and the money power of the country will endeavor to prolong its reign by working upon the prejudices of the people until all wealth is aggregated in a few hands and the republic is destroyed . . ."

This quote, which first began circulating in 1888, conveniently echoes the political philosophy of the growing Populist movement, which would reach its peak in the 1890s. It doesn't sound much like Lincoln, whose comments on the future tended to be conditional ("if God wills that it continue . . .") or alternative ("I do not expect the house to fall—but I do expect it will cease to be divided. It will become all one thing, or all the other") and not simply predictions of woe. Helen Nicolay said that this was the quote her father, Lincoln's secretary John Nicolay, was "most often called upon to deny." Robert Todd Lincoln, a member in good standing of the "money power" as a corporate lawyer, took pains to deny that his father ever said it. No original manuscript of the quote has ever been found.[16]

At the other end of the political spectrum are the words that President Ronald Reagan attributed to Lincoln in his speech at the 1992 Republican convention: "You cannot strengthen the weak by weakening the strong. You cannot help the wage-earner by pulling down the wage-payer. You cannot help the poor by destroying the rich. You cannot help men permanently by doing for them what they could and should do for themselves."

If Lincoln was not a proto-populist, neither was he the "blame the poor" Social Darwinist who wrote these lines. They were actually produced by Rev. William J. H. Boetcker and published in 1916, in the form of cards with a series of "you cannot" scoldings on one side, and a real Lincoln quote on the other side.[17] Readers who agreed with the conservative minister assumed that his words must have been Lincoln's too, and

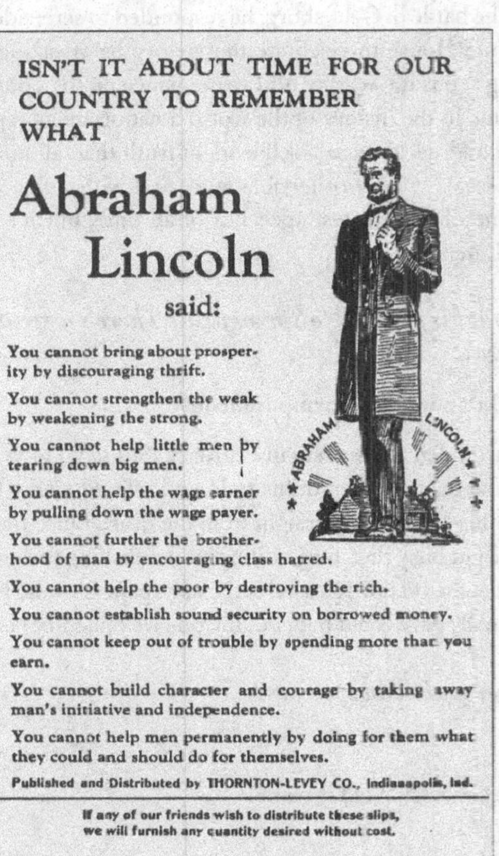
ISN'T IT ABOUT TIME FOR OUR COUNTRY TO REMEMBER WHAT

Abraham Lincoln said:

You cannot bring about prosperity by discouraging thrift.

You cannot strengthen the weak by weakening the strong.

You cannot help little men by tearing down big men.

You cannot help the wage earner by pulling down the wage payer.

You cannot further the brotherhood of man by encouraging class hatred.

You cannot help the poor by destroying the rich.

You cannot establish sound security on borrowed money.

You cannot keep out of trouble by spending more than you earn.

You cannot build character and courage by taking away man's initiative and independence.

You cannot help men permanently by doing for them what they could and should do for themselves.

Published and Distributed by THORNTON-LEVEY CO., Indianapolis, Ind.

If any of our friends wish to distribute these slips, we will furnish any quantity desired without cost.

Lincoln never said this. (Courtesy of The Lincoln Museum Fort Wayne, IN, TLM 9633)

the sayings began to appear widely in print over Lincoln's name. There being no Lincoln police to stop the spread of fraudulent Lincoln quotes, the "You Cannot" axioms eventually made their way past Reagan's research staff onto national television. With the advent of the Internet, pseudo-Lincolnian quotes like these gained a new lease on life, but you can also find many Web sites that debunk them. The struggle continues.

Was Lincoln a good extemporaneous speaker?

Not particularly.

Just after the battle of Gettysburg, he responded to serenaders who came to the White House to celebrate the victory by speaking off the cuff. "How long ago is it?—eighty odd years—since on the Fourth of July for the first time in the history of the world a nation by its representatives, assembled and declared as a self-evident truth that 'all men are created equal' [cheers]."[18] It's not terrible stuff, and with a few revisions will become one of the greatest speeches of all time, but it's not what we expect of Lincoln.

What about his farewell to Springfield? There's a great extemporaneous speech.

It's great, but not quite extemporaneous.

When Lincoln left Springfield in February 1861 to go to Washington, he stood on the rear platform of his train and offered a very brief, moving farewell to his hometown, straight from the heart. Once the train started moving, he got busy dictating, editing, and polishing the remarks he had made, so that the version released to the newspapers would be just so. The one he actually gave is not bad, but the one we remember is timeless.[19]

Did he ever make bad speeches?

Sure.

Here's the conclusion of his worst:

> I shall advert to but one more point.
>
> . . . Address *that* argument to *cowards* and to *knaves;* with the *free* and the *brave* it will effect nothing. It *may* be true, if it *must,* let it.

> Many free countries have lost their liberty; and *ours may* lose hers; but if she shall, be it my proudest plume, not that I was the *last* to desert, but that I *never* deserted her. I know that the great volcano at Washington, aroused and directed by the evil spirit that reigns there, is belching forth the lava of political corruption, in a current broad and deep, which is sweeping with frightful velocity over the whole length and breadth of the land, bidding fair to leave unscathed no green spot or living thing, while on its bosom are riding like demons on the waves of Hell, the imps of that evil spirit, and fiendishly taunting all those who dare resist its destroying course, with the hopelessness of their effort; and knowing this, I cannot deny that all may be swept away. Broken by it, I, too, may be; bow to it I never will. The *probability* that we may fall in the struggle *ought not* to deter us from the support of a cause we believe to be just; it *shall not* deter me. If ever I feel the soul within me elevate and expand to those dimensions not wholly unworthy of its Almighty Architect, it is when I contemplate the cause of my country, deserted by all the world beside, and I standing up boldly and alone and hurling defiance at her victorious oppressors. Here, without contemplating consequences, before High Heaven, and in the face of the world, I swear eternal fidelity to the just cause, as I deem it, of the land of my life, my liberty and my love. And who, that thinks with me, will not fearlessly adopt the oath that I take. Let none faulter, who thinks he is right, and we may succeed. But, if after all, we shall fail, be it so. We still shall have the proud consolation of saying to our consciences, and to the departed shade of our country's freedom, that the cause approved of our judgment, and adored of our hearts, in disaster, in chains, in torture, in death, we NEVER faultered in defending.[20]

And what was this cause for which Lincoln would defy chains, torture, and death? The survival of the Union? Government of, by, and for the people? Freedom for the slaves? No, it was the Whig Party's opposition to the government's plan to deposit federal money in various subtreasuries instead of in a national bank. Who among us would not join Lincoln in his determination to "swear eternal fidelity to the just cause" of antisubtreasuriarianism? The speech was so out of proportion to its subject that when Horace White (a journalist who accompanied Lincoln in his 1858 Senate campaign) first read it years later, he insisted, "I am sure that I never heard him say anything of the sort . . . I might add that it seems totally unlike him."[21] The only excuse one can offer for this overblown rhetorical effusion is that Lincoln was only thirty years old when he wrote it, and he may have felt that he needed to prove that he could give speeches in the traditional style of the day before he could find his own voice, like a graduate student grinding out an uninspired and unreadable dissertation in imitation of the style of the tenured professors whose approval determines his future.

What was his greatest speech?

You already know about his presidential speeches, like the Gettysburg Address and the Second Inaugural Address . . .

. . . both among the greatest prose works in the English language, so let's not discuss those yet. In Lincoln's prepresidential years, he gave a number of remarkable speeches that are less well known today, in part because they were standard-length political speeches of the time, not miniature gems like his two most famous works. Of these, the least well known (yet in some ways the most important) is the speech he gave at Peoria, Illinois, on October 16, 1854.

Lincoln's political career seemed to have hit a dead end by 1850. He had served his single term in Congress without accomplishing much. Worse, his Whig Party was losing its way. The three issues that had formed its creed from the beginning (a national bank, high tariffs, and federally funded internal improvements) had gone stale, with no realistic chance of enacting any of them in the foreseeable future. The one important national issue, the fate of slavery in the Western territories, seemed to have been settled by the Compromise of 1850, which put the institution in a position where it could spread no farther. Lincoln assumed that slavery was now safely "in the course of ultimate extinction,"[22] though the process might take many years. He turned his attention to his law practice.

In 1854, however, everything changed. Stephen A. Douglas, who had engineered passage of the Compromise of 1850, exploded a legislative bombshell in the form of the Kansas-Nebraska Act, which overturned the thirty-four-year-old Missouri Compromise and allowed slavery to expand into thousands of square miles of Western territory. "I was losing interest in politics, when the repeal of the Missouri Compromise aroused me again,"[23] Lincoln later wrote. In October, Lincoln spoke at Peoria and laid out the ideas he would use throughout the antislavery campaigns of the next six years, ending with his election to the presidency.

Lincoln opened the speech with a history of legislation designed to keep slavery out of the territories, from the Ordinance of 1787 to the Missouri Compromise to the Compromise of 1850. He then presented his own view on the spread of slavery:

> I hate it because of the monstrous injustice of slavery itself. I hate it because it deprives our republican example of its just influence in the world—enables the enemies of free institutions, with plausibility, to taunt us as hypocrites—causes the real friends of freedom to doubt our sincerity, and especially because it forces so many really good men amongst ourselves into an open war with the very fundamental principles of civil liberty—criticizing the Declaration of Independence, and insisting that there is no right principle of action but self-interest.[24]

With this, Lincoln launched a powerful attack on slavery that had the political virtue (in 1854) of ignoring the slaves themselves. Abolitionists had long opposed slavery as a violation of the principle that all men are created equal, but their rhetoric led inescapably to the conclusion that if it was wrong to deny African Americans their right to be free, it was also wrong to deny them the other rights enjoyed by European Americans, including civil and political rights. This was a conclusion that very few white Americans could stomach in 1854. Lincoln recognized this and told his audience at Peoria that he shared their views. Regarding the idea of full political and social equality, he said, "My own feelings will not admit of this; and if mine would, we well know that those of the great mass of white people will not."*

*This is a variation on the rhetorical trick Lincoln used when trying to explain his position on religion in 1846. There, he agreed with the majority view that no one should openly scoff at religion but kept his options open by never saying that he was a believer himself. Here, Lincoln acknowledges the majority view against social and political equality for all races, and although

Stephen A. Douglas and many other politicians of the era used the widespread racial bias of the voting public as a club to beat their antislavery opponents. Lincoln could not ignore this bias, but instead of exploiting it as Douglas did, Lincoln acknowledged its existence, admitted that he shared it, questioned its justice, and then moved on to criticize slavery for its effects on white people. In the passage quoted above, he said that slavery is a "monstrous injustice." We read this today as meaning an injustice to its black victims, and Lincoln undoubtedly welcomed any abolitionists who wished to so read it, but the words themselves do not specify who it is that suffers from slavery's injustice. Lincoln began to clarify this in the next sentence: slavery is bad because of what it does to the United States as a whole. It prevents the country from serving as a beacon of representative government to the world, exposes us as hypocrites when we speak of freedom, and encourages the enemies of freedom (who dominated the globe in 1854) to believe that the future was theirs.

But the worst consequence of slavery, Lincoln argued, is its effect on core American values at home. The Declaration of Independence plainly states that all men are created equal. Before 1844, Democrats had regularly included language from the Declaration in their party platforms every four years, but not after. In 1845, Governor James Henry Hammond of South Carolina (originator of the phrase "Cotton is king!") repudiated as "ridiculously absurd, that much lauded but nowhere accredited dogma of Mr Jefferson, 'that all men are born equal.' "[25] In the debate over the Kansas-Nebraska Act, Lincoln noted, Senator John Pettit of Indiana called the Declaration's premise of human equality a "self-evident lie."[26] It was to this growing rejection of the spirit of the Declaration of Independence that Lincoln referred when he said that slavery was forcing "so many really good men amongst ourselves into an open war with the very fundamental principles of civil liberty."[27]

---

he does say that his own feelings are similar, he again keeps his options open by immediately minimizing the importance of his own views, implying that they don't matter in comparison to those of "the great mass of white people." In doing so, he hints that if he did not oppose racial equality, his audience should not regard it as important. If this seems a thin defense of what appears to be an openly white supremacist remark, my only suggestion is to read Stephen Douglas's portion of his 1858 debates with Lincoln to get a sense of what real nineteenth-century white supremacism sounded like.

In place of the principle of equality, proslavery speakers advanced a number of theories as the proper basis of society, but they all (in Lincoln's view) came down to naked self-interest. To him, the implication was clear: slavery undermined the political equality of all white Americans and set the stage for a society in which there was "no right principle of action but *self-interest*."[28] Slavery, Lincoln was telling his listeners, was a threat to *your* freedom, and however little you might care about people darker than yourself, if you value your own skin then you will join me in opposing the spread of slavery now.

From there, Lincoln went on point by point to refute each of the arguments that Stephen Douglas had offered in support of the Kansas-Nebraska Act. The Peoria speech contains much that Lincoln and Douglas would say in their famous 1858 debates. Lincoln's antislavery rhetoric would continue to evolve over the intervening four years. Events like the *Dred Scott* decision would furnish new ammunition for his arguments. Increasingly, he would focus on the denial of economic opportunity to the slave as the most vulnerable point at which to challenge the institution, especially because this point could accommodate those who opposed slavery but were reluctant to concede political or social equality to black people. In outline, however, you can already find in the Peoria speech many of the arguments, and some of the most eloquent language, that Lincoln would marshal in his fight against slavery, including this:

> Our republican robe is soiled, and trailed in the dust. Let us repurify it. Let us turn and wash it white, in the spirit, if not the blood, of the Revolution. Let us turn slavery from its claims of "moral right," back upon its existing legal rights, and its arguments of "necessity." Let us return it to the position our fathers gave it; and there let it rest in peace. Let us re-adopt the Declaration of Independence, and with it, the practices, and policy, which harmonize with it. Let north and south—let all Americans—let all lovers of liberty everywhere—join in the great and good work. If we do this, we shall not only have saved the Union; but we shall have so saved it, as to make, and to keep it, forever worthy of the saving. We shall have so saved it, that the succeeding millions of free happy people, the world over, shall rise up, and call us blessed, to the latest generations.[29]

Isn't it too bad we don't have politicians today who can debate issues like Lincoln and Douglas did?

Yes, but it's also easy to romanticize the quality of those verbal encounters.

When Lincoln and Douglas debated one another seven times in the summer and fall of 1858, they each had some set pieces of rhetoric that they tended to repeat at each stop. Lincoln read whole passages from his Peoria speech. They had a lot of time to fill: an hour for the first speaker, an hour and a half for the rebuttal, then thirty minutes for the first speaker to reply. This seems long compared to the two-minute limits placed on answers in recent presidential debates, but the fact that in the 2000 season the average major league baseball game lasted two hours and fifty-eight minutes suggests that the attention span of large audiences has not changed much since the three-hour debates of 1858.

In some ways, the debates really were superior to modern presidential debates. The format allowed each candidate to develop his position in detail, without having to waste time answering absurd questions from self-important debate moderators. Stephen Douglas, for example, never had to ponder whether "If Mrs. Douglas were enslaved and murdered, would you change your mind on popular sovereignty?" But the candidates didn't spend the entire three hours in high-level intellectual combat. When they weren't reading old speeches, they both engaged in personal insult (more good-natured than vicious), ridiculed each other's arguments, and dealt with frequent interruptions from the audience.

Some of these were friendly, like those who responded to Douglas's frequent racebaiting:

> I ask you, are you in favor of conferring upon the negro the rights and privileges of citizenship? [**"No, no."**] Do you desire to strike out of our State Constitution that clause which keeps slaves and free negroes out of the State, and allow the free negroes to flow in, [**"never,"**] and cover your prairies with black settlements? Do you desire to turn this beautiful State into a free negro colony, [**"no, no,"**] . . .

Others were less so, but Lincoln usually handled them well. Here he is trying to read his Peoria speech during the first debate:

> I hope you will permit me to read a part of a printed speech that I made then at Peoria, which will show altogether a different view of the position I took in that contest of 1854.
> VOICE——Put on your specs.
> MR. LINCOLN——Yes, sir, I am obliged to do so. I am no longer a young man. **[Laughter.]**[30]

What was really remarkable about the debates, especially from Lincoln's perspective, was not so much their content as the fact that Douglas agreed to debate Lincoln in the first place. Consider that it was only two years earlier when Lincoln indulged in his self-pitying comparison of Douglas, whose "name fills the nation; and is not unknown, even, in foreign lands," with his own "flat failure."[31] It was a sign of Lincoln's rising importance as an antislavery speaker that Stephen Douglas, the most famous politician in America, felt that he could not ignore Lincoln's challenge to debate.

You seem to be saying the debates contained nothing new. What about the "Freeport interrogatories"?

Good point. Some things had changed between 1854 and 1858 . . .

. . . like the Supreme Court's 1857 decision in *Dred Scott v. Sandford.*[32] Before *Dred Scott,* Douglas had irrevocably committed himself to the doctrine of "popular sovereignty" as the solution to the problem of slavery in the West. Douglas argued that the federal government, which made the laws for new territories until they became states, should not make any laws either forbidding or allowing slavery but should let the people living in the territories make that decision for themselves. It sounds like a democratic way to resolve the issue, except that by "people" Douglas actually meant only men of European descent. It's safe to say that the idea of letting enslaved people vote on their own fate never crossed his mind.

In 1857, however, the Supreme Court came up with its own solution to the slavery question. Dred Scott, a slave whose owner had taken him into free territory, sued for his freedom in 1846. The wheels of (in)justice turned slowly, and eleven years later Chief Justice Roger B. Taney issued his opinion resolving the case. Taney stated that Scott was still a slave; that he had no right to sue, because as an African American he had "no rights which the white man is bound to respect"; and that his sojourn into free territory made no difference because Congress had no right to prohibit slavery in any federal territory.[33]

The decision was cheered by slavery's supporters, but Lincoln saw that it put Douglas in a hard place. If Congress did not have the authority to ban slavery in a territory, then how could the settlers or their territorial legislature do so, since they derived their authority from Congress? In the debate at Freeport, Lincoln put the question to Douglas as part of a series of interrogatories, like a lawyer deposing a witness: "Can the people of a United States Territory, in any lawful way, against the wish of any citizen of the United States, exclude slavery from its limits prior to the formation of a State Constitution?"[34]

Douglas was trapped. If he agreed that *Dred Scott* had ended the possibility of banning slavery in a territory, then his "gur-reat pur-rinciple"[35] of popular sovereignty was dead. If he denied that *Dred Scott* had made the West safe for slavery, he risked alienating the proslavery element in the South who had backed his Kansas-Nebraska Act. Always the gambler, Douglas took a chance and tried to please both sides. His "Freeport doctrine" (which, like most of the content of the debate, echoed points that he had made earlier in other speeches) claimed that the people of a territory could not formally ban slavery, but that they could still effectively keep it out simply by failing to pass the necessary police regulations to enforce it.

This answer doomed Douglas's future presidential hopes. It seemed a weak reed on which to rest the weight of popular sovereignty, and at the same time it outraged proslavery Southerners, who regarded Douglas as a traitor for even suggesting that slavery could be kept out of the territories. Some writers have attributed superhuman prescience to Lincoln by claiming that this was Lincoln's goal, and that throughout the 1858 Senate campaign he really had his eye on the 1860 presidential election. Lincoln was politically astute, but he did not have a crystal ball, and in any case, in 1858, he almost certainly would have preferred a seat in the Senate to one in the White House.[36]

Why would he have settled for just the Senate? Didn't he always want to be president?

No.

For most of his political career, Lincoln's highest ambition was to be a United States senator. The Senate was inhabited by giants in the 1840s, men like Daniel Webster, John C. Calhoun, and Lincoln's own "beau-ideal of a statesman," Henry Clay. They were followed by an almost equally impressive group in the 1850s, including Jefferson Davis, Thomas Hart Benton, William H. Seward, Charles Sumner, and of course Lincoln's rival Stephen A. Douglas. In contrast, the White House had never been occupied by a sorrier lot than the four nonentities between the presidencies of James K. Polk and Abraham Lincoln—how many can you name, quickly?[37]

Not until 1860, after his unsuccessful attempts to enter the Senate in 1854 and 1858, did Lincoln give any indication that he might be thinking seriously about the presidency. As late as December 1859, he wrote to a political ally, Norman B. Judd, "I would rather have a full term in the Senate than in the Presidency," and to others that "I do not think myself fit for the Presidency." His successful Cooper Union speech in New York City on February 27, 1860, was the first public sign that he might be interested in being a candidate. Finally, a few weeks before the start of the Republican convention, in a letter to Senator Lyman Trumbull, dated April 29, 1860, he confessed, "the taste *is* in my mouth a little."[38]

FOR FURTHER READING

Lincoln's famous presidential speeches have each been the subject of several books, but his earlier speeches are only starting to receive comparable coverage. The most substantial book on the topic by far is John Channing Briggs, *Lincoln's Speeches Reconsidered* (2005), which devotes chapters not only to the usual suspects (the Lyceum speech and the House Divided speech) but also the Temperance Address, the Lecture on Discoveries and Inventions, the Peoria speech, and others. Lewis E. Lehrman, *Lincoln at Peoria: The Turning Point* (2008) is the first full-length analysis of that important speech. The Cooper Union address gets a chapter in Briggs, and an entire book from Harold Holzer, titled *Lincoln at Cooper Union: The Speech That Made Abraham Lincoln President* (2004). The Lincoln-Douglas debates have been analyzed by various writers, including Harry V. Jaffa, *Crisis of the House Divided: An Interpretation of the Issues in the Lincoln-Douglas Debates* (1959); Don E.

Fehrenbacher, *Prelude to Greatness: Lincoln in the 1850's* (1962); David Zarefsky, *Lincoln, Douglas, and Slavery: In the Crucible of Public Debate* (1991); and Allen C. Guelzo, *Lincoln and Douglas: The Debates That Defined America* (2008). The debates themselves have been reprinted in various formats, but there is a need for a definitive critical text that makes clear (or as clear as possible) what the candidates actually said; current editions are largely based on one or another of the competing newspaper versions that appeared in 1858, from notes taken by reporters on the scene. Robert W. Johannsen, *Stephen A. Douglas* (1973), is the standard biography of Lincoln's great rival.

For Lincoln's speeches in general, *Lincoln's Sword: The Presidency and the Power of Words* (2006), by Douglas Wilson, reveals the president's speechwriting technique, based on an analysis of his rough drafts and final versions. Ronald C. White, *The Eloquent President: A Portrait of Lincoln Through His Words* (2005), is a close textual analysis that emphasizes the sound of Lincoln's words. Kenneth Cmiel, *Democratic Eloquence: The Fight Over Popular Speech in Nineteenth-Century America* (1990), describes the context in which Lincoln found the opportunity to develop his unique form of rhetoric.

{ CHAPTER SIX }

President

I happen temporarily to occupy this big White House. I am a living witness that any one of your children may look to come here as my father's child has.

—From a speech by Lincoln to the soldiers of the 166th Ohio Volunteer Infantry regiment, August 22, 1864[1]

How old was Lincoln when he became president?

Fifty-one when he was elected in November 1860.

He was not quite a month past his fifty-second birthday when he was inaugurated in March 1861, making "Old Abe" the third-youngest person elected to the White House up to that time.[2]

If Lincoln's whole political experience was in the Illinois state legislature, plus one term in Congress, how did he ever get elected president?

When Lincoln was nominated to be the Republican candidate in 1860, it was a surprise to everyone.

The other candidates for the nomination were much better known than Lincoln. There was Senator William Henry Seward of New York, who had coined the phrase "irrepressible conflict" to describe the standoff between the free and slave states. There was Salmon P. Chase, the governor of Ohio, who was accustomed to being the smartest person in the room and had been bitten hard by the presidential bug. There was the famously corrupt Senator Simon Cameron of Pennsylvania, whose reputation was reflected in the story of Lincoln's meeting with another Pennsylvanian, Thaddeus Stevens. When Lincoln asked him if he really

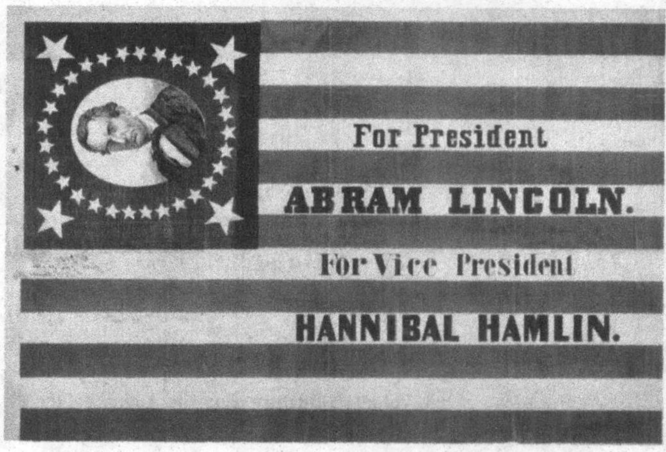

Even after he was nominated for president, Lincoln was still so obscure that his own campaign literature sometimes spelled his name wrong. (Courtesy of the Library of Congress, Prints and Photographs Division, LC-USZ62-14844)

thought that Cameron would steal, Stevens supposedly replied, "Well, I don't think he would steal a red hot stove."[3]

So bitterly did the front-runners detest one another that each of them, as he saw his own chances for the nomination fade, directed his followers to vote for the dark horse candidate Lincoln rather than one of the other leaders, until by the third ballot Lincoln had enough votes to overtake Seward and win the nomination.

How did he win the election?

By the self-destruction of his opponents, more than anything else.

Stephen A. Douglas hoped to be the Democratic nominee in 1860, but his chances were destroyed when he clung to his theory of "popular sovereignty," maintaining that slavery could still effectively be voted up or down by the inhabitants of a federal territory even after the *Dred Scott* decision held otherwise.[4] The Democrats guaranteed trouble for themselves by holding their convention in South Carolina ("too small for a republic, too large for an insane asylum"), where secessionist feeling ran high.[5] Many of the delegates who met at Charleston in April 1860 wanted Douglas, but those from several slave states refused to accept the possibility and walked out of the convention. Having failed to choose a candidate, the Democrats tried a second time in June, at Baltimore, where slave-state delegates bolted again. This time the rump of the convention went ahead and nominated Douglas. The Southern Democrats held their own meeting and nominated Vice President John C. Breckinridge of Kentucky. Whigs from the border states who were equally dismayed by Republican antislavery rhetoric and Southern Democratic talk of secession formed their own Constitutional Union party, nominating John Bell of Tennessee and Edward Everett of Massachusetts as a compromise ticket. In some Southern states, Lincoln's name did not even appear on the ballot, but with three candidates dividing the nonantislavery vote, Lincoln was able to get all the electoral support he needed from the North and Midwest.

Did he make a whistle-stop campaign?

No, it wasn't considered appropriate.

The presidency in 1860 was still considered to possess a special dignity, not to be soiled by rank electioneering. The office was supposed to seek the man, not vice versa. Lincoln accordingly stayed in Springfield and avoided public appearances. Behind the scenes, of course, he kept a close eye on the campaign conducted by his friends and supporters throughout the North. "The man who thinks Lincoln calmly sat down and gathered his robes about him, waiting for the people to call him, has a very erroneous knowledge," William Herndon observed.[6]

Stephen Douglas, in contrast, broke with tradition and made a shockingly active effort to get elected. At first he traveled by train through the Northeast, making brief speeches at each stop. He defended his unorthodox conduct by claiming that he was simply going to visit his mother and didn't want to be rude by refusing to acknowledge the crowds that met him at every station. The press treated this with the same ridicule that a future president would receive for claiming "I didn't inhale." One editorial cartoon, captioned "Stephen Finding 'His Mother,' " portrayed Mrs. Douglas in the person of Columbia, with the Little Giant over her knee getting a sound spanking for all the mischief he had caused for the country with his Kansas-Nebraska Act.

By the end of the summer, Douglas realized that Lincoln was going to win the election and that secession was a real possibility. He threw off any pretense and openly campaigned through the South, speaking not for his candidacy but for national unity. His effort was in vain, as South Carolina responded to Lincoln's election by seceding in December 1860, followed by six more states in January and February.

Lincoln did make a whistle-stop tour of sorts on his way to the White House from Springfield, that nervous February of 1861. He took almost two weeks to make the journey, with frequent stops to say a few encouraging words at the railroad station or give a more formal speech, but he made no new policy statements even as the slave states were seceding one by one. The trip was not a success; people thought he didn't understand the gravity of the situation.

Is it true that Stephen Douglas held Lincoln's hat during the inaugural ceremony?

I hope so . . .

. . . because it is such a good story. According to the anonymous *Diary of a Public Man,* Lincoln stood up to give his speech, removed his hat, and found nowhere to put it. His old rival Douglas graciously reached out and took it, holding it on his lap throughout the speech.[7] Douglas later met with Lincoln to ask what he could do to best help the Union cause and agreed to go back to Illinois to rally support for the administration. Unfortunately, Douglas had spent his last reserves of energy in the presidential campaign. He caught a cold, developed a fever, and died from various complications on June 3, 1861.

What about his cabinet? Did Lincoln really fill it with his rivals?

Yes, Lincoln chose the strongest men in the Republican Party to serve in his cabinet, regardless of their loyalty (or lack of it) to him.

These official advisers were more important to him for the political strength that they brought to his administration than for the advice they gave him. His cabinet was unusual in that it consisted not of his closest political allies but of his greatest rivals for power within his party. The Republican Party was a fragile political coalition whose members were united only on the principle that slavery must not be allowed to expand any further and who disagreed about everything else. Lincoln knew that his only hope for leading such a party was to make sure that all the other major Republican leaders were working for his administration rather than against it. He wanted his enemies where he could keep an eye on them, and in the process created one of the most effective cabinets in the history of the presidency.[8]

Specifically, he gave Seward the premier position as secretary of state. Chase became secretary of the treasury. To the dishonest but politically important Simon Cameron, Lincoln allotted what seemed at the time to be the relatively unimportant cabinet post of secretary of war. These choices had the advantage of giving Lincoln the counsel of a group of talented, strong-willed advisers. The corresponding disadvantage, of course, was that some of those advisers thought that they ought to be the president, not Lincoln. Chase still regarded himself as the smartest man in the room, a characteristic that prompted Senator Ben Wade to comment, "Chase is a good man, but his theology is unsound. He thinks there is a fourth Person in the Trinity."[9] William Seward was quite blunt about his view that he should be the leader of the government and sent Lincoln a memorandum to that effect a month after the inauguration. In it he proposed a set of policies for the administration to follow and graciously offered to carry them out, in effect making Lincoln a figurehead. Lincoln responded with a memo of his own in which he made it clear that whatever would be done, "*I* must do it."[10] He apparently never sent the memo to Seward (it was later found among Lincoln's papers), but whatever he said to the secretary must have made an impression. Within a few months Seward would write to his wife that "the president is the best of us."[11]

Did the rest of the cabinet support Lincoln?

Yes, each in his own way.

The most troublesome was always Salmon P. Chase. He ran the Treasury Department brilliantly, finding ways to finance the Union war effort without ruining the economy but never giving up the idea that he should have been in Lincoln's place. Lincoln was aware of Chase's ambition but didn't let it bother him. He told this story about it, as related later by a journalist:

> "My brother and I," he said, "were once plowing corn, I driving the horse and he holding the plow. The horse was lazy, but on one occa-

sion he rushed across the field so that I, with my long legs, could scarcely keep pace with him. On reaching the end of the furrow, I found an enormous chin-fly fastened on him, and knocked it off. My brother asked me what I did that for. I told him I didn't want the old horse bitten in that way. 'Why,' said my brother, 'that's all that made him go.'

"Now," said Mr. Lincoln, "if Mr. ——— has a Presidential chin-fly biting him, I'm not going to knock it off, if it will only make his department go."[12]

What's a chin-fly?

An equine parasite, also called the horse bot fly.

Adult chin-flies don't actually bite, but the females irritate horses by laying eggs on them.

So did Chase ever come to acknowledge Lincoln's superiority the way Seward did?

Eventually, but only because Lincoln forced him into it.

By December 1862, the war effort was in serious trouble, and Chase was actively intriguing against Lincoln by telling a group of radical antislavery senators how dysfunctional the cabinet had become. Both Chase and the senators hoped to force Lincoln to remove the moderate Seward. Lincoln finessed the problem by meeting first with the senators, who accused him of not consulting his advisers and who blamed Seward for everything wrong with the war effort. He then met with his cabinet privately, where they all agreed with Lincoln that they had been adequately consulted and were more or less in agreement on policy. Seward offered to resign to relieve the president of the pressure he was under, but Lincoln instead called a third meeting of the cabinet and the radical senators together, where he again asked the secretaries if they felt that they were being adequately consulted and working together well. Chase was checkmated; if he agreed with Lincoln, the senators would think that he had duped them, but if he made public his anti-Seward stance, he would be exposed as disloyal to his boss. He stammered and gave a sort of nonanswer, and the next day sheepishly offered to resign. Lincoln triumphantly grabbed Chase's resignation from his hand and declared, "I can dispose of this subject now without difficulty . . . I see my way clear."[13] The resignations offered by the moderate Seward and the radical Chase gave him "a pumpkin in each end of my bag."[14] He rejected both of them, thus keeping his cabinet intact, defying the Senate's attempt to dictate who would serve there and demonstrating to all who cared to notice that there was no percentage in trying to outmaneuver him, because he knew exactly what was going on around him at all times. He, not Chase or anyone else, was clearly the smartest person in the room.

Who was Lincoln's vice president?

Lincoln's first vice president was Hannibal Hamlin of Maine.

He was chosen by the Republican convention in 1860 to run with Lincoln, whom he had never met, in order to provide regional and political balance (Hamlin was a former Democrat, Lincoln a former Whig). He did not play much of a role in the administration and was so out of the loop that when Lincoln issued the Emancipation Proclamation, Hamlin doubted whether his letter of congratulation (written from Bangor, Maine) would even get past the presidential secretaries: "I do not know, as in the multiplicity of the correspondence with which you are burthened, this note will ever meet your eye."[15]

But Andrew Johnson became president after Lincoln was killed. Why the change?

Lincoln must have had his reasons . . .

. . . but nobody knows exactly what they were. For that matter, no one has been able to pin on Lincoln the decision to drop Hamlin in favor of Johnson. In 1864, the Republicans and a few War Democrats held a convention under the name "Union Party" to renominate Lincoln for president, and they voted for Andrew Johnson of Tennessee to replace Hamlin. Johnson was a Democrat and a Southerner, so he gave the ticket a veneer of national unity. No documentary smoking gun has ever been found associating Lincoln with the decision to ditch Hamlin, but it's easy to believe that Lincoln found this politically desirable and impossible to imagine the convention deciding to change vice presidents without his knowledge or approval.[16]

Why did Lincoln start the Civil War?

"When, sir, did you stop beating your wife?"

Every lawyer knows the trick of asking questions like this. The implied premise, that Lincoln deliberately started the Civil War for sinister ulterior motives, has a vocal following among neo-Confederates, but it's not accepted by any reputable historians.[17]

When Lincoln took office in 1861, he faced the greatest crisis in the nation's history: what to do about the dissolution of the Union. South Carolina had responded to news of Lincoln's election by passing an ordinance of secession in December 1860, and before Lincoln was inaugurated on March 4, 1861, a total of seven states had declared themselves out of the Union. Outgoing president James Buchanan had managed to avoid doing anything one way or the other long enough to leave the entire mess in Lincoln's hands, but Lincoln quickly discovered that he could not continue to play a waiting game. The government of South Carolina had demanded that federal troops be withdrawn from Fort Sumter in Charleston Harbor, and the cabinet was divided as to whether to reinforce the fort or give it up. Lincoln learned to his dismay that the garrison was almost out of food and would have to surrender if not immediately resupplied. Forced to make a decision on which the fate of the nation might hang, Lincoln called his cabinet together. The good news was that his advisers were no longer divided, but the bad news was that a clear majority agreed that he had to give up the fort. In the face of almost unanimous advice to the contrary, Lincoln decided that he would send food, but not military supplies or reinforcements.

It turned out to be exactly the right decision. When Confederate artillery opened fire on the fort rather than allow the supplies to arrive, the North rallied behind Lincoln and entered the war united and enthusiastic. As in 1941 and 2001, an attack on American soil mobilized citizens of all political persuasions to unite behind the flag.

Did Lincoln's presidential actions violate the Constitution?

Some of them did, as Lincoln admitted.

Lincoln was faced not only with a rebellion in the Southern half of the country that he fought openly to subdue but also with the threat of dissent, subversion, and even terrorism in the North from domestic enemies. This started as soon as the war did, when pro-Southern mobs in Baltimore blocked the streets and refused to let Northern troops pass through on their way to defend Washington. The 6th Massachusetts regiment had to fight its way through, with casualties on both sides, which prompted a committee of dignitaries from Baltimore to ask Lincoln not to send any more troops through the city. His response showed a rare flash of temper: "You, gentlemen, come here to me and ask for peace on any terms, and yet have no word of condemnation for those who are making war on us. . . . Your citizens attack troops sent to the defense of the Government, . . . and yet you would have me break my oath and surrender the Government without a blow. There is no Washington in that—no Jackson in that—no manhood nor honor in that." Just as quickly, the president regained his composure and even allowed his sense of humor to bubble up, observing that Washington was surrounded by Virginia and Maryland, and that "Our men are not moles, and can't dig under the earth; they are not birds, and can't fly through the air. There is no way but to march across, and that they must do."[18]

To be sure that there was no more trouble with communications to the North via Baltimore, Lincoln authorized his officers to suspend the privilege of the writ of habeas corpus in the area between Washington and Philadelphia. This writ is the mechanism used to enforce one of the foundations of Anglo-American civil rights, the right not to be subject to arbitrary arrest. With the writ suspended, individuals suspected of opposing the government could be arrested and detained indefinitely without being charged with a crime or even being told why they were in custody. As the war went on, Lincoln found it necessary to suspend the writ in other places and at other times, eventually making the suspension general throughout the country in September 1862 and again in September 1863.

Whether this was constitutional was unclear. The Constitution expressly provides for suspension of the writ in times of rebellion, but it doesn't say who gets to do the suspending.[19] Since the clause appears in Article I, which covers the legislative branch, the implication is that the power belongs to Congress and not the president, but the point is not certain. Legalisms aside, Lincoln defended his actions on the grounds of necessity. "Are all the laws, *but one,* to go unexecuted, and the government itself go to pieces, lest that one be violated?"[20]

Still, arresting 13,535 political prisoners is outrageous, isn't it?

It would have been, but that's not what he did.

The remarkably specific statistic of 13,535 military arrests of civilians during the Civil War has a history of its own. When historian Mark E. Neely, Jr., set out to research Lincoln's record on civil liberties, he found that this number, quoted widely in Civil War books, was based on the estimate of Colonel F. C. Ainsworth of the War Department's Record and Pension Office in 1897. In the 1980s, Neely undertook a much longer and more thorough study of what survived of the War Department records, and numerous other sources as well. What he found was that the number of civilians arrested by the military during the war was actually far more than 13,535. Most of these arrests, however, took place in the border states of Kentucky or Missouri. Some of the detainees were civilians from Confederate states, and most were suspected of such crimes as desertion, draft evasion, smuggling, defrauding the government, and other activities that would hardly qualify their perpetrators for political prisoner status. The number of Northerners arrested for expressing political views opposing the war was much smaller than 13,535, perhaps less than 1 percent of that number.[21]

What happened to those who did get arrested for opposing the war?

Most were held for a time and then released, but one posed a special problem.

The arrest of Clement L. Vallandigham put the president in a particularly awkward position. Vallandigham was an Ohio politician whose antigovernment rhetoric came close to crossing the line into subversion. In 1863, he was a powerful voice in the Democratic Party in Ohio and drew large crowds whenever he spoke. The officer in charge of military security in Ohio at the time was the luckless Ambrose Burnside, who had led the Union Army of the Potomac to a shattering defeat at Fredericksburg the previous December and had been put out to pasture with a rear area command where it was imagined that he could do little further harm. Burnside, perhaps eager to do something to redeem his reputation, took it upon himself to suppress the virulently anti-Lincoln tirades coming from Vallandigham. In doing so, however, he played right into his target's hands. He sent guards to arrest Vallandigham at his home, where the clever agitator waited behind a series of locked doors that the soldiers had to break down before taking Vallandigham literally from the arms of his family. Continuing to spin the incident for all it was worth, Vallandigham smuggled letters to his followers out of the posh Cincinnati hotel where he was held, in which he characterized himself as a prisoner in an American "bastille."

For all of Vallandigham's theatrics, he had a good point. Arbitrary arrest was the tool that autocratic European governments traditionally used to suppress legitimate protest, and Vallandigham had done no more than express his opposition to the government's policies, as any citizen was entitled to do. To release Vallandigham would be an embarrassing confession of error that would humiliate General Burnside and undercut the government's authority. To hold him would be not only unjust but also dangerous politically, making Vallandigham into a martyr and strengthening his position as leader of the anti-Lincoln voters of Ohio. Lincoln, as he so often did, hit upon the middle solution: he ordered Vallandigham banished to the South. This turned the situation around. The Confederates were not sure what to do with him, as they had plenty of anti-Lincoln orators of their own. If they accepted him, he would become the Jane Fonda of his generation, viewed by many in the North as an enemy of his country instead of a loyal American who simply opposed the current administration. If they rejected him, where would he go? He ended up leaving the South at the first opportunity, taking a ship through the Union naval blockade and sailing to Canada, where he launched his campaign for governor of Ohio in 1864. He returned to the United States in June 1864, but this time Lincoln made sure that his officers did not take the bait, and Vallandigham was allowed to make all the speeches he wanted, including the keynote address at the Democratic convention in August 1864, where his presence hurt more than it helped by tarring the Democrats with the brush of disloyalty.

Throughout the war, Lincoln's handling of civil liberties remained one of his most glaring political vulnerabilities. Along with suspending the privilege of the writ of habeas corpus, he was willing to go further if necessary, at one point authorizing General Winfield Scott to bombard cities in Maryland rather than allow its legislature to enact a resolution to secede. But he was always sensitive to the charge that he was unnecessarily infringing on Americans' rights and took care to defend himself. In 1863 he wrote an open letter to Erastus Corning, president of the New

York Central Railroad and a critic of the administration, in which he laid out two of the main elements of his defense. The first was that it was not only necessary to national security to arrest antigovernment agitators, but that doing so prevented worse consequences. "Must I shoot a simpleminded soldier boy who deserts, while I must not touch a hair of a wiley agitator who induces him to desert?"[22] It was thus better to arrest Vallandigham, who urged citizens not to enlist, than to punish those who listened to him and deserted after enlisting. Sympathetic and easy to understand, like many of Lincoln's arguments, it posits only two options: shooting simpleminded soldier boys or arresting agitators, leaving the listener in no doubt as to which is better.

The second defense was still more problematic. Lincoln acknowledged that his actions infringed on civil liberties but argued that they were temporary wartime measures only and would be removed as soon as possible at the end of hostilities. It was unlikely, Lincoln said, that these temporary measures would lead to the permanent loss of the "right of public discussion, the liberty of speech and the press, the law of evidence, trial by jury, and Habeas corpus . . . any more than I am able to believe that a man could contract so strong an appetite for emetics during temporary illness, as to persist in feeding upon them through the remainder of his healthful life."[23] But one could make an equally apt comparison to a person who, during temporary illness, is given powerful narcotics to which he becomes addicted and which he persists in consuming long after the original medical justification is gone. Fortunately, the American body politic proved sufficiently resistant. Like the Alien and Sedition Acts of the quasiwar with France in the 1790s, the Espionage and Sedition Acts of World War I, and the internment of Japanese Americans during World War II, various elements of Lincoln's wartime infringements of civil rights were afterward either struck down by the Supreme Court or voluntarily removed by the government.[24]

Is it true that Lincoln had an arrest warrant made out for the chief justice of the United States?

No, but he might have fantasized about doing so.

The rumor that Lincoln did this is based on a single comment to that effect in the papers of Ward Hill Lamon, a friend of Lincoln from Illinois who served as his unofficial White House bodyguard.[25] Lamon was close to Lincoln, but his reliability as a source of information is less than solid. In the absence of any other hint of Lincoln's intention to have the chief justice arrested, the scholarly consensus is that no such warrant was ever prepared.

This is not to say that Lincoln would have minded seeing Roger B. Taney behind bars. Taney had written the worst opinion in the history of the Supreme Court in the 1857 *Dred Scott* case (narrowly edging out *Plessy v. Ferguson*),[26] and once the war had started he did what he could to make winning it more difficult for Lincoln. The most notable example of this, and the one that led to the mythical warrant, was his handling of the case *Ex parte Merryman,* which involved the arrest of a Confederate sympathizer in Maryland. Taney issued a writ of habeas corpus for John Merryman, requiring his jailer to bring him into court and explain to Taney why he was being held. Lincoln, however, had suspended the privilege of the writ of habeas corpus in the area north of Baltimore where Merryman was arrested, so the military officer holding the prisoner refused to honor the chief justice's writ, and Merryman stayed in custody. Taney published an opinion that only Congress had the power to suspend the writ, but as he had no troops at his call and Lincoln had several hundred thousand, it was game, set, and match to the president.

Lincoln had no use for Taney, but having won the political battle he had no legal reason to have him arrested. Even if he had, it is inconceivable that such a skilled politician would have risked conferring martyr status on the aged judge by sending a squad of police to haul him out of his chambers.

Was Lincoln responsible for the income tax?

Yes . . .

. . . in the sense that he signed into law the first federal income tax in American history, on August 5, 1861. It was a bill passed by Congress, not something that Lincoln declared unilaterally like the Emancipation Proclamation, so he can't get all the blame (or credit). The 1861 law exempted all incomes below $800 per year, at a time when the per capita income nationally was about $300. Higher incomes were to be taxed at 3 percent.

Before the law could be generally enforced, Congress passed the Internal Revenue Act of 1862, which revised the income tax by lowering the exemption to $600, taxing the amount between $600 and $10,000 at 3 percent, and taxing income above $10,000 at 5 percent. The act also established the Bureau of Internal Revenue and levied a series of other taxes, on luxuries, inheritances, vices (alcohol and tobacco), corporations and their dividends, and so on. By the judicious use of taxation, borrowing (through bond sales), and paper money (greenbacks), the federal government managed to pay for the Civil War while keeping inflation under control, something the Confederate government was unable to do.

Congress ended the income tax in 1872, then passed another version in 1894 that was ruled unconstitutional by the Supreme Court in 1895. The modern income tax began after the Constitution was amended to allow it in 1913.

Did Lincoln make Thanksgiving a national holiday?

He helped, but the real credit goes to Sarah Josepha Hale . . .

. . . the poet who wrote "Mary Had a Little Lamb." She was also the editor of *Godey's Lady's Book*, the most influential women's magazine of the era, and she had a bee in her bonnet about the United States having a national day of thanksgiving. She went from governor to governor trying to get them to issue thanksgiving proclamations for their states, until she finally hit upon the idea of going over their heads to the White House. In the fall of 1863, Lincoln was preoccupied with other matters, like the address he was writing to deliver at Gettysburg on November 19, but he agreed to sign a Proclamation of Thanksgiving drafted by his secretary of state, William Seward. He might have forgotten about his pledge to Hale to declare the holiday annually had she not reminded him in 1864, when he issued another proclamation.[27]

Lincoln issued a number of thanksgiving proclamations, usually tied to events in the war. The one associated with the last Thursday in November was actually the second one of 1863, the first having been issued in July and designating August 6 as a day to give thanks for recent Union victories at Gettysburg and Vicksburg. Had there not been a second proclamation, we might today be playing football and eating too much turkey in the heat of early August every year.[28]

Did Mary remodel the White House without telling him?

She did it without telling him what it cost.

Back in Springfield, when the Lincolns outgrew the modest story-and-a-half cottage on the corner of Eighth and Jackson, Mary used money from her inheritance to add a full second story, supposedly without her husband's prior approval. In the White House, Mary built on this precedent to go on a redecorating spree, using $20,000 that Congress allocated for the purpose. To be fair, the place needed it, as the prior tenant had been a bachelor who did not keep things up as well as he might. New paint and furniture were long overdue, to repair the "faded, worn, untidy look" that presidential secretary William O. Stoddard found in 1861. Mary Lincoln's cousin Elizabeth wrote that the "deplorably shabby" furniture in the family's rooms looked as if it had been there since Washington was president.[29]

For Mary Lincoln, refurbishing the White House represented an important opportunity to establish herself as the "First Lady," a term first applied to her. To the doubting doyens of Washington society who regarded her as an uncouth frontier woman, Mrs. Lincoln intended to demonstrate the sophistication of her taste. She ordered expensive new carpets, wallpaper, and china, the latter trimmed in a fashionable new shade of reddish purple called solferino, after the battle of Solferino in 1859.* Her taste was so lavish that she managed to overspend her appropriation by more than $6,000, a fact she was unable to hide from the president. When he found out, he was outraged. Imagining the political response, he said that "it would stink in the land" to ask Congress for more money "when the poor freezing soldiers could not have blankets," and vowed to pay the costs himself rather than approve any more bills for "*flub dubs for that damned old house!*" especially since it was already furnished "better than any house *they* had ever lived in."[30]

With help from her friend Charles Sumner, Mary eventually got the money from Congress anyway. On February 5, 1862, she held a grand dinner for five hundred invited guests to show off what she had accomplished. The evening was a great success. There were a few minutes of confusion when the doors to the dining room failed to open at 11 p.m. as scheduled (the steward had mislaid the key), but all was forgotten when the guests saw the "magnificent supper" provided by Maillard of New

*The battle, fought by France, Austria, and Sardinia, was part of the war for Italian independence, which also featured the battle of Magenta (June 4, 1859), inspiration for another high-fashion color.

York, including confectionary models of Fort Sumter and a steamship. The party lasted until three in the morning, but unfortunately, Mary and her husband were unable to enjoy her triumph. They spent the evening slipping away in shifts to sit at the bedside of their son Willie, who had contracted typhoid fever and would live only two more weeks.[31]

Did Lincoln appear before a Congressional committee to defend his wife's loyalty to the Union?

No, but there's a story out there that he did.

It has the Joint Committee on the Conduct of the War, which regularly met in secret to oversee Lincoln's actions, questioning his wife's patriotism. After all, the committee thinks, Mary Todd Lincoln of the slave state of Kentucky has a brother and three half brothers serving in Southern armies. In 1863, she allowed her half sister Emilie Todd Helm to stay at the White House after Emilie's husband, Brigadier General Benjamin Hardin Helm, was killed at Chickamauga—fighting for the South. But before the committee can even begin calling witnesses to start the inquisition, the president arrives unexpectedly, stands before them with hat in hand, declares his unequivocal faith in Mary's loyalty, and leaves.

In the story, this dramatic testimony puts the kibosh on any further Congressional speculation about Mrs. Lincoln. In real life, it never happened.[32] No president before Gerald Ford ever appeared formally in front of a Congressional committee. The constitutional separation of powers generally makes it unthinkable that a president would deign to testify before Congress. Only under the extraordinary circumstance of President Ford's pardon of former president Richard Nixon did a sitting president agree to such a procedure.[33]

What gives this Lincoln legend particular interest is that historians have had the opportunity to see it grow before their eyes, like geologists studying the birth of a volcanic island. It may have begun as a confused version of Lincoln's meetings with Republican members of the House Judiciary Committee in 1862 over suspicions that Mary Lincoln was involved in leaking the president's 1861 Annual Message to Congress to the *New York Herald;* these meetings were misreported in the *New York Tribune,* as though Lincoln had formally testified before the committee.[34] Whatever the source, the story of Lincoln suddenly showing up before the Committee on the Conduct of the War first appeared in a newspaper article published around 1905, then as a pamphlet in 1916, as part of a book in 1931, and in Carl Sandburg's famous 1939 biography (*The War Years,* vol. 2, p. 200, published in 1939). Many people read it there, but it still lay beneath the surface of public consciousness. Finally, in 1973, it erupted. During the Watergate hearings, Senator Lowell Weicker read Sandburg's account aloud in an effort to persuade Richard Nixon to appear before Congress voluntarily and explain himself. Now everyone "knew" that Lincoln had gone hat in hand to stand in front of Congress when the good of the country required it. Although Lincoln experts immediately pointed out that there was no evidence to support the story, the cat was out of the bag, and the legend continues to circulate today.[35]

Since the last decade of the twentieth century, the Internet has made it possible for conscientious writers to check the validity of Lincoln stories like this one before incorporating them into speeches, books, or other publications. It has also made it possible for sloppy or malicious writers to create and spread new Lincoln legends much faster than ever before. In December 2003, for example, a magazine columnist who thought antiwar members of Congress should be "exiled, arrested, or hanged" attributed those words (wrongly) to Abraham Lincoln. The new quote immediately began circulating below the scholarly radar, appearing on Web sites some 18,000 times over the next three years, until it finally burst into the view of the mainstream when a Representative from Alaska read it on the floor of Congress. Retractions and corrections followed, but the damage was done, and the quote has become part of the ever-increasing stock of things that Lincoln didn't really say.[36]

Did the Lincolns have a secret summer home?

The Lincoln version of Camp David was a retreat called the Soldiers' Home, but it wasn't secret then.

Everybody knew that in the summer, the president and his family lived in a spacious "cottage" on a hill in northwest Washington, on the grounds of the Soldiers' Home, some three miles from the White House.* In

*The Soldiers' Home complex is still there on Rock Creek Church Road, near the campus of Catholic University. Known since 2001 as the Armed Forces Retirement Home, it has more than 1,200 residents and its own golf course.

1861, the Lincolns stayed in town, but one D.C. summer without air-conditioning was enough for them, and the next three years saw them moving to the breezy heights of the Soldiers' Home, where summer temperatures are today as much as ten degrees cooler than those of downtown Washington.[37] Lincoln commuted to work on horseback or in a carriage.

After the war, the Soldiers' Home campus continued to fulfill its original function as a home for disabled veterans. The house where the Lincolns stayed, which came to be known as the Anderson Cottage, served as a presidential retreat until the 1880s. It was later converted to office space and eventually fell into neglect, its historical importance largely forgotten until 1995, when historian David E. Long proposed a preservation effort that ultimately led to the creation of the President Lincoln and Soldiers' Home National Monument in 2000.

What was a typical day like for President Lincoln?

Busy.

Lincoln got up early to get a head start on his paperwork, signing appointments and commissions, then met visitors for most of the day. He was by far the most accessible president the country had ever had, and long lines of people waited in the halls of the White House to ask him for a job, beg for a favor, complain about some injustice, or just shake his hand. He met with whoever came to see him, from cabinet officers to farmers, from housewives to Harriet Beecher Stowe,[38] from General Tom Thumb (two feet nine inches tall) of P. T. Barnum's circus to Senator Charles Sumner (about six feet four, a fraction below Lincoln), from Stephen Douglas to Frederick Douglass.

To prevent him from spending all his time in this fashion, his secretaries John Nicolay and John Hay tried to limit his visiting hours and establish some routine. "It was a four years' struggle on Nicolay's part and mine to get him to adopt some systematic rules," Hay wrote. They learned, as Billy Herndon had in the Springfield law office, that Lincoln "had no managing faculty nor organizing power."[39] He did meet with his cabinet two afternoons each week, and he tried to take time for a carriage ride before dinner each day, accompanied by his wife or a political friend, but otherwise he usually made himself available to the public, despite the attempts of his secretaries to give him some peace and quiet. There were no polls or surveys to tell Lincoln what his constituents wanted, and he relied on his "*public-opinion baths*" to keep his finger on the pulse of the body politic.[40]

How big was his White House staff?

Tiny.

In addition to Nicolay and Hay, his personal secretaries, there was just William O. Stoddard (later replaced by Edward Neill), supplemented by other clerks.[41] Nicolay, Hay, and Stoddard were all younger than thirty years old when they came to the White House. There was also a domestic staff of cooks, servants, and the doorkeeper, "Old Edward" McManus. It wasn't much.

How much mail did he get?

More than two hundred pieces a day.

Did Lincoln answer his own mail?

Some of it . . .

. . . although his secretaries only let him see a few letters each day. They screened the nut mail, for instance. William O. Stoddard recounted how a White House visitor with rising anger watched him as he read and discarded incoming letters. Finally the visitor could not stand it and began to berate him for denying the people their right to communicate with the chief executive. Stoddard handed the man a sample of the worst threats and abuse from that morning's mail and asked him to read it. In a few moments, the visitor gasped, "Young man! You are right! He ought not to see a line of that stuff! Burn it, sir! Burn it! What devils there are!"[42]

Lincoln often relied on Hay or Nicolay to draft replies for him to sign.[43] On at least one occasion, however, Lincoln did the reverse, drafting a reply for Nicolay's signature. In response to a crank telegram from a constituent who insisted that "White men is in class number one & black men is in class number two & must be governed by white men forever," Lincoln allowed himself the luxury of venting his spleen with a sarcastic reply:

> The President has received yours of yesterday, and is kindly paying attention to it. As it is my business to assist him whenever I can, I will thank you to inform me, for his use, whether you are either a white man or black one, because in either case, you can not be regarded as an entirely impartial judge. It may be that you belong to a third or fourth class of *yellow* or *red* men, in which case the impartiality of your judgment would be more apparant [*sic*].[44]

Why didn't Lincoln sign every letter himself?

Because he knew better than to write his name under anything that he did not want to see in the paper the next day.

Once in a while, however, his caution slipped. He responded to a letter from James H. Hackett, a famous actor, with an enthusiastic discussion of Shakespeare in which he offered his opinion that Claudius's "O, my offence is rank" is a greater soliloquy than Hamlet's "To be, or not to be." Lincoln perhaps assumed that a fellow celebrity would be willing to exchange private correspondence, but if so, he underestimated the power of his own aura and the desire of others to bask in it. Hackett leaked the letter to a reporter, and the press erupted in mockery of the idea that the uncultured buffoon in the White House should presume to engage in Shakespeare criticism, something like the way their twenty-first-century successors guffawed at the news that George W. Bush was spending his 2006 summer vacation reading French existentialism at his Texas ranch.[46] When Hackett apologized in a second letter, Lincoln brushed off the matter in classic form: "I have endured a great deal of ridicule without much malice; and have received a great deal of kindness, not quite free from ridicule. I am used to it."[47]

Did one of his secretaries write the Bixby letter?

Probably.

The most famous and controversial example of ghostwriting in the Lincoln White House is the letter of condolence to Mrs. Lydia Bixby, a widow from Boston:

> Dear Madam—I have been shown in the files of the War Department . . . that you are the mother of five sons who have died gloriously on the field of battle.

> I feel how weak and fruitless must be any words of mine which should attempt to beguile you from the grief of a loss so overwhelming. But I cannot refrain from tendering to you the consolation that may be found in the thanks of the Republic they died to save.
>
> I pray that our Heavenly Father may assuage the anguish of your bereavement, and leave you only the cherished memory of the loved and lost, and the solemn pride that must be yours, to have laid so costly a sacrifice upon the altar of Freedom. Yours, very sincerely and respectfully, A. LINCOLN.[47]

The letter was, in the words of author William E. Barton, "a beautiful blunder." Mrs. Bixby turned out to be a Southern sympathizer and possibly the keeper of a house of ill-repute. She had lost two sons in the war, not five, and two of her surviving boys had deserted. Most important, from a literary point of view, Lincoln's secretary John Hay was probably its author, not Lincoln. Suspicion that Hay wrote the letter arose with Barton's 1926 book but subsided until the 1990s when Michael Burlingame reopened the case, using textual analysis (Hay often used the word "beguile" in writing; Lincoln never did) and circumstantial evidence (a clipping of the letter appears in Hay's scrapbook). The original letter, which would at least indicate who had actually penned the words, if not who had composed them, has long been lost; all that survive are copies of a forged version, which have been reproduced many times and are widely available.[48]

The scholarly consensus, which has swung back and forth since 1926, now seems to be on Hay's side as the author of the letter. Regardless of their authorship, the words retain their power and supplied the inspiration and concept for the 1998 movie *Saving Private Ryan.*

What was the "Blind Memorandum" that Lincoln wrote?

It was a document that he asked his cabinet secretaries to sign without reading.

In August 1864, Lincoln looked ahead to the November presidential election and saw no chance of winning. The previous summer's victories at Gettysburg and Vicksburg had not brought the war to an end, and this year's campaigns to capture Richmond and Atlanta had yet to show any results other than casualty lists of unprecedented size. Expecting not to be reelected, Lincoln wanted to be certain that his advisers were ready to follow him with blind loyalty, even to the point of committing themselves in writing to a policy they had not read. All of them signed.

What did it say?

"This morning, as for some days past, it seems exceedingly probable that this Administration will not be re-elected. Then it will be my duty to so co-operate with the President elect, as to save the Union between the election and the inauguration; as he will have secured his election on such ground that he can not possibly save it afterwards."[49]

In other words, Lincoln knew that signing an armistice that would end the war and permanently divide the Union would be at the top of his successor's to-do list, but that there would still be four months between the election and the inauguration in which he could make a last desperate effort to prevent that from happening.

Why not just postpone the election?

"We can not have free government without elections" . . .

. . . he said in November 1864, after victories at Atlanta, Mobile, and the Shenandoah Valley had secured his reelection, "and if the rebellion could force us to forego, or postpone a national election, it might fairly claim to have already conquered and ruined us." By risking electoral defeat, Lincoln helped vindicate the idea of democracy, and "demonstrated that a people's government can sustain a national election, in the midst of a great civil war. Until now it has not been known to the world that this was a possibility."[50]

FOR FURTHER READING

An excellent place to start is Phillip Shaw Paludan, *The Presidency of Abraham Lincoln* (1994). Mark E. Neely, Jr., *The Last Best Hope of Earth* (1993), is a succinct summary of the Lincoln presidency. James Randall, *Lincoln the President: Midstream* (1952) is a classic account. *Lincoln: A Life of Purpose and Power* (2006), by Richard Carwardine, is a biography that focuses heavily on the presidential years, with an emphasis on Lincoln's religious sensibilities. William Lee Miller, *President Lincoln: The*

Duty of a Statesman (2008) analyzes ethical issues of the Lincoln presidency with insight and wit.

For Lincoln and his cabinet, Doris Kearns Goodwin, *Team of Rivals: The Political Genius of Abraham Lincoln* (2005), is outstanding; if that piques your interest, read the diaries of Treasury Secretary Chase and Navy Secretary Welles, both available in libraries. Mark E. Neely, Jr., *The Fate of Liberty: Abraham Lincoln and Civil Liberties* (1991), deserved its Pulitzer Prize for the prodigious research that went into it. For life in the Lincoln White House, a good summary is Ronald Rietveld's article "The Lincoln White House Community" in the *Journal of the Abraham Lincoln Association* 20, no. 2 (summer 1999), available online. Michael Burlingame has edited numerous works by Nicolay, Hay, and Stoddard that give the inside view on the official workings of the White House. For the Soldiers' Home summer residence, read Matthew Pinsker, *Lincoln's Sanctuary: Abraham Lincoln and the Soldiers' Home* (2003). Harold Holzer, *Dear Mr. Lincoln* (1993) and *The Lincoln Mailbag* (1998), sample the incoming mail at the White House. The election of 1864 is analyzed in David E. Long, *The Jewel of Liberty: Abraham Lincoln's Re-election and the End of Slavery* (1994); a similar volume on the 1860 election is long overdue.

CHAPTER SEVEN

Commander in Chief

Thus often, I who am not a specially brave man have had to sustain the sinking courage of these professional fighters in critical times.

—Lincoln to his secretary John Hay, 1864[1]

Before Lincoln became commander in chief, did he have any military experience?

Yes, he served for not quite three months in the Black Hawk War.

In 1832, the Sac and Fox people followed their leader Black Hawk across the Mississippi River from what is now Iowa into Illinois. In the eyes of Illinois settlers it looked like an invasion, and the governor called out the militia, which included Lincoln and most of the other boys of New Salem. He enjoyed his brief active service and especially valued the respect shown by his fellow soldiers when they elected him captain of their company, but he remained immune to the lure of martial life. Sixteen years later, he gave a speech in Congress opposing the war with Mexico, in which he made light of his service and condemned President Polk for trying to distract the public with dreams of military glory, "that attractive rainbow, that rises in showers of blood—that serpent's eye, that charms to destroy."[2] In an era when men traditionally carried titles with them long after leaving office (Stephen Douglas was known as "Judge Douglas" even after he became a senator), Lincoln chose to shed his military rank and go back to being Mister, not Captain, Lincoln.[3]

Were Lincoln and his men sworn into service in the Black Hawk War by Jefferson Davis?

No. Lincoln and Davis were in the war at the same time, but they didn't meet.

Davis, the future president of the Confederate States of America (so-called), was an officer in the First Infantry Regiment of the Regular Army, serving under a future U.S. president, Colonel Zachary Taylor, whose daughter he would marry. Davis and Lincoln didn't cross paths, contrary to what the second Mrs. Davis (not the colonel's daughter) wrote in her memoir of her husband's life.[4] Lincoln might have met Zachary Taylor, and he did meet Lieutenant Robert Anderson, who would be the commander of the garrison at Fort Sumter when Lincoln became president in March 1861. It was a much smaller country then.

Did he teach himself military strategy when he became president?

Not really. He borrowed a military textbook from the Library of Congress in 1862 . . .

. . . but his purpose was probably less to teach himself strategy than to learn the meaning of technical military terms like "mamelon" and "ravelin." As a lawyer, Lincoln knew the power of professional jargon as a tool to intimidate the uninitiated, and he was not about to let any of his generals attempt to talk down to him.[5] Borrowing a single book on the subject (Henry Halleck's *Elements of Military Art and Science*) was the full extent of Lincoln's formal military self-education.[6]

Was Lincoln a military genius?

As of now, yes. But the answer to this question has changed before and could change again.

During the first two years of the war, almost no one (including Lincoln) would have characterized him as a military genius. The Union war effort under Lincoln's leadership floundered, as he sought vainly to find generals of the same caliber as their Confederate opponents. This was especially the case in Virginia, where the series of leaders he appointed met defeat again and again. These men included Irvin McDowell (who lost at Bull Run), George McClellan (lost the Seven Days' Battles), John Pope (lost Second Bull Run), McClellan again (unable to crush Lee's army at Antietam, even though his army was much larger, and he possessed a copy of Lee's secret campaign plan), Ambrose Burnside (lost Fredericksburg), Joseph Hooker (lost Chancellorsville), and finally George Meade. At Gettysburg, Meade brought Lee's invasion of Pennsylvania to a halt, but when he encouraged his men to "drive from our soil every vestige of the presence of the invader," Lincoln was exasperated by Meade's limited vision. To John Hay, Lincoln complained, "Will our Generals never get that idea out of their heads? The whole country is *our* soil."[7]

Eventually Lincoln found the right commanders, in Ulysses S. Grant and William T. Sherman. Victories followed, but Lincoln's military reputation remained spotty. Until the early twentieth century, most writers pictured him as a civilian bumbler who only succeeded when he stepped aside and let Grant do the job. Grant's memoirs, though generally favorable to Lincoln, reinforced this portrait of a president who wisely deferred to professional soldiers. Then came World War I, when civilian leaders allowed their military counterparts to butcher an entire generation of European youth in the trenches of Flanders and the forests of Russia, for no political gain to anyone. Afterward, when Georges Clemenceau was credited with saying that war was "too important to be left to the generals," Lincoln came to be seen as the model for strong civilian control over the military. After World War II, historian T. Harry Williams took the case for Lincoln as military genius a step further by arguing that even after the appointment of Grant, Lincoln remained firmly in control of Union military strategy, and that he directed this strategy with consummate skill. Williams's argument was so persuasive that it remains the orthodox view today, but as historian Richard Current observed, writing in 1958 of the debate over Lincoln's military skill, "Since the points at issue are matters of *judgment* rather than of *fact,* it will probably go on forever."[8]

You said Lincoln "eventually" found the right commanders—why did it take so long?

A lot of people wanted to know the same thing in 1862.

After the first major battle of the war, at Bull Run in July 1861, Lincoln sacked the commander of the defeated Army of the Potomac and replaced him with George B. McClellan, the "Young Napoleon." He was a brilliant organizer and motivator who drilled the Army of the Potomac until it was honed to a fine edge.

Then he kept on honing, and drilling, and organizing, and motivating, until Lincoln (and many others in the North) wondered if he were ever going to attack. Lincoln at first showed the general great deference when they met to discuss strategy, and McClellan said all the right things in return, but in private he repaid the president with contempt, calling him an "idiot" and a "baboon."[9] Sometimes McClellan let slip his mask of civility. On November 13, 1861, Lincoln and Secretary of State Seward, with John Hay, went to McClellan's house, only to find the general out. They waited for him to return, but when he did he refused to see the president, sending a servant to deliver the message that the general had gone to bed and could not be disturbed.

Lincoln kept his temper, saying on another occasion that he would be willing to hold McClellan's horse if it would lead to victory. He tried to exercise his authority as commander in chief, issuing "President's General War Order No. 1" on January 27, 1862, which called for "a general movement of the Land and Naval forces of the United States against the insurgent forces" on February 22, in a grand military celebration of Washington's birthday—but McClellan ignored it.[10] In March 1862, McClellan finally moved, transporting his enormous army by sea to

Lincoln and McClellan at Antietam, October 3, 1862 (Courtesy of The Lincoln Museum, Fort Wayne, TLM O-62)

Fortress Monroe, on the tip of the peninsula formed by the York and James rivers southeast of Richmond. It was a clever move that outflanked the rebel defenses near Manassas and offered the possibility of a quick seizure of the Confederate capital, but by this time Lincoln had little faith left in Little Mac.

So why did he put up with McClellan?

Because he had no one who could replace him.

As dilatory as McClellan was, Lincoln recognized that he was very popular with his troops (in part because he was so sparing with their lives), and that he was a man of rare administrative talent. Civil War buffs tend to regard McClellan with scorn, but many of us struggle trying to get the luggage and family packed into the minivan so four people and a dog can leave on time for vacation; McClellan moved more than 100,000 men from Washington, D.C., to the Virginia Peninsula smoothly and efficiently in March 1862. If he were going to replace the popular and technically competent McClellan, Lincoln would need somebody who was not only aggressive but also at least reasonably skilled and well liked by the soldiers. To a Republican senator who was dissatisfied with both McClellan's lack of zeal for fighting and his tender regard for the property rights of the civilian slaveholders in his army's path, Lincoln asked who should take his place. "Anybody!" was the answer, but that was just the problem. "*Anybody* will do for you, but not for me," Lincoln replied. "I must have *somebody*."[11]

In 1862, there were very few somebodies available within the Army of the Potomac. None of the next four highest-ranking officers below McClellan were reasonable candidates (if you can name two of them, it's time to get a new hobby).[12] Outside the Army of the Potomac, Lincoln was having just as much trouble trying to goad into action the commanders of his Western armies, Henry Halleck and Don Carlos Buell, the latter described by historian T. Harry Williams as "McClellan without charm or glamor."[13] It's easy today to compare McClellan to Sherman or Grant and say that he does not measure up well, but Lincoln could only measure McClellan against his available replacements, and in early 1862 there weren't many. Lincoln left McClellan in command until he was defeated in the Seven Days' Battles and then recalled him to command after John Pope was defeated at Second Bull Run.

How did he finally get rid of McClellan?

He waited until after the November elections.

In September 1862, McClellan obtained a copy of Lee's campaign orders and used it to maneuver the rebel army into battle at Antietam but still could only manage a draw against a much smaller Confederate force. Lincoln urged him to pursue Lee, but McClellan offered nothing but excuses, including the fatigued state of his horses. "Will you pardon me for asking what the horses of your army have done since the battle of Antietam that fatigue anything?" Lincoln replied, with unusual sharpness.[14] Having visited the army to be sure that its men would not mutiny upon removal of their beloved leader, and after waiting for the Congressional elections to pass, Lincoln replaced McClellan on November 5, 1862.

Did McClellan and Lincoln know each other before the war?

Yes, but not well.

McClellan lived in Chicago and worked for the Illinois Central, the same railroad that Lincoln represented in the McLean County case and later sued for his fee. According to Herndon, when Lincoln presented the railroad with a bill for $4,000, it was rejected by the company's representative, who happened to be George McClellan. "This is as much as Daniel Webster himself would have charged," is what Herndon has McClellan saying, and it made Lincoln so mad that he increased the bill to $5,000 and sued the railroad. It's a good story, but McClellan was in Europe observing the Crimean War on behalf of the War Department when the case was decided in 1856.[15]

The facts are that McClellan did not start working for the Illinois Central until 1857. Lincoln might have encountered him in New York the following year, when he went there to try to collect his fee, and they saw each other a number of times during the 1858 Illinois senatorial campaign (McClellan supported Douglas and gave him use of a private railroad car), but that was the limit of their contact.

How about Confederate General George Pickett, of Pickett's Charge fame—wasn't he an old friend of Lincoln?

Mrs. Pickett said he was . . .

. . . but you just can't believe that old liar LaSalle Corbell Pickett. The story comes from her 1917 memoir, *What Happened to Me,* which contains an imaginative account of the events of April 3, 1865, the day after Lee's army retreated from Richmond. According to Mrs. Pickett, when Abraham Lincoln made his famous visit to the city, accompanied only by a few sailors and his young son Tad, he stopped in at her house to pay his respects and kiss the couple's new baby. "Tell your father, the rascal," Lincoln supposedly said to George, Jr., "that I forgive him for the sake of your bright eyes." The story is inherently improbable, and none of the other thousands of people who saw Lincoln in Richmond that day seem to have noticed any side trips to the Pickett household.

The story still occasionally surfaces, however, because Mrs. Pickett was skilled at promoting her husband's reputation by using just enough of the truth to keep things plausible. In the 1840s, George Pickett did spend some time studying law with an uncle named Andrew Johnston in Quincy, Illinois. Lincoln knew Johnston and might well have met young George. When Pickett sought an appointment to the U.S. Military Academy, it was Lincoln's old law partner John Todd Stuart who arranged it. It's certainly possible that Lincoln knew who George Pickett was. Perhaps he even remembered meeting the man who gave his name to the fabled, doomed charge that ended rebel hopes for victory at Gettysburg. When Sally Pickett described this tenuous relationship as a friendship, however, she was exaggerating at best; when she described Lincoln's visit to her home amid the ruins of Richmond, she was concocting a fantasy.[16]

Didn't he once ask General McClellan if he could borrow the army, since McClellan was not using it?

Probably.

That particular line supposedly comes from the Peninsula campaign in the spring of 1862. When Lincoln visited the army after Antietam, he remarked that it was not really an army at all, just McClellan's bodyguard.[17] On several occasions he seriously considered invoking his constitutional power as commander in chief and taking personal control of the army. One of these was immediately after the battle of Gettysburg, in order to complete the pursuit and destruction of Lee's forces. General George Meade failed to do that, Lincoln told his son Robert, but "If I had gone up there, I could have whipped them myself."[18]

Was he serious?

I think so. Most writers have assumed that Lincoln was just venting . . .

. . . but he made comments about taking command on more than one occasion, enough times to think that he at least considered the idea.[19] Fortunately, Lincoln had the self-awareness to know that the battlefield was not the place for him.

Why not? Didn't he understand military strategy at least as well as people like McClellan?

Yes, but war is more than an elaborate chess game.

A lot of spotty thirteen-year-old fanboys (and some girls) spend enough time playing video war games to understand the principles of strategy pretty well, but that doesn't mean they would make good generals. It's true that Lincoln demonstrated an intuitive grasp of such strategic concepts as interior and exterior lines (January 1862: Lincoln urges Halleck and Buell to coordinate their attacks); maintenance of the objective (June 1863: Lincoln reminds Hooker that defeating Lee's army, not capturing Richmond, should be his goal); and the value of the offensive (August 1864: Lincoln tells Grant to "Hold on with a bull-dog gripe [*sic*], and chew & choke, as much as possible").[20] Lincoln also had the self-confidence and moral courage to make difficult decisions and to stand behind them and accept the consequences. In this, Lincoln outdid most of his generals, especially the ones who led his armies in the first two years of the war.

The problem is that being a great general and a great political leader require different skills. Had Lincoln taken the field as a literal commander in chief, he would have found little further use for the political skills that made him great. His ability to negotiate, to see the other side's point of view, to find a favorable middle ground, to use humor to soothe injured feelings, all would have been useless to him in the world of war, where intense single-mindedness of purpose and iron conviction in one's own military ability were the hallmarks of successful generals like Grant, Stonewall Jackson, and Sherman. Leading the Union war effort from the White House took its toll on Lincoln, as can be seen in the difference between photographs taken in 1860 and 1865. Had he shouldered the even more direct burden of watching as thousands of men went into battle to be killed or maimed, it is hard to imagine that he still could have maintained the reservoir of humanity that allowed him to call for peace "with malice toward none; with charity for all" in 1865.

Did he ever see a battle?

Yes.

In 1864, Grant was hounding Lee's army in the bloody battles of the Wilderness, Spotsylvania, and Cold Harbor, while constantly maneuvering closer to Richmond. To relieve the pressure, Lee sent a force under Jubal Early into the Shenandoah Valley, hoping that it would distract the War Department's attention and perhaps fool Lincoln into pulling resources away from Grant, just as he had done to McClellan in response to Stonewall Jackson's Valley campaign of May 1862. Early's small force marched through the valley, crossed the Potomac north into Maryland,

The toll of war: June 1860 and February 1865 (Courtesy of The Lincoln Museum, Fort Wayne, IN, TLM O-25 and TLM O-116)

ABRAHAM LINCOLN, Pres't U. S.
Entered according to Act of Congress, by Alex. Gardner, in the year 1865, in the Clerk's Office of the District Court for the District of Columbia

and approached Washington, but it was not nearly large enough to break through the powerful fortifications surrounding the capital. Still, Early was determined to draw a reaction, so on July 12 and 13 he probed the defenses near Fort Stevens, not far from the Soldiers' Home on the outskirts of the city.

Lincoln could not resist the opportunity to go and see the fighting, which he watched from a parapet. A military surgeon standing near Lincoln was wounded in the leg, and Lincoln was quickly told to take cover, which he did. There are conflicting accounts as to who ordered the commander in chief not to stand up under enemy fire, one claimant being a young officer named Oliver Wendell Holmes, Jr. (the future Supreme Court justice), who later wrote that he did not recognize Lincoln and yelled, "Get down, you fool!"[21] Even though there is no evidence to corroborate Holmes's version of the incident, the story is so irresistible that it appears in many Lincoln biographies. Less well known is Lincoln's other personal military encounter with the Confederacy, when he conducted a Navy SEAL–style reconnaissance of an enemy shoreline in 1862.

For real? Lincoln was involved in a dangerous military operation?

Absolutely.

When McClellan's forces were inching their way up the Peninsula toward Richmond in May 1862, Lincoln visited the army to see what was taking so long. One obstacle to their progress was the threat of the Confederate ironclad C.S.S. *Virginia* (née U.S.S. *Merrimac*), based at the navy yard in Norfolk, Virginia, across the James River from the Peninsula. If Union troops could land on the south bank of the James, they could force the Confederates to abandon Norfolk and leave the *Virginia* with no base from which to operate. No such amphibious operation had been planned, however, because the Union generals and admirals in charge believed that there were no suitable landing sites. To get them off the dime, Lincoln decided to see for himself. Accompanied by Edwin Stanton and Salmon Chase, Lincoln sailed in a revenue cutter close to the enemy shore. Lincoln and Stanton then transferred to a smaller boat and actually landed on the beach. The secretary of war on a personal reconnaissance of enemy territory must have been the second-most surreal sight of the entire war, surpassed only by that of the president of the United States walking point on the same mission. The next day, using the information Lincoln and Stanton had collected, soldiers crossed the James (led by Chase) and took Norfolk from the rebels, who blew up the *Virginia* to save it from capture.[22]

Did Lincoln hire a substitute to fight for him?

Yes.

After the initial flood of volunteers dried up, both sides in the Civil War started drafting men into their armies. The federal government was not particular about whom it got, so if your name came up you could put on the uniform or hire someone to do it for you. The draft law also provided the option of paying a $300 commutation fee, which got you out of the immediate draft but left you eligible for the next. The idea behind the fee was to prevent runaway inflation in the price of substitutes, who otherwise might ask for thousands of dollars.

Abraham Lincoln, as commander in chief, was exempt from the draft, but he nonetheless hired a substitute, John Summerfield Staples of Pennsylvania, to serve in his stead. He also found a place for his oldest son, Robert, to serve (on the staff of General Grant), much against Mary Lincoln's wishes. Both were symbolic gestures of Lincoln's willingness to subject his family to the same demands that the war was inflicting on so many hundreds of thousands of others.

Didn't one of his generals plan to replace him and take over the government as a dictator?

Actually there were two of them who did . . .

. . . or at least who thought about it. It's too much to say that either George McClellan or Joseph Hooker actually got to the planning stage, but each believed that it might not be a bad idea if he took over the government as a temporary strongman, on the model of an ancient Roman dictator. McClellan wrote to his wife after he was appointed to command the Army of the Potomac in July 1861, "I almost think were I to win some small success now I could become Dictator."[23] His inability to win any such successes largely precluded that possibility, but Lincoln always remained conscious of the danger posed by the intense loyalty that McClellan's troops held for their leader. As for Joseph Hooker, he openly spoke of the need for a dictator to replace the imbeciles in Washington who were botching the war effort. Lincoln went ahead and promoted Hooker to lead the Army of the Potomac but did so with a letter warning him that Lincoln knew what he was thinking:

> I have heard, in such way as to believe it, of your recently saying that both the Army and the Government needed a Dictator. Of course it was not *for* this, but in spite of it, that I have given you the command. Only those generals who gain successes, can set up dictators. What I now ask of you is military success, and I will risk the dictatorship.[24]

Didn't Lincoln offer to send a barrel of Grant's whiskey to his other generals?

No, but he appreciated the joke, which was circulating even then.

When the war began, Grant was an obscure, underemployed loser with a West Point ring and a rumored drinking problem. Not surprisingly, he was not given a high command at first. His performance in small battles like the one at Belmont, Missouri, and larger ones like the capture of Forts Henry and Donelson led to the opportunity to command an army at Shiloh, where he was taken by surprise and nearly defeated. Although he recovered and won the battle, he was punished afterward by his superior, Henry Halleck, who effectively removed him from field command. The story that Lincoln defended Grant by saying, "I can't spare this man: he fights," is almost certainly a myth, but it captures the fact that Grant's aggressiveness set him apart from other generals.[25] The president eventually gave him a series of increasingly important assignments, culminating in command of all Union armies in March 1864.

After the Union defeat at Fredericksburg in December 1862, which cost the Army of the Potomac some 12,000 men, Lincoln made a brutal assessment of the military situation. The Confederates had suffered fewer than half the losses of the Union army in that battle, but they had fewer men in their army to start with. If a series of Fredericksburgs could be fought in a week, Union losses would be enormous, but Lee's army would run out of men first. In the long run, Lincoln noted, this would actually save lives by shortening the war, since more men died of disease in camp than from bullets on the battlefield. It was not a pretty way to win, but it would get the job done, if only someone would do it. "No general yet found can face the arithmetic," Lincoln concluded sadly. Grant, although he was far more than the military butcher described by his detractors, turned out to be the general who could face the arithmetic.[26]

Did he pardon a soldier who was about to be executed for sleeping on duty?

He pardoned a lot of soldiers . . .

. . . much to the distress of some of his generals, who thought that it undermined discipline to have such a softhearted man at the top of the chain of command. The story of the sleeping sentinel, William Scott of the 3rd Vermont regiment, was simply the most famous. In August 1861, Scott was found sleeping while on guard duty, a crime punishable by death under military law. A popular poem written by Francis de Hayes Janvier in 1863 described how, just before Scott was to be executed, Abraham Lincoln arrived "rolling through a cloud of dust" in a "stately coach" to grant Scott a pardon. A book written in 1891 contained another version of the story, in which Lincoln paid Scott a visit the night before the execution, to assure him that the sentence would not be carried out if Scott would promise to be a good soldier. In both versions, Scott dies heroically at the battle of Lee's Mill a few months later.[27]

Lincoln scholars long assumed that the story was pure myth, but in 1997, the pardon document was found in the National Archives. Lincoln didn't visit Scott or show up at the last second, but he did sign a pardon for Scott, who was in fact killed in action at Lee's Mill in April 1862. Further, Scott was only one of seventy-eight "sleeping sentinel" cases that Lincoln is known to have reviewed—he pardoned them all.[28] He insisted on personally reviewing every case of capital punishment, as well as many other court-martial sentences, and he frequently granted clemency. It was one of the few moments of relief he experienced as president, he told a friend. "Some of my generals complain that I impair discipline by my frequent pardons and reprieves; but it rests me, after a day's hard work, that I can find some excuse for saving some poor fellow's life."[29]

Lincoln did not grant pardons to everyone, however. In the aftermath of the Sioux rebellion of 1862, a military commission passed death sentences on 303 captured warriors. Lincoln ordered the cases reviewed, to distinguish those who had committed war crimes against civilians from those who had simply fought against soldiers. He pardoned all but thirty-eight; but this still resulted in the largest mass hanging in American history.[30] Another prominent case was that of Nathaniel Gordon, caught by the U.S. Navy in 1860 with a ship full of slaves from Africa, in violation of the ban on importing slaves that Congress had passed in 1808. Lincoln made a point of refusing to grant clemency, and Gordon was hanged in February 1862.

Did Lincoln try to have Jeff Davis killed?

No, not explicitly, but some historians think that he had it in mind.

The argument is based on Lincoln's authorization of the infamous Dahlgren raid of 1864, an unsuccessful cavalry expedition that was supposed to ride into Richmond, Virginia, free the Union prisoners of war held there (who would then burn the city to the ground), and kidnap Jefferson Davis and his cabinet. To historian David E. Long, Lincoln's sanction of an attempt to kidnap the feisty Confederate president implied acceptance of the possibility that Davis would be killed while resisting, and thus Lincoln's willingness to go ahead with the plan was tantamount to authorizing the murder of Davis. In Long's view, Lincoln was a fierce warrior, dedicated to the survival of the Union at any price. In 1862, Lincoln calculated the daily cost of the war, as a way of demonstrating that it would be a bargain to secure the loyalty of the border states by paying for and emancipating the slaves who lived there; if he could do that, then surely he could have calculated the savings in lives that would follow an early end to the war, which in turn would justify killing the one man who was doing the most to keep it going, Jefferson Davis.[31]

There are, however, two problems with this argument. The first is that there is only circumstantial evidence that Lincoln approved of the Dahlgren raid. For many years historians even doubted that the raiders intended to kidnap Davis at all. The documents found on the body of Union officer Ulric Dahlgren that called for arson and kidnapping seemed to be forgeries, with Dahlgren's signature misspelled. More recently, historians have generally come to accept the argument of Confederate General Jubal Early, confirmed in the 1980s by James O. Hall, that the signature was not misspelled and only appeared so because of ink soaking through from the reverse of the page, but the authenticity of Dahlgren's documents still does not necessarily implicate Lincoln. They were not written or signed by him, and there are no documents in Lincoln's papers at the Library of Congress that clearly link the president to the raid.

Against this, those who believe Lincoln knew of the raid's goals can only point to his friendship with Dahlgren's father, Rear Admiral John Dahlgren, which implies that he would have known what Ulric was up to. They also note that Lincoln's papers passed through the hands of his son Robert and his loyal secretaries Hay and Nicolay after his death, so the absence of incriminating documents means only that the papers must have been "sanitized" before they were donated to the Library of Congress. Both points are true, but they prove nothing. The claim that Lincoln knew of the plan to kidnap Davis is not implausible, but it's based on speculation rather than firm evidence.

The second problem is that even if Lincoln did know of the plan, this does not make him guilty of attempting to kill Jeff Davis. In legal terms, it is not true that any act that is undertaken knowing it will result in death is necessarily a murder. For example, a philanthropist who generously finances the construction of a great public building may know that it is statistically certain that one or more workers will be killed in the process, but this obviously does not make the donation an act of murder. If Lincoln did order the capture of Jefferson Davis, even suspecting that Davis might resist at the cost of his life, this is not the same as ordering an assassination. Lincoln made a similar point metaphorically in 1860, describing the argument of secessionists who warned against electing a Republican president: "In that supposed event, you say, you will destroy the Union; and then, you say, the great crime of having destroyed it will be upon us! That is cool. A highwayman holds a pistol to my ear, and mutters through his teeth, 'Stand and deliver, or I shall kill you, and then you will be a murderer!' "[32]

Did Lincoln have something to do with machine guns?

Yes.

The Civil War was fought in an era of rapid and unpredictable technological change, and Lincoln was fascinated by the possibilities. He personally funded the purchase of a set of primitive machine guns for the army, after the director of ordnance decided against them as impractical. He occasionally went down to the Mall in Washington to test fire new rifles, as in those days the Mall was a swampy wasteland, not full of tourists or craft fairs as it generally is today.[33] Among his many other cares, Lincoln took the time to grant personal audiences to inventors and scientists who had ideas that they thought would help the Union win the war. Some were cranks, like the inventor Edward Tippett, who wrote of his gravity-powered "self-moving machine." which letter Lincoln filed away with the notation "Tippett: Crazy-Man."[34]

Others were not, like John Ericsson, a Swedish inventor and naval architect who proposed that the Union navy build a radical new warship that looked like a raft, riding barely a foot above the water, with no superstructure except a single revolving turret holding two enormous cannon.

At a meeting of Navy Department officers, Lincoln spoke up for the idea. "All I have to say is what the girl said when she put her foot into the stocking, 'It strikes me there's something in it.' "[35] The *Monitor* would be built just in time to contest for naval supremacy with the Confederate ironclad *Virginia/Merrimac.*

Intoxicated with the idea that the North now possessed an invincible new technology, Lincoln and his secretary of the navy embraced the idea of sending a whole fleet of "monitors" to sail into heavily defended Charleston Harbor and intimidate the city into surrendering without firing a shot. "The sublimity of such a silent attack is beyond words to describe," wrote one official.[36] The reality proved less sublime. When seven of the new ironclad wonder weapons attacked Charleston on April 7, 1863, their limitations were painfully revealed. Smokestacks, pilot houses, and lifeboats were shot away; turret turning gears and gunport shutters were jammed; sailors were shocked and deafened by the concussion of cannonballs denting the iron plating. After two hours, the fleet withdrew sullenly. Instead of a technological triumph, the president was handed a humiliating defeat. There was no technological shortcut to victory.

What did the soldiers think of Lincoln?

They laughed at his appearance . . .

. . . but they became increasingly devoted to him as the war progressed. "I have seldom witnessed a more ludicrous sight than our worthy Chief Magistrate presented on horseback," a Connecticut chaplain wrote in 1862. "It did seem as though every moment the Presidential limbs would become entangled with those of the horse he rode. . . . That arm with which he drew the rein, in its angles and position, resembled the hind leg of a grasshopper. . . . But *the boys* liked him, in fact his popularity in the army is and has been universal."[37] The "boys" in this case were McClellan's men, observing Lincoln's visit to the Army of the Potomac at Harrison's Landing near Richmond in July 1862. As much as they loved Little Mac, the soldiers ultimately proved more loyal to Lincoln. When McClellan ran for president in 1864, the soldiers' vote (in all the Union armies) ran about four to one in favor of reelecting "Father Abraham."[38]

FOR FURTHER READING

There are a number of excellent books and essays on various aspects of Lincoln as commander in chief, but no single volume dominates the field. For an introduction, William E. Gienapp, *Abraham Lincoln and Civil War America: A Biography* (2002), tells Lincoln's life story with emphasis on Lincoln's role as military leader during the Civil War. On Lincoln and his generals, the aptly titled *Lincoln and His Generals* (1952), by T. Harry Williams, is a highly readable classic but now outdated. *Lincoln's Generals* (1994), edited by Gabor S. Boritt, is a collection of thoughtful essays by Boritt, Stephen Sears, Mark Neely, Michael Fellman, and John Y. Simon. Ethan Rafuse, *McClellan's War: The Failure of Moderation in the Struggle for the Union* (2005), is especially interesting on the prewar relationship between Lincoln and McClellan. The memoirs of McClellan (modestly titled *McClellan's Own Story*) and Grant give very different perspectives on Lincoln from the two generals closest to the commander in chief.

Two good essay collections devoted in part to Lincoln as commander in chief are *The Lincoln Forum: Rediscovering Abraham Lincoln* (2002), edited by John Y. Simon and Harold Holzer, and James McPherson's *Abraham Lincoln and the Second American Revolution* (1991). For Lincoln's relationship with the men who served in the Union armies, see William C. Davis, *Lincoln's Men: How President Lincoln Became Father to an Army and a Nation* (1999). Thomas P. Lowry catalogs hundreds of court-martial cases that Lincoln reviewed in *Don't Shoot That Boy! Abraham Lincoln and Military Justice* (1999). Craig L. Symonds examines Lincoln's role as admiral in chief in his forthcoming *Lincoln and His Admirals* (2008). Robert V. Bruce, *Lincoln and the Tools of War* (1956), is still the standard account of Lincoln and military technology. Tom Wheeler, *Mr. Lincoln's T-Mails: The Untold Story of How Abraham Lincoln Used the Telegraph to Win the Civil War* (2006) retells some familiar stories in a breezy, journalistic style.

{ CHAPTER EIGHT }

Gettysburg

The world will little note, nor long remember, what we say here.

—From the Gettysburg Address, November 19, 1863[1]

Did Lincoln really think the world would not remember what he said at Gettysburg?

Perhaps. But he was certain that "it can never forget what they did here."

When the battle of Gettysburg ended on July 3, 1863, it was the moment for which Lincoln had been waiting two long years. Robert E. Lee's rebel army had finally been defeated. One more attack against Lee's weakened forces before they could retreat south of the Potomac, and the war would be over. There was no question that Gettysburg could be the decisive battle of the war.

But the Union army had suffered greatly as well. Its cautious commander, Major General George Meade, pursued Lee at a respectful distance, and the Confederates were able to escape. Lincoln was so disappointed and upset that Meade offered to resign, adding to Lincoln's troubles. He could not afford to lose the services of the only general who had not been intimidated by Robert E. Lee, so he immediately sat down to write Meade a conciliatory letter. He began by thanking Meade for his success and apologizing for offending him, but he soon came to the topic that was really on his mind: Why did you let Lee go? Lincoln hurled a series of rhetorical questions at Meade, like a parent berating a sulky teenager: "If you could not safely attack Lee last monday, how can you possibly do so South of the river?" He tried to make Meade feel as bad as he did: "Again, my dear general, I do not believe you appreciate the magnitude of the misfortune involved in Lee's escape." He laid on the guilt, pointing out that Meade's failure meant that now "the war will be prolonged indefinitely."[2] The next hundred thousand deaths will be *your* fault, General Meade.

It was a harsh letter, and a masterpiece of emotional manipulation. It must have made Lincoln feel a good deal better to have unburdened himself of all the anger and frustration the campaign had brought him, and to unload it on poor George Meade. Having obtained the release he needed, Lincoln then filed the letter away, unsigned and unsent. Meade's resignation was quietly refused, and he went on to serve with distinction until the end of the war.

Did Lincoln write the Gettysburg Address on the back of an envelope, on the train to Gettysburg?

(FRANK & ERNEST: © Thaves/Dist. by Newspaper Enterprise Association, Inc.)

No.

This may be the most famous and most persistent of all Lincoln myths. An early version appeared in Isaac Arnold's 1866 biography, in which Lincoln was not even notified that he would be expected to speak until he got on the train. The legend was popularized by *The Perfect Tribute*, a story by Mary Raymond Shipman Andrews published in *Scribner's* magazine in 1906, in which Lincoln wrote the address on a torn piece of brown wrapping paper, then crumpled it and dropped it on the floor of the train car in disgust. In that version, he repents of his littering, retrieves the scrap, and eventually reads it to the audience, which responds with complete silence, leaving him to conclude that the speech was a complete failure (another myth).[3]

In fact, the train ride would have been too bumpy to do any writing.

You can test this yourself by trying to write out the first sentence of the address while riding in a car. Even in a modern automobile, with rubber tires, coil springs, and hydraulic shock absorbers, you will have a hard time duplicating the clear, even penmanship that is found on all five surviving copies of the speech in Lincoln's hand. Now picture yourself on the rickety railroads of 1863, in a bouncing and swaying train car with rudimentary suspension. According to presidential secretary John Nicolay, who was there, Lincoln did no writing on the way to Gettysburg, "the rockings and joltings of the train, rendering writing virtually impossible."[4]

More important, Lincoln did not put off writing the address until the day before he gave it. Everything about his trip to Gettysburg to speak at the dedication of a national cemetery shows that he took it very seriously. It was a crucial opportunity to crystallize the meaning of the conflict for a war-weary Northern public, and he put a great deal of effort into choosing his words. He wrote the first page of an early draft on Executive Mansion stationery, not the back of an envelope. The neatness of even the earliest of the five surviving drafts implies that there may have been earlier compositional drafts in which Lincoln worked out his thoughts. He rarely left Washington, D.C., during the war, but for this occasion he planned to travel to Gettysburg a day ahead of time, even though it lay less than eighty miles away, so that his trip would not be "a mere breathless running of the gauntlet."[5] A few days before the trip his youngest son Tad became seriously ill, driving Mary almost hysterical with fear that he would follow his brother Willie into the grave, yet Lincoln went ahead with the trip as scheduled. In Gettysburg he stayed at David Wills's house and worked on the address further, both the night before and the morning of the dedication.[6] This was not an extemporaneous outpouring.

Yet the train/envelope story persists in spite of all the evidence against it. Its appeal is that it makes Lincoln's immortal words into a gift from the gods, a product of sudden inspiration instead of weeks of hard work. This is comforting, because it holds out the possibility that any one of us might be struck by a similar bolt of inspiration, perhaps while driving to work one day. The subtext of the story is one of anti-intellectualism; it exalts Lincoln as a genius at the same time that it devalues him as an intellectual laborer. It makes great ideas into something to be won in a cosmic lottery, rather than something earned by years of painstaking reading, arguing, speaking, and thinking. Lincoln himself would surely have rejected such an idea, just as he would have rejected this particular myth, which tells us much more about ourselves than it does about Abraham Lincoln.

So the train ride was too bumpy to write with a pen. Could he have done it if he had a laptop computer?

Yes, but with dire results.

If Lincoln had PowerPoint, the Gettysburg Presentation would have ended like this:[7]

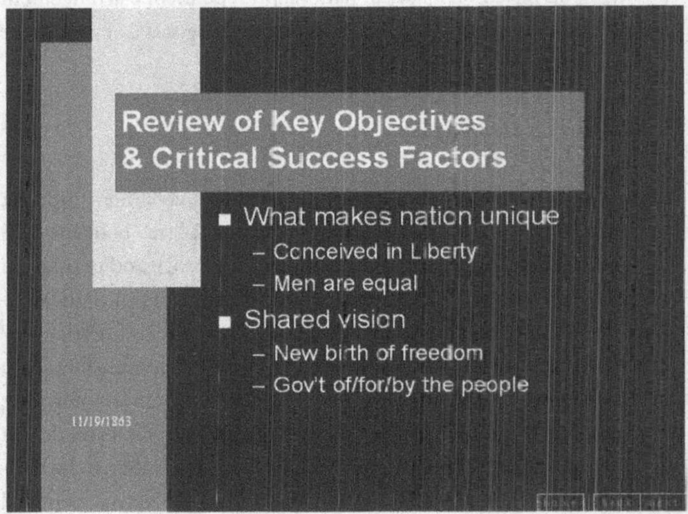

(Courtesy of Peter Norvig)

Rewriting the Gettysburg Address in another style is a staple of American cultural humor. Here's 1950s hipster Lord Buckley:

> *Four big hits and seven licks ago,*
> *our before-daddies swung forth upon this sweet groovy land*
> *a jumpin', wailin', stompin', swingin' new nation,*
> *hip to the cool sweet groove of liberty.*[8]

Late twentieth-century corporate jargon:

Within the parameters of an 87-year time period, our progenitors engendered on the Atlantic Rim, a state-of-the-art political paradigm, prioritized in personal empowerment, with an upfront sign-off on the mandate of a level playing field.[9]

President Eisenhower at a press conference:

I haven't checked these figures but 87 years ago, I think it was, a number of individuals organized a governmental set-up here in this country, I believe it covered certain Eastern areas, with this idea they were following up based on a sort of national independence arrangement and the program that every individual is just as good as every other individual.[10]

Calling the local pizza place:

Four score and seven minutes ago, our founding fathers brought forth upon the telegraph an order for a new pizza, conceived in hunger, and dedicated to the proposition that sausage and pepperoni would hit the spot . . . But, in a larger sense, we can not dedicate—we can not consume—we can not inhale—this pizza. The delivery driver, living or dead, who isn't here yet, is preventing us, far above our poor power to get the pie. The world will little note, nor long remember what we say here, but you will deeply regret it if you do not get our order here, pronto. It is for you the manager, rather, to be dedicated here to the unfinished work which your driver has screwed up . . .[11]

Didn't the Gettysburg dedication committee almost forget to invite Lincoln?

No.

It's another myth that the Gettysburg Address came about only because Lincoln was invited as an afterthought, and that he surprised everyone with the brevity of his talk after the main speaker's tedious and overblown two-hour stem-winder of an oration.* In fact, everything at the Gettysburg ceremony went more or less according to plan, which was unusual for any large-scale Civil War activity, civilian or military. The committee wanted to recognize the event with appropriate solemnity, so to give a speech they invited Edward Everett, a man who today is forgotten by everyone but Lincoln buffs and graduate history students. Everett, however, was very well known in 1863. He had been a U.S. senator, secretary of state, governor of Massachusetts, minister to England, president of Harvard University, and candidate for vice president in 1860. He was widely recognized as the foremost orator in America. The committee made no mistake in inviting Everett to give the main oration at Gettysburg.

Nor was Everett's speech at Gettysburg too long, at least as far as those who heard it were concerned. The audience expected him to provide a full afternoon's entertainment. Lincoln's speech, on the other hand, was not supposed to be a speech at all. Everyone who could read the program knew that he was supposed to be brief. Lincoln was there on behalf of the federal government, just to give the dedication; the actual "Gettysburg Address," as far as everybody there was concerned, was the oration by Everett. The next day Lincoln received a note from Everett praising his remarks, and he replied in kind, adding "you could not have been excused to make a short address, nor I a long one."[12]

If everyone there knew that Lincoln's presence was not just an afterthought but an appropriate part of the ceremony, how did this myth get started?

The primary suspect is Clark E. Carr . . .

. . . a member of the organizing committee from Illinois. In 1900, he wrote that "in considering the program of exercises it was suggested that

*Stem-winding watches (as opposed to those requiring keys to wind) were the latest in technology in 1863, and "stem-winder" became a metaphor for a rousing speech. In the late twentieth century, when battery-powered watches made stem-winders seem old-fashioned, the term began to acquire the opposite meaning, referring to a speech so long and boring that time seems to stand still and people in the audience keep winding their watches to be sure they are still working. It is used here in the latter sense, although Edward Everett's listeners would have described his speech with the former.

Mr. Lincoln be especially asked to speak." But six years later, Carr gave a speech in which he said that "it did not seem to occur to anyone that he could speak on such an occasion" and "the proposition to ask Mr. Lincoln to speak at the Gettysburg ceremonies was an afterthought." Later in 1906, Carr said in an interview that "there was immediate and vigorous objection" to the idea of Lincoln speaking, when it was proposed to the committee. A few years after that, Carr recalled that the committee objected to the idea, but "they finally yielded to my demands" that Lincoln speak. Had Carr lived much longer, we may suppose that he would have recalled supplying the envelope for Abe to write on, if not actually penning the address himself.[13]

So Lincoln didn't think the speech was a failure?

"Lamon, that speech won't *scour*" . . .

. . . is what he supposedly said to his bodyguard and marshal of ceremonies for the day, Ward Hill Lamon, as they left the stage.* According to some accounts there was no applause, and *The Perfect Tribute* has Lincoln responding to an attempted compliment from Everett by saying, "This isn't the first time I've felt that my dignity ought not to permit me to be a public speaker."[14]

Of course, the idea of Lincoln disavowing his ability to speak in public after a lifetime as a lawyer, legislator, and politician is absurd on its face. Sources conflict regarding the audience's response, with the primary newspaper account recording several instances of applause during and after Lincoln's words. Even if there were no applause at the end of the speech, which dedicated a cemetery for fallen heroes, this might have simply been appropriate behavior. People don't generally applaud at funerals either. As for the "scour" comment, the only source for it is the unreliable Lamon. If there is any real evidence that Lincoln was displeased with his effort, it is in his reply to Everett's complimentary note, where he wrote, "I am pleased to know that, in your judgement, the little I did say was not entirely a failure."[15]

*A plow that "scours" cuts through the ground smoothly, with no clumps of soil sticking to the moldboard. The quote is from Ward Hill Lamon, *Recollections of Abraham Lincoln 1847–1865* (1895), 171.

What did others think of it?

Press reports were mixed . . .

. . . as they were about every political event. One review that reappears every so often in articles about inaccurate media predictions reads: "The cheek of every American must tingle with shame as he reads the silly, flat and dishwatery remarks." It's allegedly from the *Chicago Times,* although no date for the article appears in Carl Sandburg's biography, and most other sources that quote it refer only to Sandburg. Still, it's not out of character for the partisan journalism of the era. If Jesus of Nazareth had descended from the sky and given the Sermon on the Mount at Gettysburg, on the same bill with Lincoln, it is safe to say that the virulently pro-Democratic, anti-Lincoln *Chicago Times* would have found fault with His presentation. Republican papers, on the other hand, loved the speech. Josiah Holland, later to write a biography of Lincoln, called it "a perfect gem" in the *Springfield* (Mass.) *Daily Republican.* James B. Angell, later president of the University of Michigan, asked in the *Providence Daily Journal,* "Could the most elaborate and splendid oration be more beautiful, more touching, more inspiring than those few words of the President?"[16]

The speech was thus not a failure, but it did take some time before it became one of the fundamental texts of American democracy. Lincoln's original manuscript of the Emancipation Proclamation was sold for three thousand dollars (the money went to benefit Union soldiers), but a handwritten copy of the Gettysburg Address found no buyers at a similar auction in 1864. Before the war was over, printmakers offered numerous editions of the Emancipation Proclamation for people to hang on their parlor walls, but for twenty years, Lincoln was correct in his prediction that his words at Gettysburg would be little noted, nor long remembered. Only after the failure of Reconstruction began to make the promise of freedom for the former slaves seem hollow did the Gettysburg Address begin to replace the Emancipation Proclamation in the public mind as Lincoln's most significant document.[17]

My kid's textbook has the Gettysburg Address in it, and they took out the phrase "under God." Can't these revisionists leave Lincoln's words alone?

It was Lincoln himself who couldn't leave his words alone.

There are five known different versions of the Gettysburg Address, all handwritten by Lincoln. The oldest version (known as the Nicolay copy) was written before he gave the speech and does not include the phrase "under God," nor does the second draft (the Hay copy). When he gave the speech, news reports confirm that he delivered the line "that the nation shall, under God, have a new birth of freedom." Over the next four months, he had occasion to make three additional copies (the Everett, Bancroft, and Bliss copies), all of which include "under God," but in a slightly different place: "that this nation, under God, shall have a new birth of freedom." The change is small, but powerful. Lincoln was a consummate craftsman who could not resist trying to perfect his work.[18]

Where are the copies now?

The Library of Congress (Nicolay and Hay copies), the White House (Bliss copy), Cornell University (Bancroft copy), and the Abraham Lincoln Presidential Library and Museum in Springfield (Everett copy).

Some historians believe that Lincoln read the address from the Hay copy (the second draft), but witnesses describe Lincoln as taking a folded sheet from his pocket that day, and the Hay copy has never been folded. Many others regard the Nicolay copy (the first draft) as the reading copy, but this would mean that Lincoln ad-libbed the phrase "under God" at the cemetery, then left it out of the subsequent Hay copy. There is also the tantalizing possibility that Lincoln read the speech from another, unknown copy that is still out there somewhere. Check your attic.[19]

When I heard the actor Sam Waterston recite the address, he emphasized "people" in the last line: "of the PEOPLE, by the PEOPLE, for the PEOPLE," instead of "OF the people, BY the people, FOR the people," the way it's usually done. Why did he do that? Does he know something the rest of us don't know?

Yes.

Waterston was the definitive portrayer of Lincoln in the late twentieth century, replacing Henry Fonda and Raymond Massey. In the early 1990s, he adopted this reading of the Gettysburg Address. Perhaps he discussed it with fellow actor George Clooney, whose father once wrote a newspaper column that described how a ninety-year-old Union veteran who had been a drummer boy at the time of the address insisted that he had heard Lincoln deliver it with the emphasis on "people."[20] Considering what Lincoln was trying to do, it certainly makes more sense to read it this way.

What was he trying to do?

Scholars disagree, but it was something big.

On one hand, Garry Wills's *Lincoln at Gettysburg: The Words that Remade America* claims that all Lincoln was doing was changing the meaning of America in 272 words by smuggling the concept of equality out of the Declaration of Independence (written four score and seven years earlier), past the Constitution (which merely sets up political processes that can be used for good or ill, like protecting slavery), and into the pantheon of modern American values. Allen Guelzo, on the other hand, could not agree less with what he calls Wills's "misbegotten book"; in his view, Lincoln saw no conflict between the Declaration and the Constitution and compared them to an "apple of gold in a picture of silver," the Constitution being the picture frame that was created to adorn and enhance the golden Declaration, both made by the same Founding Fathers and partaking of the same values. Far from rejecting the Constitution as merely a neutral set of procedures that needed to be displaced in Americans' hearts by the equality-promoting Declaration, Lincoln at Gettysburg, according to Guelzo, was trying to create a sense of America as a "nation" rather than a mere Union of disparate states and interest groups.[21]

It is one of the unique qualities of the Gettysburg Address that it can be plausibly subjected to such differing interpretations without losing its core identity, like the elephant examined by the blind men. It does not belong to any one time or place but speaks to universal human ideals and problems. Stylistically, it has nothing in common with conventional nineteenth-century political oratory (like Everett's speech), but neither did it create a new model for political discourse, so that today it sounds neither old-fashioned nor trite. By writing something that does not belong to the rhetorical tradition of either its own time or ours, Lincoln paradoxically created a document that remains as accessible, comprehensible, and dramatic as the day it was written.

He further rendered his words timeless by carefully avoiding any specificity in his references to the occasion of the speech. He is not at Gettysburg, Pennsylvania, but at "a great battlefield of that war." It is not 1863, but four score and seven years after an event of universal importance (echoing the biblical description of "three score and ten years" as the life span of man). There are no Yankees or rebels, only "they who fought here," and "those who gave the last full measure of devotion." There is no North or South, only "this nation." From the Hay draft, Lincoln amended "that this government of the people . . ." to "that government of the people . . . shall not perish from the earth," so that it applied not just to this one case but to the very concept of self-government. Lincoln lifted the speech out of its specific occasion and made it something that could be applicable to all peoples, at all times.

This was no accident. Lincoln needed to attach a timeless, mythic meaning to what had happened at Gettysburg. He had called on hundreds of thousands of Northern boys to fight and give their lives in battle against hundreds of thousands of Southern boys, whom Lincoln regarded as equally his people, loyal Americans temporarily deluded by a slaveholding aristocracy that would stop at nothing to preserve its exploitative, corrupt way of life. After two and a half years of fighting, the war seemed little closer to an ending than when it had first begun. Why should the people of the North continue to make these sacrifices? Was it worth it just to drag the unwilling Southern states back into a Union of which they wanted no part? Lincoln saw the address as an opportunity to redefine the war, not just for the Northern public (though that was his primary audience) but for posterity. He was keenly aware that "we cannot escape history," and that his actions would be remembered long after he had passed from the scene. "The fiery trial through which we pass, will light us down, in honor or dishonor, to the latest generation," he had told Congress in December 1862.[22] At Gettysburg, Lincoln strove to explain to those future generations, as well as to his constituents, why the war was worth continuing.

The purpose that he came up with, and the only one great enough to be commensurate with the slaughter the nation had endured, was "a new birth of freedom." The war would not merely reunite North and South but would re-create the United States as a new nation, with a new dedication to the ideals expressed in the Declaration of Independence. To achieve this, the sacrifices of both North and South were prices that had

to be paid to expunge the sin of slavery, even if "every drop of blood drawn with the lash, shall be paid by another drawn with the sword," as Lincoln would say in his Second Inaugural Address. Thus it was perfectly fitting and proper to pay tribute to all the men killed at Gettysburg, Northern and Southern alike, for participating in the mythic purification and rebirth of America's experiment in human freedom, whatever political goals they may have imagined they were fighting for. This national redemption—and not the idea that such great thoughts could be scribbled on an envelope—is the real miracle of the Gettysburg Address.

FOR FURTHER READING

Gabor Boritt, *The Gettysburg Gospel* (2006), replaces Garry Wills, *Lincoln at Gettysburg: The Words that Remade America* (1992), as the first book to read, if you are going to read only one book about the speech, but read both. If you are going to read only one chapter, choose "The Gettysburg Address" from Douglas Wilson, *Lincoln's Sword: The Presidency and the Power of Words* (2006). For the battle of Gettysburg, there are hundreds of books from which to choose, but the classic remains Edwin B. Coddington, *The Gettysburg Campaign: A Study in Command* (1968); the best modern synthesis is Steven E. Woodworth's *Beneath a Northern Sky: A Short History of the Gettysburg Campaign* (2003).

{ CHAPTER NINE }

Emancipator

If my name ever goes into history it will be for this act.

—Lincoln, just before signing the final Emancipation Proclamation, January 1, 1863[1]

Washington owned slaves, right? Jefferson owned slaves, right?

Right.

Did Lincoln own slaves?

No, but people keep asking.

The facts are clear enough. Lincoln never lived in a slave state after leaving Kentucky at the age of seven, spending most of his adult life in the free states of Indiana and Illinois. He never said a good word about slavery. He made his first public statement on the subject in 1837, after the Illinois General Assembly responded to the murder of abolitionist Elijah Lovejoy with a resolution that the right to own slaves was "sacred" to the slaveholding states; Lincoln and one other legislator protested that "slavery is founded on both injustice and bad policy."[2] After 1854, he reentered politics to combat the expansion of slavery. His basic views on slavery were so consistent throughout his life that he could write in 1860 that they had not changed since his antislavery protest in 1837.[3] In 1864, he wrote, "I am naturally anti-slavery. If slavery is not wrong, nothing is wrong. I can not remember when I did not so think, and feel."[4] As president, he issued the Emancipation Proclamation, which sounded the death knell of slavery in America, and he worked hard for the passage and ratification of the Thirteenth Amendment, which permanently banned it. Many people, if asked for one fact they know about Abraham Lincoln, will reply, "He freed the slaves."

Yet the question persists: "Did Lincoln own slaves?" It is the historical equivalent of the teenage slasher movie villain who is shot, stabbed, drowned, and otherwise repeatedly dispatched, yet somehow continues to rise up at the most inopportune moment to torment the heroine. Lincoln hated slavery; he didn't live in slave territory after the age of seven; he was a lawyer, not a planter, so he had little use for a slave. No matter how many times facts or logic are driven into its heart, the question Did Lincoln own slaves? refuses to die.

I heard it at Fort Wayne's Lincoln Museum over the nine years I worked there, both from visitors who knew nothing about Lincoln and from those who knew plenty. It was not a frequent question, nor usually a loud one (although sometimes it was one teacher proclaimed to her students that Lincoln had owned slaves and absolutely refused to accept the staff's assertions to the contrary—she just knew that he did). Instead it was a persistent question, an undertone, sometimes expressed as an explicit query, sometimes conveyed more subtly by a murmured aside or a rolling of the eyes in response to a docent's enthusiastic description of Lincoln's antislavery virtues.

The question is hardly limited to Lincoln Museum visitors. When Tony Horwitz toured the South gathering material for his insightful *Confederates in the Attic*, he encountered high school students who insisted that Lincoln had owned slaves.[5] I have heard the same as a question, or an assertion, from my own students at universities in Indiana and North Carolina, and from audiences I have addressed throughout the Midwest. No matter how many times it is answered, you can still find people who ask, and expect a positive answer, to the question Did Lincoln own slaves?

Why doesn't the question go away?

The easy answer is to blame the historical ignorance of the public.

This is best done with a dismissive remark accompanied by a wry condescending smile and a slow shaking of the head from side to side, while savoring the smug pleasure of superior knowledge. As satisfying as this may be, however, it's not a very Lincolnian response. Lincoln understood that in a democracy the public mind, right or wrong, had to be respected. In 1854, when he established himself as a powerful antislavery voice with his Peoria speech, he also rejected the possibility of social and political equality among the races. The reason he gave for this was that equality was unacceptable to the feelings of "the great mass of white people." He observed, "Whether this feeling accords with justice and sound judgment, is not the sole question, if indeed, it is any part of it. *A universal feeling, whether well or ill-founded, can not be safely disregarded*" (emphasis added).[6] In his 1862 open letter to Horace Greeley defining his position on emancipation, and in many places elsewhere, Lincoln consistently distinguished between his responsibility to the public, whether the public was right or wrong, and "my oft-expressed *personal* wish that all men every where could be free."[7] Frederick Douglass recognized this when he acknowledged that Lincoln "was bound as a statesman to consult" the public's views on the issue of slavery, even if it meant going slower toward emancipation than Douglass, and perhaps Lincoln, would have liked.[8]

Historians, I believe, would do well to keep the same principle in mind. Those of us in the tenured elite can in theory afford to ignore the rest of the world altogether, at least until state legislators and tuition-paying parents get fed up with our self-indulgent arrogance, but historians who work in museums and other public venues know (or ought to know) that smug contempt toward visitors is not a viable long-term strategy for institutional growth. If lots of people keep asking a question, no matter how absurd it may appear, that question deserves consideration.

So consider it. What's the reason for asking if Lincoln owned slaves?

First, there's logic.

We live in an iconoclastic culture. We're suspicious of heroes. We used to revere Washington and Jefferson, but now we also think of them as slaveholders, and in Jefferson's case a slaveholder who fathered children by one of his slaves. If we used to revere Lincoln too, then there must also be something wrong with him; he must have owned slaves too.

But you already established that he didn't. There must be some other justification for the question, no?

Here's one: he didn't own slaves, but it's possible he may have rented one.

In other words, the question is factually not quite as absurd as it appears at first blush. The Lincolns may have never owned a slave, but to the African American students who argued with Tony Horwitz in an Alabama classroom, that didn't matter: "He was probably paying blacks so little that they might as well have been slaves."[9] In fact, the Lincoln family in Springfield sometimes had no domestic help at all, black or white, due to Mary Lincoln's unsound management practices. But usually they did, and some of their hired servants were of African descent.[10]

One of these servants, Ruth Burns Stanton, gave an interview in 1894 describing her work for the Lincolns in the 1840s. Burns (her name at the time) actually worked for another family but was sent over every Sunday to assist Mrs. Lincoln, who had no other help. In 1849, at the age of fourteen, Burns was sent to live with the Lincolns and stayed for about one year. This is significant because although she was not a slave, it is not altogether clear that she was a free person either.[11]

To clarify this, consider the history of the state of Illinois. In the eighteenth century, when the land that would become Illinois was under French authority, slavery was legal. An enterprising settler brought in five hundred slaves for sale, and their distribution gave the institution a foothold throughout the area. Slavery was banned in Illinois by the Northwest Ordinance of 1787, but there was confusion over whether the law applied retroactively to the so-called "french slaves" and their descendants already in the territory. Many Illinoisans wanted slavery legalized, in order to attract settlers from the South. In 1807, a law was passed under which individuals could be indentured to their employers, maintaining the fiction of freedom while allowing slaveholders to bring their slaves into the territory and have them sign (voluntarily, in theory) ninety-nine-year indentures that made them slaves in all but name.[12]

Gradually, Illinois began to rid itself of this system. In 1828, the Illinois Supreme Court invalidated the 1807 indenture law as contrary to the Northwest Ordinance, but it upheld any existing indentures under Article VI, section 3, of the state constitution of 1818. Ironically, that provision had been meant to limit the use of indentures, as it declared all indentured servants free when they reached the age of twenty-one for men or eighteen for women. It is thus possible that Ruth Burns was indentured, with freedom awaiting her at eighteen, when she worked for the family of John Bradford, who in turn lent her to the Lincolns. The Illinois Supreme Court had ruled that indentured servants could be bought, sold, inherited, or otherwise alienated like other forms of property. It's not clear if the Lincolns paid Burns's wages directly to her or to her masters the Bradfords (assuming she was indentured to them). If the latter, then Tony Horwitz's students were right after all: the Lincolns paid so little to their servant that she might as well have been a slave.

In addition to Burns, we know beyond doubt that there were other people in the Lincoln household who were less than completely free. The most obvious one is Mary Lincoln. She was not Abraham's slave, but she was his inferior in legal and social rights, most obviously lacking the right to vote. The Lincoln children were even more legally disabled than Mary. This is not a trivial point. It illustrates that the boundaries between freedom and nonfreedom are not static and rigid, but fluid and flexible. If Lincoln did not own slaves in the sense that Thomas Jefferson owned slaves, he did partake of freedom more fully than did his contemporaries who were not white adult males.

Lincoln could not avoid participating in his era's hierarchy of race, gender, and age, for good or ill, any more than we can avoid ours. He participated in 1841 when he was subject to the "continual torment" of seeing enslaved families on a steamboat being sent down the Ohio River to a life of unrewarded toil. He participated in 1849 when his father-in-law Richard Todd died, and through his wife's inheritance he obtained some fraction of the wealth realized by the liquidation of the estate, including the sale of slaves. He participated in 1857 when he tried unsuccessfully to persuade the governor of Illinois to intervene in the case of a free African American from Springfield who had gone to Louisiana and been illegally imprisoned; Lincoln and Herndon then raised funds to buy his freedom.[13]

So we end up with another ambiguous answer to another Lincoln question. The details of Lincoln's employment of Ruth Burns or the payment of a ransom to rescue someone from slavery, however, are not what people want to hear about when they ask if Lincoln owned slaves. What they are really asking is a surrogate for a larger, much more substantial question.

And what is the big question about Lincoln and slavery?

"Was Lincoln really the Great Emancipator that we have traditionally been brought up to admire, or was he just a clever, lying, racist, white

male politician who had no interest in the well-being of black America other than when it served his political interests?" That's what they're asking.

Which was he—the "Great Emancipator" or a clever, lying racist?

Neither, fully, but more of the former.

Let's look at the question in its historical context. In 1854, Lincoln threw himself into the antislavery fight. In his speech at Peoria, he condemned the expansion of slavery, but he denied the possibility of political and social equality. As a practical political matter, this made sense. Racial equality was a radical idea, held by a few cranks on the abolitionist fringe, with no realistic hope of coming to pass in American society, at least not in Lincoln's lifetime. It wasn't necessary to the antislavery argument—you can oppose slavery for many reasons without believing in racial equality. More to the point, equality is just what Stephen Douglas always accused Lincoln and the "Black Republicans" of secretly desiring. If you're opposed to the expansion of slavery, he claimed, that must mean that you are in favor of full racial equality, and especially racial intermarriage.

Just as Douglas tried to make racial equality the heart of Lincoln's position, some modern critics have tried to do the opposite, making the preservation of white supremacy Lincoln's main goal. Both miss the point that Lincoln regarded race as a red herring in the slavery argument. Africans might (or might not) be inferior in some ways, compared to Europeans, but the essence of slavery was not race but power. In a fragmentary note on the essence of slavery, Lincoln made these logical observations:

> If A. can prove, however conclusively, that he may, of right, enslave B.—why may not B. snatch the same argument and prove equally that he may enslave A.?—
>
> You say A. is white, and B. is black. It is *color,* then; the lighter, having the right to enslave the darker? Take care. By this rule, you are to be slave to the first man you meet, with a fairer skin than your own.
>
> You do not mean *color* exactly?—You mean the whites are *intellectually* the superiors of the blacks and, therefore, have the right to enslave them? Take care again. By this rule, you are to be slave to the first man you meet, with an intellect superior to your own.

> But, say you, it is a question of *interest;* and, if you can make it your *interest,* you have the right to enslave another. Very well. And if he can make it his interest, he has the right to enslave you.[14]

Lincoln saw that it was not color, or intellectual capacity, or anything but the raw self-interest of the masters that "justified" their enslavement of Africans, and raw self-interest was no basis for a principled society.

In his 1858 debates with Stephen Douglas, Lincoln repeatedly denied the possibility of political and social equality between the races, in response to Douglas's repeated play of the race card. Here's Douglas at Ottawa, Illinois:

> If you desire negro citizenship, if you desire to allow them to come into the State and settle with the white man, if you desire them to vote on an equality with yourselves, and to make them eligible to office, to serve on juries, and to adjudge your rights, then support Mr. Lincoln and the Black Republican party, who are in favor of the citizenship of the negro. For one, I am opposed to negro citizenship in any and every form. [Cheers.] I believe this government was made on the white basis. ["Good."] I believe it was made by white men, for the benefit of white men and their posterity for ever, and I am in favour of confining citizenship to white men, men of European birth and descent, instead of conferring it upon negroes, Indians and other inferior races. ["Good for you." "Douglas forever."][15]

Lincoln's reply is worth quoting at length, because parts of it are so frequently quoted out of context:

> I have no purpose to introduce political and social equality between the white and the black races. There is a physical difference between the two, which in my judgment will probably forever forbid their living together upon the footing of perfect equality, and inasmuch as it becomes a necessity that there must be a difference, I, as well as Judge Douglas, am in favor of the race to which I belong, having the superior position. I have never said anything to the contrary, but I hold that notwithstanding all this, there is no reason in the world why the negro is not entitled to all the natural rights enumerated in

> the Declaration of Independence, the right to life, liberty and the pursuit of happiness. [Loud cheers.] I hold that he is as much entitled to these as the white man. I agree with Judge Douglas he is not my equal in many respects—certainly not in color, perhaps not in moral or intellectual endowment. But in the right to eat the bread, without leave of anybody else, which his own hand earns, *he is my equal and the equal of Judge Douglas, and the equal of every living man.* [Great applause.][16]

The thrust of Lincoln's statement, delivered to a partly hostile, mostly racist, and almost all-white audience, was to contradict Douglas on the issue of equal natural rights. His concession of the minor point in order to give force to the major was a rhetorical device that he used often in court, with great effect. Lincoln's twenty-first-century critics tend to focus on the concession instead of the conclusion. The conclusion speaks for itself; what is more significant is that in discussing race, when Lincoln was at his worst (by the standards of our time), he was still extremely careful, specific, and limited, by the standards of his. Consider each of his propositions:

> **1.** There is a physical difference between the races, which Lincoln does not define but which will, in his estimation, prevent them from ever living together in "perfect equality." This is a prediction, not a prescription—Lincoln does not argue against perfect equality; he simply says he doesn't think it's going to happen. Unfortunately, more than 150 years later, we have yet to prove him wrong.
>
> **2.** If there cannot be perfect equality in society, then one group must hold a position superior to the other. In mathematical terms, if *A* is not equal to *B*, then either *A* is greater than *B*, or *B* greater than *A*. Lincoln, who took up the study of Euclidean geometry in the early 1850s, is citing an intuitive property of quantities that appears in Euclid's *Elements*, Book 1, Proposition 6.[17]
>
> **3.** If either $A > B$ or $B > A$ must be true, but not both, then as a member of *A*, Lincoln says that he prefers $A > B$. He does not say, as Douglas does, that *A* is inherently better than *B*, only that if equality

is not an option, then out of open self-interest he prefers *A* to *B*. Implicitly, he recognizes that a member of *B* would prefer *B* > *A*, which in turn implies inevitable conflict between *A* and *B*.

4. Lincoln stops to point out that whatever inequalities may exist, they have no effect on the fact that "the negro is . . . entitled to all the natural rights enumerated in the Declaration of Independence."

5. He continues by analyzing the nature of the inequalities between the races, the first of which is that the black man is not the equal of the white man in color. It would be more precise to use the concept of identity rather than equality here, but the point is simple enough: people are not all the same color.

6. While people are "certainly" not equal in color, they are also "perhaps" unequal "in moral or intellectual endowment." Lincoln comes closest here to saying that there is a nontrivial difference between the races that might justify different treatment by society, but he qualifies it with "perhaps," and then closes his argument with a restatement of his fourth point: whatever differences may exist, they do not justify the enslavement of one group by another. Even if there are inequalities in moral and intellectual endowment (a point that Lincoln does not actually concede, though he knows that his audience does), natural rights are unchanged. Slavery is still wrong.

What Lincoln was doing here is clear. He believed that slavery was incompatible with republican self-government, and he wanted to prevent it from spreading. To do this, he had to persuade an audience that shared his opponent's unquestioning belief in white supremacy. Lincoln recognized the existence of political and social white domination (how could he not?) and had no objection to benefiting from it, but unlike Douglas he did not believe that it was rooted in an inherent natural order, one in which only people of European descent possessed natural rights. Douglas tried to conflate the issues of natural rights and civil rights at every opportunity. Lincoln wanted to keep them as separate as possible, because only then could his antislavery argument (based on natural rights) hope to prevail. One way of demonstrating this separation was by proclaiming his view in favor of one but not the other. He offered voters a model that would allow them to join him in opposing the spread of slavery without giving up their belief in white supremacy and especially without endorsing social and political equality (including black voting and racial intermarriage).

So, Lincoln was a racist. Everybody knows that now anyway. Why is he still called "the Great Emancipator"?

As the great Lincoln scholar James G. Randall observed, "what everybody knows" about Lincoln changes over time.

"A certain idea gets started in association with an event or figure. It is repeated by speakers and editors. It soon becomes a part of that superficial aggregation of concepts that goes under the heading 'what everybody knows.' " Author Joshua Shenk has cited this phenomenon in connection with Lincoln's mental health, but it applies equally well, if not more so, to the much more critical question of Lincoln and race.[18] In the years immediately following his assassination, Lincoln was remembered predominantly as the Great Emancipator. When African Americans raised money for a statue of Lincoln in 1876, the work they commissioned portrayed a beneficent Emancipator granting freedom to a shackled slave crouching at his feet. The defeat of Reconstruction and the institution of Jim Crow laws by the end of the nineteenth century seemed to mock the achievement of emancipation, and by the time the Lincoln Memorial was dedicated in 1922, Lincoln was remembered more for saving the Union than for helping to end slavery. The Second Reconstruction of the 1950s and 1960s might have revived interest in Lincoln as an antislavery icon, but the disillusionment and backlash that followed the end of the civil rights era instead led to bitter attacks on Lincoln for his failure to measure up to contemporary standards.[19]

The argument that Lincoln should not be viewed as the Great Emancipator has gained a great deal of traction since the late 1960s. One method commonly used to attack Lincoln on this score is to quote bits and pieces of his words, particularly those from his debates with Stephen Douglas, without providing their historical context. Barbara Fields, a commentator in Ken Burns's *The Civil War* television series, did this; libertarian anti-Lincoln zealots like Thomas DiLorenzo do it regularly; and even the National Park Service did it, at the Fort Sumter Visitor Education Center, where the two Lincoln quotes that appear in the exhibit

Postwar emancipation images gave all the credit to Lincoln—slaves appeared only as grateful recipients of a gift they did nothing to earn, even in this statue by Thomas Bell that was commissioned by freed slaves. By the end of the twentieth century, such paternalistic images had contributed to a decline in Lincoln's reputation among African Americans. (Courtesy of The Lincoln Museum, Fort Wayne, IN, TLM 747)

(drawn out of eight volumes of Lincoln's writings) are the two most negative things Lincoln ever said relating to slaves and slavery.*

As is the case with many of those who advocate nontraditional views regarding Lincoln's sexuality, many of those who attack Lincoln on race

*One is the quote from the debates with Douglas discussed above, and the other is the letter to Horace Greeley, discussed below. A park ranger at Sumter told me that the negative take on Lincoln's slavery policy in the exhibit (which is otherwise very professional) was a concession to local interests, who would have preferred that the issue of slavery not be mentioned at all.

use "the Great Emancipator" as a vehicle for pursuing their own ideological agendas. For example, some libertarians have fastened on to Lincoln as the source of everything they hate about the federal government in the twenty-first century. They despise him for presiding over its expansion during the Civil War. Obsessed as they are with the issue of government power, they assume that Lincoln was too and that he only used the issue of slavery as a political front. These critics tend to be so far off base historically that one is tempted to dismiss them out of hand, but their persistence, resistance to evidence, conspiratorial paranoia, and ability to whip one another into rhetorical frenzies via the Internet all indicate that they are not going to go away easily.

Curiously, these extremists share many arguments in common with Lincoln's opponents at the opposite end of the political spectrum, although the latter's positions tend to have greater historical coherence and more popular impact. The leading voice on this flank has been that of Lerone Bennett, author of *Forced Into Glory: Abraham Lincoln's White Dream.* Bennett formulated his views on Lincoln in the mid-1960s, when he set out to educate himself on the subject by reading the eight volumes of Lincoln's collected works, going to the source instead of learning about Lincoln through biographies. As a result, he developed a unique, nonmainstream interpretation of Lincoln. Bennett concluded that Lincoln was not interested in emancipation nor in the well-being of the slaves, and that to the extent he opposed slavery, he did so only as far as it would benefit white America. Bennett wrote an influential article published in *Ebony* in 1968, "Was Abe Lincoln a White Supremacist?" and then elaborated on his theme for another thirty years, eventually publishing *Forced Into Glory* in 2000.[20]

Unlike Larry Kramer, who admitted that he placed ideology above history, or Thomas DiLorenzo, whose work reveals the same, Bennett actually read everything Lincoln wrote and used much of it in his analysis. One of his approaches was to deconstruct what he called the "feel-good" approach to Lincoln, in which biographers have taken Lincoln at his word whenever he expressed his personal wish that everyone could be free or otherwise said anything progressive about race and slavery but discounted as mere politics anything Lincoln said to the contrary, like his rejection of equality in the 1854 Peoria speech and the debates with Douglas. Bennett simply reversed the process, using what could be called a "feel-bad" technique. He took as Lincoln's real views those expressed in his occasional jokes about black people, his replies to Stephen Douglas's race baiting in 1858, and every other bad thing Lincoln ever said; the noble sentiments of the Gettysburg Address and Second Inaugural, for Bennett, were merely politics in which Lincoln engaged to cover his true feelings.[21]

What comes out of this interpretation is a sort of anti-Lincoln, the opposite in every way from the one we think we know, but surprisingly consistent with himself. It's not an accurate view, but it is one that has resonated with many Americans. It has tapped into an unexpected vein of pent-up resentment toward the traditional image of Lincoln the Great Emancipator, Lincoln patronizingly bestowing freedom on a hapless kneeling slave, or even more grating, Lincoln the benevolent emancipator sitting complacently in his memorial, gazing contentedly at a nation where few of his fine words have turned into reality. This is the Lincoln who for 150 years has allowed white Americans (particularly those in the North) to feel good about race relations in this country, when so many black Americans have had powerful reasons to feel otherwise. It is largely because of this image, I believe, that so few African Americans visit Lincoln museums or attend the annual Lincoln Forum in Gettysburg or otherwise show interest in a man who was once regarded in the African American community as practically a savior on earth.

Lincoln is still called "the Great Emancipator" on stone memorials and in the pages of old books, but the title rarely appears in new publications without quotation marks. Even those who regard him as the individual most responsible for emancipation acknowledge that he didn't do it alone. Emancipation was the act of millions of people, including abolitionist radicals, moderate antislavery politicians, petition-signing housewives, angry editors, brave Underground Railroad stationmasters, clergy of many denominations, endless regiments of Union soldiers and the families that supported them, and most of all, the slaves themselves. References to Lincoln as the Great Emancipator (without quotes) are a legacy not only of an era of Dead White Male history written from the top down but also of what the poet Robert Penn Warren described as the North's "treasury of virtue" syndrome: the idea of contemporary white Northerners treating the sacrifices of their forebears, including Lincoln, as such an enormous contribution toward a more just society that they need do nothing more themselves.[22] There are good reasons to look on

This wartime image prefigures the modern view of emancipation as a drama with many players: Lincoln (whose words are being read aloud), the slaves who can scarcely dare to believe what they are hearing, and the soldiers whose bayonets will enforce the Proclamation. (Courtesy of The Lincoln Museum, Fort Wayne, IN, TLM 536)

the term "Great Emancipator" as a relic of another day—but not because Lincoln has been called a racist.

So Lincoln was not a racist?

He believed that there were certain differences between the races . . .

. . . as he said when debating Douglas. Lincoln did not share the modern ideals of political and social equality that *we* hold today or even those that were held by more progressive thinkers in his own time (Charles Sumner, Frederick Douglass, George Julian, William Lloyd Garrison, the Grimké sisters, to name a few). Lincoln's critics can justly say that he could have done better at imagining a multiracial future for the nation.

He was a president, however, not a visionary, and as he told Congress in December 1862: "It is not 'can *any* of us *imagine* better?' but 'can we *all* do better?' "[23] As far as that went, no one *did* better than he did to dismantle the institution of slavery.

It is also worth noting that as president, Lincoln's views of equality broadened. Before the war he favored the idea of colonizing freed slaves to Central America or Africa, consistent with his fear that the races could not live in harmony together. Over time, however, he gave up the idea, especially after the large-scale enlistment of African American soldiers in 1863. On August 26, 1863, he lectured white antiwar Northerners that when peace came, "there will be some black men who can remember that, with silent tongue, and clenched teeth, and steady eye, and well-poised bayonet, they have helped mankind on to this great consummation, while, I fear, there will be some white ones, unable to forget that, with malignant heart, and deceitful speech, they have strove to hinder it." In contrast to his prewar opposition to political equality, in 1864 he proposed to the Union governor of Louisiana that the vote be extended to some African Americans. The actions of black Americans who fought for the Union at places like Fort Wagner had an impact on him, and in his last public speech, he became the first president to express public support for black suffrage.[24]

That Lincoln did much to end slavery, or that his views evolved toward equality over his lifetime, is not to say that those who criticize Lincoln's record are all wrong. One of the long-standing weaknesses in Lincoln scholarship is the defensiveness with which many of his biographers have responded to any criticism of their hero at all. For example, Lerone Bennett's *Forced Into Glory* has been widely derided within the Lincoln community for the distortions, exaggerations, and misuse of evidence in its anti-Lincoln arguments. Bennett's book is indeed guilty on these counts, but as he argues convincingly, so are those of many other authors who write about Lincoln, only in the other direction.

To take another example, most traditional biographers have paid no attention to Lincoln's own racial identity. White men themselves, they took whiteness as a norm, not a characteristic worth analyzing. Bennett, in contrast, looked at every bit of evidence of Lincoln's racial awareness that he could find, from his attendance at minstrel shows, to his telling of racial jokes, to his interactions with individual African Americans. If Bennett's conclusion that Lincoln was a deep-dyed white supremacist does not seem borne out by what he found, he has at least forced future scholars to recognize that Lincoln's whiteness cannot be taken for granted.[25]

Over time, the analysis of Lincoln's racial views is bound to move beyond simplistic, politically motivated attacks and counterattacks. An essay published in 2007 by James Leiker (whose previous scholarship, significantly, had nothing to do with Lincoln) built on the point that whiteness is an important concept and that Lincoln identified himself as a white person, but went from there to argue that Lincoln expanded the definition of whiteness in his time to encompass previously excluded ethnicities. In contrast to Stephen Douglas, who believed that "all men are created equal" applied only to Englishmen and their descendants, Lincoln believed that freedom should be extended to all people, and that political rights should be extended to all white people, or as he put it, America should be "an outlet for *free white people everywhere,* the world over—in which Hans and Baptiste and Patrick, and all other men from all the world, may find new homes and better their conditions in life." Those words sound ugly to us today, defining America as a haven for white males, but Lincoln's emphasis (Leiker argued) was to extend the boundaries of whiteness, not to limit the opportunities of black people.[26]

Lincoln was not a rainbow warrior who secretly wished for a twenty-first-century multicultural society, but neither was he a lying, racist hypocrite. By the standards of his own time, Lincoln's views on race were progressive but not radical. With the benefit of all that has taken place since Lincoln's lifetime, Americans generally have come to accept ideas about race that would have been considered excessively egalitarian in the 1850s. One can only speculate how Lincoln, given the same additional experience, would have moderated his own views. It is true that he expressed a belief that white Americans and black ones could never learn to transcend race and live together in harmony, but if he could have somehow known of events to come, of *Brown v. Board of Education,* of the March on Washington, of African Americans demanding and receiving political rights and social equality to a degree few could imagine in his day, surely his surprise would have been a pleasant one.

Did Lincoln use the n—— word?

Yes.

To the discomfort of anyone who turns to Lincoln seeking a model for contemporary race relations, he did. The *Collected Works* include several examples from his debates with Stephen Douglas, for example.[27] He used it much less frequently than Douglas, who was so profligate with the term that fellow senator William Seward once allegedly warned him that no one could hope to become president who spelled "negro" with two *g*s. That many (not all) other white politicians used such language is no excuse, however, as David Donald has noted.

How often Lincoln said it is less clear, as it is sometimes difficult to tell from contemporary newspaper reports if a speaker said "negro" or its offensive variation. Douglas clearly used the latter throughout the debates, but some editors consistently changed it to "negro" for their readers. Lincoln gave a speech at Hartford, Connecticut, in 1860 in which one newspaper quoted him as saying "negro" except when he was paraphrasing Douglas, while another newspaper had him using "negro" in every case; one of them had to be wrong.[28]

Lincoln did not use the word in public speech after he became president, although he apparently did so on some occasions in private. As with his views on race generally, Lincoln was amenable to change. In 1864, speaking with a group of advocates who wanted equal pay for civilians employed by the army, regardless of race, Lincoln said, "Well, gentlemen, you wish the pay of 'Cuffey' raised." One of the delegation, Henry Samuels, replied, "Excuse me, Mr. Lincoln the term 'Cuffey' is not in our vernacular." Lincoln acknowledged his error: "I stand corrected, young man, but you know I am by birth a Southerner and in our section that term is applied without any idea of an offensive nature." More important, he promised to equalize the pay.[29]

The Emancipation Proclamation wasn't announced until September 1862. If Lincoln cared about the slaves, why didn't he free them as soon as he became president?

There are several reasons.

The first is that he did not believe the Constitution gave the federal government the authority to interfere with "domestic" arrangements within the states, including slavery. As the war went on, Lincoln would find in the war powers of the president the extraordinary authority he would need to issue the Emancipation Proclamation as a wartime action designed to weaken the enemy.

The second reason is that it would have done no good. Four slave states remained in the Union in 1861 (Maryland, Kentucky, Missouri, and Delaware), and their continued loyalty was critical to the outcome of the war. Lincoln supposedly once said, "I hope to have God on my side, but I must have Kentucky." He definitely did say, "I think to lose Kentucky is nearly the same as to lose the whole game. Kentucky gone, we can not hold Missouri, nor, as I think, Maryland."[30] The surest way to lose any or all of the border states was to alienate the slaveholders living there, which emancipation would certainly do. Lincoln thus not only did not free the slaves in 1861, but when Major General John C. Frémont declared the slaves of rebels in Missouri to be free, Lincoln overruled him.

The Frémont incident, and a similar occasion involving David Hunter in South Carolina in 1862, has led Lerone Bennett to argue that Lincoln actually prolonged the existence of slavery. Bennett echoes the impatience of wartime radicals who thought emancipation and Union victory were just a matter of will, and could not understand Lincoln's failure to exercise it. Lincoln, however, was fully aware of the practicalities of the matter and knew that if the Confederacy became independent because of a premature emancipation, its slaves would remain in bondage indefinitely.

Speaking of indefinitely, what about the constitutional amendment Lincoln favored that would have protected slavery indefinitely?

In 1861, an amendment was proposed to try to head off the disaster of civil war.

Seven states had declared themselves out of the Union by the time Lincoln was inaugurated. War was a real possibility. To prevent it, Lincoln repeated something he had said many times over the past decade, that the federal government had no authority to interfere with slavery in states where it already existed. In his First Inaugural Address, he said that he understood there was an amendment, passed by Congress, which would expressly and permanently prohibit federal interference with slavery in the states. Since that already was what the Constitution implied, Lincoln said, "I have no objection to its being made express, and irrevocable." Of course, he also knew that no amendment could really be irrevocable; any future generation could use the same amendment process to change it. The amendment was never ratified, and the war came.[31]

Didn't he once say that he wanted to win the war, whether or not he freed the slaves?

Yes . . .

. . . in an open letter to Horace Greeley, editor of the *New York Tribune.* In August 1862, Greeley wrote an editorial called "The Prayer of Twenty Millions," in which he argued for immediate emancipation. Lincoln responded with a letter for Greeley to publish. In it, he said: "My paramount object in this struggle *is* to save the Union, and is *not* either to save or to destroy slavery. If I could save the Union without freeing *any* slave I would do it, and if I could save it by freeing *all* the slaves I would do it; and if I could save it by freeing some and leaving others alone I would also do that."[32]

As he had done in his debates with Stephen Douglas, Lincoln in this letter conceded abstractions in order to achieve real results. He was willing to concede political and social equality in 1858, because neither was a potential reality. When he wrote to Greeley, he was willing to concede the possibility that he would save the Union without freeing any slaves, because he knew that the possibility no longer existed. By August 1862, he had already written the Emancipation Proclamation and showed it to his cabinet. On Secretary of State Seward's advice, he was simply waiting for a Union battlefield victory so that he could issue it from a position of strength and not have it sound like a "last *shriek*, on the retreat."[33] He knew there would be a negative backlash against the proclamation from many Northerners, and he sought to preempt as much of their criticism as he could. If that meant convincing some people that any emancipating would be done for the sake of the Union and not for the slaves, he was more than willing to do so.

Isn't it true that the Emancipation Proclamation didn't really free any slaves at all?

A number of historians have said that, but they're wrong.[34]

It's true that the proclamation only applied to places that were actively in rebellion. It excluded the border slave states and some portions of Confederate states that had been occupied by federal troops. Since rebel slaveholders in the areas affected by the proclamation were hardly likely to obey Lincoln's edict, it would seem that it must not have affected anyone. In fact, however, the lack of immediate enforceability had no effect on the legal validity of the proclamation. Laws are still laws, even if they are not immediately enforceable. On January 1, 1863, every slave in rebeldom became "thenceforward, and forever free" in the eyes of the law, and their former owners were thenceforward guilty of kidnapping and false imprisonment if they did not release them.

The Emancipation Proclamation also clarified the ambiguous legal status of slaves escaping from their masters. At the beginning of the war, under the Fugitive Slave Act, Union officers were theoretically obligated to return escaping slaves to their Confederate masters. This made no sense in a war, so Union soldiers began to retain escaped slaves as "contraband of war," an ingenious theory promulgated by General Benjamin Butler. The problem with this theory was that if the federal government could retain escapees the same way it could seize the horses and cannon of the enemy, then the federal government was now the largest slaveholder in the world. The proclamation guaranteed that any future slaves coming into federal hands were doing so as free people, not as property.

The real importance of the proclamation was that it set the federal government squarely against slavery, in contrast to the policy advocated by George McClellan and others that it adopt a neutral stance, protecting the institution where it existed and doing nothing to encourage slaves to escape. The proclamation also affected foreign relations (making it virtually impossible for Britain or France to recognize a Confederacy now indelibly associated with the preservation of slavery), allowed the recruitment of 180,000 African American soldiers and sailors, and gave the millions still held in bondage an incentive to escape. But these were incidental to its main effect: it put the Union on the side of freedom, and gave the war a new moral dimension.

As momentous as it was in practice, in theory the Emancipation Proclamation rested on shaky ground, and Lincoln knew it. Since he issued it based on his war powers as commander in chief, what would happen when the war was over? What if Congress passed a contradictory law? What if a future president rescinded the proclamation? And what about all the slaves in the border states and other areas not covered by the document? That's why he was so eager to see slavery permanently ended by the ratification of the Thirteenth Amendment to the Constitution, which he called a "King's cure for all the evils."[35]

Did Lincoln write the Thirteenth Amendment?

No, but he took the unusual step of signing his name . . .

. . . to the Congressional resolution that sent it to the states for ratification. The power to propose constitutional amendments lies with Congress, not the executive branch, and Lincoln was criticized for signing the Thirteenth Amendment after Congress passed it, as though he were implying that presidential approval was part of the process. In fact, he simply wanted to be part of the historic moment.

Did Lincoln bribe Congressmen to get them to vote for the Thirteenth Amendment?

There were long-standing rumors to this effect.

According to a thirdhand account written more than thirty years after the fact, the amendment was "passed by corruption, aided and abetted by the purest man in America."[36] The leading historian of the Thirteenth Amendment, Michael Vorenberg, found that several of Lincoln's political allies, including Secretary of State Seward, pulled strings and made deals to get votes for the amendment, but he found no evidence of Lincoln himself engaging in any corrupt behavior.

Did Lincoln make Nevada a state just so it could ratify the Thirteenth Amendment?

It makes a good story, but no.

Lincoln signed off on Nevada's statehood in October 1864, in time for the presidential election that year, leading some to believe that he was eager for the three electoral votes the state would be able to cast but which proved unnecessary to his reelection.

The Thirteenth Amendment was not passed by Congress until January 1865. Three-quarters of the states (twenty-seven, if the Confederate states counted) were needed for ratification, which took place when Georgia approved the amendment in December 1865.[37]

Why didn't Lincoln offer to pay the slaveholders for their slaves? That would have been easier than fighting a war.

That's a Yankee notion.

There was never a realistic possibility that the slaveholding aristocrats of the South would sell out their bid for independence, and the bedrock of their way of life, just for cash. As Confederate Vice President Alexander Stephens declared, slavery was the "cornerstone" of the Confederacy.[38] Lincoln understood enough about Southern concepts of honor and race to know how an offer like that would go over.

What about paying slaveholders not in the Confederacy, like the ones in Kentucky or Missouri?

He tried to do that, on several occasions, but the slaveholders were not interested.

Lincoln could do his sums as well as the next person, and in 1862, he calculated that for the same cost in dollars (to say nothing of lives) as eighty-seven days of prosecuting the war, the federal government could buy all the slaves still in the Union (i.e., in Kentucky, Missouri, Maryland, Delaware, and the District of Columbia) at four hundred dollars each. It didn't happen, because Congress wouldn't authorize the money and because the slaveholders of Kentucky told Lincoln that they weren't interested, even after he presciently warned them that no matter what he did, the institution of slavery would soon be destroyed "by mere friction and abrasion—by the mere incidents of the war."[39]

How did he come up with the value? Did slaves really cost four hundred dollars?

Four hundred dollars is on the low side.

A male in the prime of life could command as much as two thousand dollars before the war, while slaves who were very old, very young, or in poor health brought much less.[40] In 1956, Lincoln experts Ralph Newman and

Robert E. Bennett were defeated on a television game show, *The $64,000 Question,* when they were unable to answer how much Abraham Lincoln was willing to pay per head to compensate slaveholders. Bennett protested that the question was "irrelevant" and "not pertinent."[41] It is a sign of changing historical interests since the 1950s that a Lincoln specialist could at one time regard the historical price of enslaved African Americans as "irrelevant."

Did Lincoln want to send blacks back to Africa?

Yes, at one time.

Was he serious?

Ultimately, no, despite what some writers have said.

First, the idea of sending anyone "back to Africa" was a misnomer, as the importation of slaves had been banned by Congress in 1808. The great majority of people living in slavery in Lincoln's lifetime were born in the United States and logically could not go back to a place where they had never been.

Logic aside, the idea of sending African Americans "back" to Africa, or to Central America, or anywhere out of the country, did have a certain amount of support in the decades before the Civil War. The American Colonization Society was founded in Washington, D.C., in 1816, when enlightened statesmen in the South still viewed the ownership of slaves, in Jefferson's words, as holding "a wolf by the ears, and we can neither hold him, nor safely let him go."[42] Colonization seemed to offer a solution that would end slavery without subsequent racial slaughter. Lincoln's political role model Henry Clay was a proponent of colonization, and in a eulogy for his hero Lincoln quoted Clay's description of the "moral fitness in the idea of returning to Africa her children, whose ancestors have been torn from her by the ruthless hand of fraud and violence."[43]

Lincoln's view that complete equality was not possible implied that emancipation would inevitably be followed by some other form of oppression. In the 1850s, he belonged to the Illinois State Colonization Society. During the Civil War he invited a delegation of African American leaders to the White House (the first president to do so) to urge them to accept colonization. "Your race are suffering, in my judgment, the greatest wrong inflicted on any people," he said, but the end of slavery would still leave them in a society where black people would be treated as inferior. "I do not propose to discuss this, but to present it as a fact with which we have to deal. I cannot alter it if I would."[44]

Lincoln's visitors listened politely but showed no interest in leaving the country. Their unfavorable response, together with the corruption of the agents Lincoln hired to organize such colonies, pushed Lincoln toward the realization that colonization was impractical, while the service of black soldiers beginning in 1863 convinced him that it was unjust. His secretary, John Hay, wrote in 1864, "I am glad the President has sloughed off that idea of colonization."[45]

Traditional historians have long tried to minimize Lincoln's support for colonization, which they found embarrassing and inconsistent with their own values. More recently, writers such as Lerone Bennett and Michael Lind have swung to the opposite tack, overemphasizing Lincoln's dedication to colonization to show that white supremacy was, in Bennett's words, the "center and circumference of his being."[46] The truth, as is so often the case, lies between the extremes. Lincoln wanted to end slavery and incidentally thought that in the aftermath of its demise it would be a good idea to separate white and black Americans, since the alternative of a peaceful, harmonious, multiracial postslavery society existed nowhere on earth and did not seem likely to begin here.

By analogy, consider vegetarianism. There are some people today who believe that all forms of animal life deserve the same dignity as do humans and thus refuse to eat meat. The great majority of us, however, do eat meat. We've always done so and haven't thought about it much. As part of the meat-eating majority, I enjoy a good hamburger too—but I am not an "advocate" or "proponent" of meat eating. Meat is not the "center and circumference of my being" (although it contributes to the latter). If I were to be transported two hundred years into the future, where no one eats meat and the practical problems of a nonmeat diet have been solved, I would have no objection to going vegetarian. I don't have any moral commitment in favor of killing animals for consumption; I just live in a world where that is commonly done and where only people with an advanced moral sense (or kooks, depending how you wish to characterize them) believe that "meat is murder."

Likewise, Abraham Lincoln lived in a world of white supremacy. In his lifetime, there was no practical political possibility of black social or political equality taking hold in any part of the country that had a substantial black population. When Lincoln told the audiences in his debates with Douglas that he had no intention of introducing such equality, he might as well have added that he did not favor reorganizing society on the same basis as the free-love commune at Oneida, New York; that wasn't going to happen either. But if we could put Lincoln in a time machine and show him the multiracial, multicultural society of America today, I believe that he would respond like the omnivore transported to a vegetarian future: surprised but willing to accommodate to the changed conditions, for they would violate none of his basic precepts. Lincoln was deeply dedicated to the survival of representative government and the spread of economic opportunity; the existence of white supremacy, in contrast, was simply a condition in which he lived, one in which he did not choose to engage in quixotic battle over (though fortunately there were others who did) and the disappearance of which he would hardly have mourned.

Did he know any African Americans personally?

Yes, but not many.

There were a number of black people living in Springfield in the 1850s, including "Billy the Barber" (William Fleurville), who probably cut Lincoln's hair.[47] The Lincolns had black servants at times, like Ruth Burns and Maria Vance. William Johnson went with Lincoln to the White House as his valet, where the lighter-skinned servants objected to his dark presence. Lincoln found a different job for Johnson in the Treasury Department, but he continued to serve as Lincoln's valet until he contracted smallpox while accompanying Lincoln to Gettysburg in 1863. He died the next year.

Not all of Lincoln's contact with the African American community was through servants and barbers. As president, he occasionally met with black leaders, including the most prominent African American of his generation, Frederick Douglass. He conferred with Douglass on several occasions, once inviting him to visit at the Soldiers' Home, and Douglass later wrote an often-quoted passage praising Lincoln as the "the first great man that I talked with in the United States freely, who in no single instance reminded me of the difference between himself and myself, of the difference of color."[48] This perhaps says more about the many other great men whom Douglass met over the course of his career, all apparently unable to refrain from bringing up race whenever they talked with him.

What did Lincoln think about women's rights?

It's tempting to see Lincoln as a pioneer of gender equality . . .

. . . considering what he wrote when running for the state legislature in 1836: "To the Editor of the Journal. I go for all sharing the privileges of the government, who assist in bearing its burthens. Consequently I go for admitting all whites to the right of suffrage, who pay taxes or bear arms (by no means excluding females.)"[49]

The problem is that irony does not always travel well through the centuries. The number of females who bore arms in 1836 (in the constitutional sense of being part of a well-regulated militia) was zero, and the number who paid taxes was exceedingly small, as the only way for a woman to own a substantial amount of property in her own name at that time was (in most states) to inherit it from her husband and not remarry. Lincoln never seriously endorsed female suffrage, which was an idea well outside the political mainstream in 1836, far more so than immediate abolition, which Lincoln also abjured at that time.

Was Lincoln black?

Some people thought he was.[50]

In fact, nobody was. White and black, then as now, were social constructs rather than objective facts. Lincoln was not literally white, like the pages of this book, any more than Frederick Douglass was literally black, like the ink of these letters. Human skin can be found in various shades of brown, tan, cream, pink, and so on, and it is only by convention that we group everyone on one side of a mysterious yet universally understood border as "white," and everyone on the other as "black" (or "colored" or "Negro" or "African American"). If we did the same thing with height, our driver's licenses would describe everyone north of five feet nine inches as "tall" and everyone else as "short," instead of giving one's actual height. In time, we could come to identify ourselves by strict height categories and learn to hate, fear, and oppress those on the wrong side of the line.

Of course, nowhere in American history has height had the same

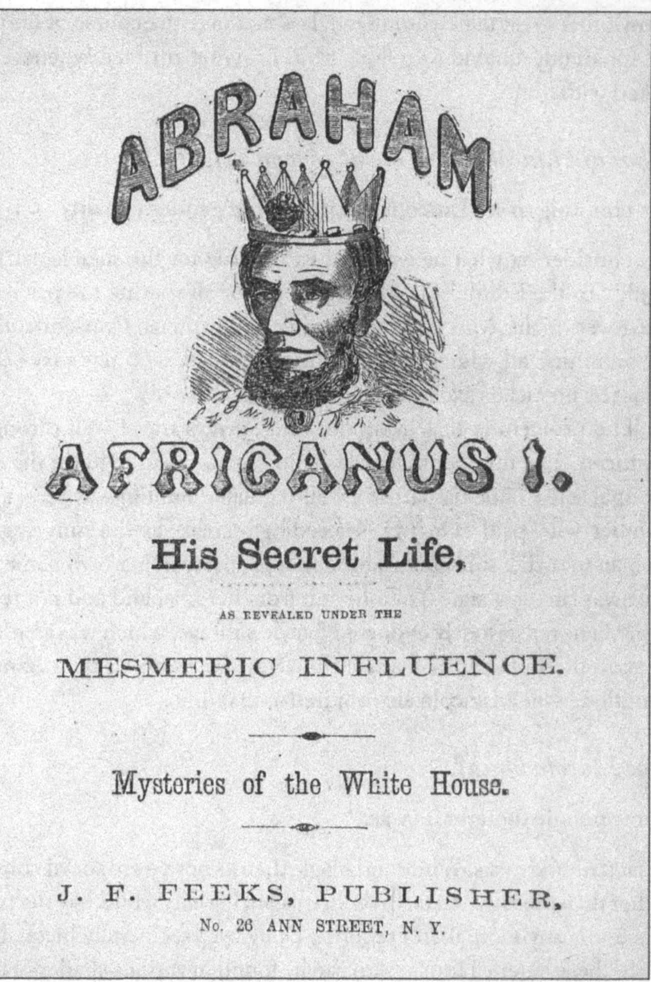

Anti-Lincoln political literature from 1864. (Courtesy of The Lincoln Museum, Fort Wayne, IN, TLM 3330)

polarizing effect as skin color. People in Lincoln's time felt no need to create a limited number of distinct categories of height or to identify people by their size. Color, on the other hand, mattered. Lincoln's opponents sometimes accused him of being "black," by which they meant to say that he had a single African ancestor somewhere in his family tree.

Lincoln was part of this world. He identified himself as "white" and stated that if there must be inequality between "white" and "black," he favored his race having the superior position. In that sense, Lincoln's views differed from those of most modern Americans, who would disagree with his premise that equality is not a reachable goal. To take from this, as some writers have done, that Lincoln was dedicated to the proposition of white supremacy is no more accurate than portraying him as a modern multiculturalist, and less true to his nature. Lincoln was a casual white supremacist by accident of birth, not by intellectual or moral choice. He was aware of the Darwinian pseudoscientific arguments for racial inequality that were gaining popularity in his time (he was born on the same day as Charles Darwin), but he never echoed them and had little patience for those who did. "Let us discard this quibbling . . . about this race and that race and the other race being inferior," he told an audience in 1858, "until we shall once more stand up declaring that all men are created equal."[51]

What do you think Lincoln would have said about the idea of reparations for slavery?

We know the answer to this one, because he gave it in his Second Inaugural Address.

Slavery was a national sin, not a Southern one, in Lincoln's view. As early as the Peoria speech of 1854, he stressed that the North had no claim to moral superiority over the South because of slavery. Southerners "are just what we would be in their situation. If slavery did not now exist amongst them, they would not introduce it. If it did now exist amongst us, we should not instantly give it up." He returned to this theme at the end of the Civil War in his attempt to understand the meaning of the conflict. "The Almighty has His own purposes," and one of them has been to give "to both North and South, this terrible war" as joint punishment for the national offense of slavery. "Fondly do we hope—fervently do we pray—that this mighty scourge of war may speedily pass away," Lincoln begged, but then he accepted that the reparation must be paid: "Yet, if God wills that it continue, until all the wealth piled by the bondman's two hundred and fifty years of unrequited toil shall be sunk, and until every drop of blood drawn with the lash, shall be paid by another drawn with the sword, as was said three thousand years ago, so still it must be said 'the judgments of the Lord, are true and righteous altogether.' "[52]

Together, the white North and South together paid in blood and treasure for all they had ever gained from the exploitation of black America, in the holocaust of civil war. For the country to suffer the same casualties today, as a proportion of the population, would be to lose more than five million American lives. The judgment of the Lord, Lincoln believed, was paid in full.

Tragically, a new scourge would fall upon African Americans in the aftermath of slavery and war. The judgment of the Lord was paid, but not to them. Instead of the rumored "forty acres and a mule" that many of them imagined they might receive, the former slaves found themselves with nothing but freedom at the end of the Civil War. Lincoln's hope for a future with malice toward none and charity for all would be betrayed by the restoration of white supremacy and a century of Jim Crow apartheid, marked by legal segregation and separate drinking fountains in the South, and "sundown towns" and restricted neighborhoods in the North. What reparations should be paid for that crime, and to whom, are questions to ask of ourselves, not of Abraham Lincoln.

FOR FURTHER READING

The best way to get to know Lincoln's thinking on race, slavery, and emancipation is to read his own writings, picking through the eight volumes and two supplements for the bits and pieces that reveal something of his views. For those without the time for such a project, start with *Big Enough to Be Inconsistent: Abraham Lincoln Confronts Slavery and Race* (2008) by George M. Fredrickson, which offers a concise, balanced summary of recent scholarship. From there, read *Lincoln's Emancipation Proclamation: The End of Slavery in America* (2004), by Allen Guelzo, the first scholarly study of that critical document since John Hope Franklin's brief classic *The Emancipation Proclamation* (1963). For criticism of Lincoln's role, see Lerone Bennett, *Forced Into Glory: Abraham Lincoln's White Dream* (2000); it's not the place to start for a balanced view of Lincoln, but it is an insistent, passionate, erudite book that demands the attention of everyone who has already read a traditional Lincoln biography or two. I find that I can only read a few pages at a time before I have to stop and marshal my thoughts. Brian R. Dirck, ed., *Lincoln Emancipated: The President and the Politics of Race* (2007), offers recent scholarship on the subject.

Phillip Shaw Paludan gives an excellent summary of how Lincoln scholars have dealt with the unsettling issue of colonization and suggests a way forward, in "Lincoln and Colonization: Policy or Propaganda?" in the *Journal of the Abraham Lincoln Association* 25, no. 1 (winter 2004). Michael Vorenberg's *Final Freedom: The Civil War, the Abolition of Slavery, and the Thirteenth Amendment* (2001) is the most in-depth study of the Thirteenth Amendment. The Second Inaugural has been the subject of several insightful books, including Lucas E. Morel, *Lincoln's Sacred Effort* (2000), and Ronald C. White, Jr., *Lincoln's Greatest Speech: The Second Inaugural* (2002).

CHAPTER TEN

Lincoln the Man

If any personal description of me is thought desirable, it may be said, I am, in height, six feet, four inches, nearly; lean in flesh, weighing, on an average, one hundred and eighty pounds; dark complexion, with coarse black hair, and grey eyes—no other marks or brands recollected. Yours very truly A. LINCOLN

—In response to a request for an autobiographical sketch, 1859[1]

How tall was he?

"Six feet, four inches, nearly"; so maybe six feet three and seven-eighths.

Since the average height of a Union soldier was about five feet eight inches,[2] he was pretty tall for his time.

What was his shoe size?

Fourteen. His right foot was actually twelve and one-quarter inches long, a quarter inch longer than his left.[3]

Did people think he was ugly?

Some did, like Nathaniel Hawthorne, who called him "the homeliest man I ever saw."[4]

When he was elected president, he received a letter addressed to "Deformed Sir," which announced, "The Ugly Club, in full meeting, have elected you an Honorary Member of the Hard-Favored Fraternity," and declared him "the Prince of Ugly Fellows."[5]

But such talk never bothered Lincoln. From the time he was a young man, he told jokes about his appearance. There was the one about the time he met a man who pointed a gun at him and said that he had always promised himself that if he met a man uglier than himself, he would shoot him. Lincoln looked at the stranger's face and replied, "If I'm uglier than you, fire away." Then there was the story of the ugly man who encountered a farm woman who stared at him and said she had never seen a man so ugly before. "But what can I do about it, Ma'am?" asked the ugly man. "Well, you could stay home," was the answer. And there was also the response Lincoln supposedly gave when he was accused by a political opponent of being two-faced: "If I had two faces, would I wear this one?" Perhaps Lincoln realized that even those who regarded him as superficially ugly could see through his appearance and recognize his character. Nathaniel Hawthorne, for instance, considered him homely but also said that his face was "by no means repulsive or disagreeable" and that it was "redeemed, illuminated, softened, and brightened by a kindly though serious look out of his eyes, and an expression of homely sagacity."[6]

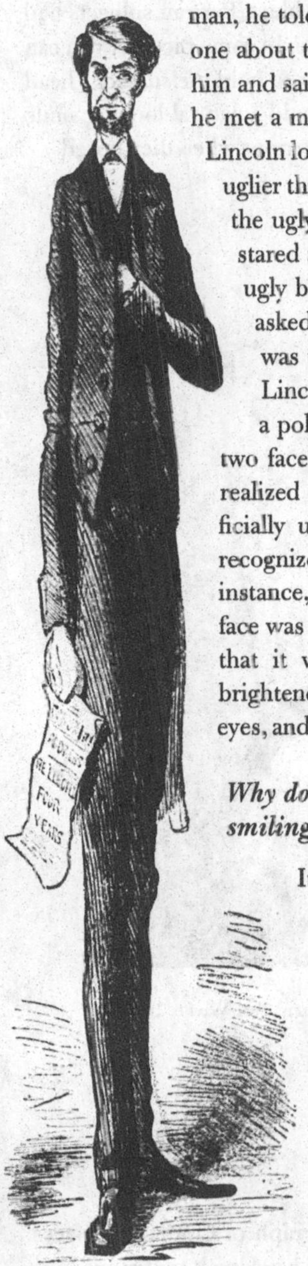

Why don't any photographs of Lincoln show him smiling?

It's the camera's fault.

The primitive photographic equipment of Lincoln's day required prolonged exposures to produce an image. That's why there are plenty of photos of the Civil War, but no action shots of battles; the moving

"Long Abe a little longer" was the original caption of this drawing in Harper's Weekly, *when Lincoln was reelected in 1864.* (Courtesy of The Lincoln Museum, Fort Wayne, IN, TLM 1942)

figures would have appeared as nothing but blurs. Portrait subjects had to hold absolutely still for as long as a minute. In some pictures you can even see the brace used by the photographer to hold the subject's head motionless. Since it's almost impossible to hold a natural-looking smile for more than a few seconds, people looked serious when they posed.

What's the worst photograph of him?

This one:

February 1865. (Courtesy of The Lincoln Museum, Fort Wayne, IN, TLM O-103b)

What's the first one?

This one:

Every now and then a new "first photograph of Lincoln" surfaces. The owners of one such daguerreotype tried hawking it to various insti-

1846. (Courtesy of The Lincoln Museum, Fort Wayne IN, TLM O-1)

tutions for many years, but despite their best efforts, most experts remained unconvinced that it really was an image of Lincoln. In 1998, it was displayed at the Old State Capitol in Springfield, where visitors were invited to express their views on its authenticity. The publicity stunt backfired, as the public voted almost three to one against it. The picture was put up for auction in October 1998, but bidding did not reach the reserve price.

Another candidate is the Kaplan daguerreotype, which surfaced in a New York gallery in 1977. There's certainly a resemblance, but there is no evidence of Lincoln posing for a daguerreotype in 1841 (the approximate date of the image). There were no photographers in Illinois at all at that time, and there is absolutely no provenance (chain of possession) to explain what happened to the picture between 1841 and 1977. The person who found it in 1977 speculated that Lincoln had it made when visiting Joshua Speed in Louisville and that he gave it to the Speeds, who

Young Lincoln? (Courtesy of Albert Kaplan/Hulton Archive/Getty Images)

kept it for years (which is plausible), but then it somehow ended up in New York City, with no information attached (which is not plausible, at least not if it's really a Lincoln photo).[7]

What's the last photograph of Lincoln?

There is a beautiful, haunting portrait of the war-scarred president that was made by Alexander Gardner on February 5, 1865.

It occasionally appears in books labeled as the last photo, erroneously dated to April 1865. In fact, a less well-known set of three photographs (two of which survive) was made on March 6, 1865. Even these are not the last images of Lincoln, however, as another photograph was taken in New York City on April 24, 1865, of the president's body in its coffin. This was contrary to the wishes of Secretary of War Edwin Stanton, who ordered the plates destroyed but retained a single print in his files. Years later, Stanton's son sent the print to John Nicolay, who was working with John Hay on a ten-volume Lincoln biography. Eventually the photograph ended up in the Hay-Nicolay papers in the Illinois State Historical Library, still unknown to the world, until July 20, 1952.

On that day, a fourteen-year-old boy named Ron Rietveld came across it while going through the files. He was already enough of a Lincoln buff to know that there were no known pictures of Lincoln's corpse and that what he had found was a big deal. The discovery appeared in *Life* magazine, and the picture was published in a photobiography by Stefan Lorant. Unlike the lottery winners who end up back in the trailer park a few years later, Rietveld overcame his early good fortune and went on to a productive career as a noted Lincoln scholar.[8]

What's the best Lincoln photo?

There are a number of famous ones taken during his presidency that could claim that title . . .

. . . but there is one pre-presidential beardless photo that stands out:

Photograph by Alexander Hesler, 1857. (Courtesy of The Lincoln Museum, Fort Wayne, IN, TLM O-2)

When Lincoln had his first portrait taken, Mary was present to supervise his hair. For this one, made in 1857, Lincoln was on his own. The photographer attempted several times to slick his subject's hair down, but each time, Lincoln ran his fingers through it and restored it to its natural state. The result was a picture that captured more of the essence of Lincoln than any previous image. Lincoln considered this picture "a very true one," but he admitted that Mary did not like it, because of "the disordered condition of the hair."[9]

Separate photos of the Lincolns combined to appear as one. Given the difference in their heights, a real picture like this one could only have been taken if Mary were standing on a box, or Abe in a trench. (Courtesy of The Lincoln Museum, Fort Wayne, IN, TLM 1794)

Are there any photographs of Lincoln with his wife?

No.

They never posed together. Any photo with both of them is a composite.

When did he decide to grow a beard?

In 1860, after a little girl told him to.

When he was running for president, he received a letter from eleven-year-old Grace Bedell of Westfield, New York. She suggested that "if you will let your whiskers grow . . . you would look a great deal better for your face is so thin." The politically astute Miss Bedell understood that women were restricted from participating directly in the election ("if I was a man I would vote for you"), but pointed out that they could aid Lincoln's election in other ways: "All the ladies like whiskers and they would tease their husband's to vote for you and then you would be President."

Lincoln wrote back with one of his characteristic rhetorical strategies, that of playing devil's advocate: "As to the whiskers, having never worn any, do you not think people would call it a piece of silly affect[at]ion if I were to begin it now?" Four months later, when his inaugural train stopped in Westfield on February 16, he called for Grace to come forward so he could show her his new beard.[10]

Of course, no story this sweet can be without its tawdry and bitter aftermath. Decades later, Robert Lincoln's wife gave Grace's letter to Republican Congressman George Dondero, with instructions to return it to Grace, then in her eighties. When he did, she gave it back and asked him to keep it, and he passed it on to his son Robert Lincoln Dondero, who donated it to the Detroit Public Library after his father's death in 1968. The letter reposed there in peace for nearly forty years, when Bedell's descendants began to agitate for its return to her family, alleging that Grace had wanted to keep the letter, but Congressman Dondero, the old rascal, had stolen it from her. Given the value of such a document, we can look forward to many years of legal wrangling over its ownership.[11]

How was Lincoln's health?

Generally very good.

The only time he was too ill to work in the White House was after his return from Gettysburg in 1863, when he came down with varioloid, a mild form of smallpox. He could not see visitors because the disease was contagious, but he was still well enough to joke that he could finally satisfy the usual horde of office seekers who came to the White House, because now he had something he could give everybody.[12]

Didn't he have some kind of genetic disease that would have eventually killed him?

If you mean "Lincoln's disease," there is only a 25 percent chance that one of his grandparents passed it on to him.

The disorder, called hereditary ataxia, causes a loss of muscle control and coordination that can make the victim appear intoxicated. There are no descriptions, however, of Lincoln behaving in such a manner. The condition is sometimes referred to as "Lincoln's disease" because it continues to affect a substantial percentage of the descendants of his grandparents, Abraham and Bathsheba, along with more than 150,000 others in the United States today. The gene that causes the disease was identified in 2006.[13]

Interesting, but that's not the one I mean. What about the one that makes people really tall?

That's called Marfan syndrome . . .

. . . and he probably didn't have that either. Marfan syndrome manifests itself in unusual height and long, spidery fingers and toes. Lincoln was unusually tall for men of his era, but the casts of his hands made by Leonard Volk in 1860 show that his fingers were strong and well proportioned, not thin and spidery, so the outward physical evidence is inconclusive at best.

Could his DNA be studied to find out if he had either of these conditions?

It could . . .

. . . but whether it should is another question. Since the 1970s, scientists have made dramatic progress in DNA research, untangling the double helixes that apparently hold the keys to much of the body's size, shape, and health. In 1986, the public became aware of Marfan syndrome when an Olympic athlete named Flo Hyman died suddenly as a result of conditions associated with it. Within a few years, some people began calling for an analysis of Lincoln's DNA, to see if he had it too. A panel consisting mostly of scientists, with token representation from the historical world, was convened to decide whether it would be appropriate to crush some of the bone fragments preserved in the National Museum of Health and Medicine, ghastly relics of Lincoln's assassination that were kept by the doctors who attended the president that night in Ford's Theatre, or who performed the autopsy. The panel did not have the expertise to determine the historical value of whatever information could be derived from testing the bone fragments, but they nonetheless recommended against testing, because the technology did not yet exist to guarantee conclusive results.[14]

The questions of hereditary ataxia and Marfan syndrome thus remain unanswered. There is no reason, however, why they need to be answered. The most important effect of Marfan syndrome is that it tends to weaken the aorta, leading to the possibility of rupture and sudden, unpredictable death, as happened to Flo Hyman in 1986. If Abraham Lincoln had this condition, it might or might not have limited his life expectancy. Likewise, if he had hereditary ataxia, it might or might not have shown itself later in his life. But in either case he was surely unaware of any anomalies in his genes, and if they were present they had no effect on his day-to-day health, either physical, mental, or emotional. They did not influence the decisions he made. They had no impact on history, and a finding that Lincoln had latent Marfan or ataxia would not lead to any reinterpretation of anything that he said or did. The desire to learn these deeply personal facts about the health of a man so intensely private, so "shut-mouthed" (as Herndon called him), represents historical voyeurism at its worst. Just because we live in an age when no question is too intimate to be asked of our public figures is no reason to violate the privacy of those, like Lincoln, who lived in a more discreet time.

In any case, the Marfan question has fallen out of the top ten in recent years, replaced by the manic-depressive question.

Was he manic-depressive?

He wasn't manic, but he did experience at least two major episodes of what today would be diagnosed as clinical depression.

That Lincoln sometimes appeared deeply depressed has always been a part of his image. "Melancholy dripped from him as he walked," according to William Herndon.[15] In January 1841, with his engagement to Mary Todd called off and his best friend Joshua Speed about to move away and get married, Lincoln described himself as "the most miserable man living. If what I feel were equally distributed to the whole human family, there would not be one cheerful face on the earth. Whether I shall ever be better I can not tell; I awfully forebode I shall not. To remain as I am is impossible; I must die or be better, it appears to me."[16]

Was this depression? The question is worth asking. In contrast to Marfan syndrome, where little would be gained by learning if Lincoln had the condition, the state of Lincoln's emotional and mental health was clearly relevant to his decision making and leadership. Now that doctors recognize clinical depression as a treatable disorder, not simply a mood, it's possible to review the descriptions of Lincoln in his depressed periods, written by him and by others, and compare them to known symptoms of clinical depression.

Lincoln's two major depressions occurred after the death of Ann Rutledge in 1835 and after the "fatal first of January" in 1841. Traditionally, historians have focused on what caused Lincoln's behavior to change so radically each time. Much of the case for a Lincoln-Rutledge romance rests on the idea that since he was so depressed after her death, he must have really loved her. But as Joshua Shenk has pointed out in his study of Lincoln's depression, such a reaction can be triggered by small events as well as great ones. Lincoln's breakdown in 1835 began, not immediately with Ann's death, but with the heavy rain that followed.[17] The winter of 1840–41 was filled with so many troubling events (struggles in the legislature, the tumultuous courtship with Mary Todd, and the imminent departure of Joshua Speed) that no one knows for certain which was the one that pushed Lincoln to the brink. What we do know is that in both instances, he exhibited the classic signs of a major depressive episode, including the inability to get out of bed and what his friends perceived as contemplation of suicide. While we do not have the evidence to identify the specific triggers of these two depressions, it is significant that they occurred in turbulent times and were not simply the products of random chemical fluctuations in his brain. Lincoln may have been prone to depression, but he was not "manic."

If Lincoln went into a suicidal tailspin just because of bad weather in 1835, isn't that pretty manic?

It wasn't just any bad weather, it was the idea of rain falling on Ann Rutledge's grave.

Through the rest of his life, the image would suggest to Lincoln the finality of death. He used it in 1864, when political opponents were attacking him for his behavior during a visit to the Army of the Potomac after the battle of Antietam. He had asked his bodyguard Ward Hill Lamon to sing a ballad, and political opponents spun the incident to portray a callous Lincoln asking for comic songs while riding over the corpses of Union soldiers. Lamon was so upset that he drafted an angry denial, which Lincoln rewrote. It was published over Lamon's name, but the last line contained an unusual turn of speech that was pure Lincoln: "No dead body was seen during the whole time the President was absent from Washington, nor even a grave that had not been rained on since the time it was made."[18]

Was he depressed when he was president?

After 1841, Lincoln never again suffered so dramatically from depression.

It is less certain whether Lincoln thereafter suffered from a chronic low-grade version of the malady or that he had to save the Union "while struggling to fight off a thick gray fog of biochemical depression."[19] One of the most debilitating symptoms of low-grade depression is the victim's lack of interest in ordinary activities and an absence of motivation to accomplish anything. If Lincoln ever felt this way, he never expressed it, nor did he allow it to interfere with the prodigious labor of being president, working long hours in his White House office, eating and sleeping but little.

We also know that Lincoln had the gift of what psychologists call "emotional intelligence," which enabled him to identify and understand feelings in others and in himself. This quality is obvious in his writings, nowhere more so than in his heartbreakingly beautiful letter of sympathy to Fanny McCullough on the death of her father in 1863.[20] He was keenly aware of his own moods, and he anticipated by more than a century the idea that depression is not simply a moral failing that can be willed away, writing to Joshua Speed's sister Mary in 1841 that "[A] tendency to melancholly . . . let it be observed, is a misfortune not a fault."[21] Had Lincoln suffered the chemical imbalances of serious chronic depression, surely at some point he would have described in himself (or recognized in someone else) the sensation that Sylvia Plath identified as feeling "blank and stopped as a dead baby" in a bell jar. This he never did.

Instead, by the time he became president, Lincoln had learned to control (but not crush) his emotional self, depression and all. He took no time off during the war, seldom leaving Washington and then only to visit the troops. Even when his beloved son Willie died in 1862, he was able to compartmentalize his grief. "I was lying half asleep on the sofa in my office when his entrance roused me," wrote his secretary. " 'Well, Nicolay,' said he, choking with emotion, 'my boy is gone—he is actually gone!' and, bursting into tears, turned and went into his own office."[22] For a time he spent Thursdays, the day of the boy's death, in solitary mourning, but eventually he put that behind him as well.

Did he take anything to treat his depression, like after Willie's death?

No, and it's a good thing, too . . .

. . . because nineteenth-century medicines were often more dangerous than the illnesses they were intended to cure.

Is it true that he once took mercury pills? Aren't they dangerous?

Yes, and yes.

Billy Herndon noted his partner sometimes took a pill for constipation, called "blue mass." He apparently continued to take them for a short period after he was elected president but stopped because they made him irritable.[23]

The decision to stop may have saved the nation, as a "blue mass" pill contains about nine thousand times more mercury than is now considered safe to ingest. Mercury was common in nineteenth-century medicine.* James Henry Hammond, the planter who coined the phrase "Cotton is king!" took a mercury-based medicine for years to help him perform a daily evacuation, which he considered necessary for health, right up to his death from mercury poisoning in 1864 at the age of fifty-seven.[24] Lincoln occasionally took blue mass in the 1850s, and his behavior at the time occasionally showed signs of mercury poisoning, including rage, depression, and an awkward gait (the same symptom others have claimed could have been a sign of ataxia). Evidence of how much he took is limited. There exists at least one prescription written for Lincoln that could shed light on the matter, but the doctor who owns it refuses to make it public, in a refreshing display of respect for patient confidentiality. Since mercury leaves the body over time (the last traces usually disappear from the hair within a year or so), there is no way to test Lincoln's remains to confirm that he stopped taking blue mass, but had he died mysteriously of mercury-related symptoms, there would have been a very good reason to test surviving hair samples.[25]

Other than from mercury poisoning, did Lincoln ever lose his temper? He always seems so calm in photographs.

Everyone looks calm in photographs from Lincoln's era . . .

. . . because with exposure times as long as sixty seconds, it was impossible to capture momentary flashes of emotion. But even when he wasn't posing, Lincoln's temperament was well controlled. For a chapter titled "Lincoln's Anger and Cruelty" in his book *The Inner World of Abraham Lincoln,* historian Michael Burlingame combed the archives for every mention of Lincoln showing his temper, and he found more than a few examples. Reading these out of context, one might assume that Lincoln was a raging cauldron of unbridled anger, but to anyone who knows how much has been written about Lincoln, the catalog of tantrums produces the opposite effect. As Burlingame concludes, "the remarkable thing about Lincoln's temper is not how often it erupted but how seldom it did."[26]

*The neurological damage, memory loss, and other dangers of mercury exposure were not widely recognized until the latter half of the twentieth century. Older readers may be able to recall happy times playing with drops of liquid mercury in science class, but those who did this too often may not.

Further, those occasions when he "rather gave my temper the rein" instead of holding it in check were sometimes intentional acts, not breakdowns of self-control.[27] One might, with only a bit of a stretch, compare Lincoln's use of anger to the fighting that takes place in professional hockey games. To the uninitiated, these fisticuffs look like the results of tempers boiling over, but in fact they are almost always calculated events, intended to send a psychological message to the opposing team. Thus fights frequently take place early in matches, or near the end of lopsided defeats, but almost never late in close games. Similarly, Lincoln's occasional displays of temper were more likely to be tactical maneuvers than emotional outbursts.

Did Lincoln hate anyone?

No. "He was certainly a very poor hater" . . .

. . . according to fellow lawyer Leonard Swett.[28] He did not carry grudges, as he demonstrated famously in the case of Edwin Stanton. He met Stanton when they both went to Cincinnati as cocounsels in the case of *McCormick v. Manny* in 1855, where the much more sophisticated and famous Stanton snubbed and insulted the funny-looking hick from Illinois. Lincoln was hurt, but seven years later, when he needed an efficient and honest man to replace Simon Cameron as secretary of war, he let bygones be bygones and chose Stanton, who served him loyally.

To take another example from his cabinet, Lincoln knew well that his secretary of the Treasury, Salmon Chase, wanted to be president and sometimes thought Lincoln's policies "idiotic."[29] Lincoln also knew that Chase wanted to be chief justice if he couldn't be president, so he waited patiently for Chase to overplay his hand and for the sitting chief justice (the superannuated Roger Taney) to meet his reward. When both happened in 1864, Lincoln accepted Chase's resignation from the cabinet, on the grounds that their personal relations had "reached a point of mutual embarrassment," but he did not allow his personal feelings to get in the way of appointing Chase to be the next chief justice.[30]

So Lincoln got along with everyone he met?

Superficially, yes. On a deeper level, he had almost no real friends.

Although he once wrote, "The better part of one's life consists of his friendships,"[31] Lincoln had only one soulmate in his life, Joshua Speed. His correspondence with Speed is on an order of magnitude more personal and intimate than anything he wrote to anyone else, including Mary Lincoln. In Illinois he enjoyed the male camaraderie of the lawyers riding the circuit, and in Washington he spent time with Senator Orville Browning and liked to tell jokes and stories with William Seward, but he "never had a confidant and therefore never unbosomed himself to others," at least not after he and Speed went their separate ways. He tended to rely on the company of the younger men with whom he spent much of his working days, including Herndon (author of the observation that Lincoln had no confidant) and John Hay. They could be counted on to hear his troubles, if he chose to share any, and not to burden him with their own.[32]

I heard that he wrote some poetry. Is it any good?

Early in his life he sometimes expressed his emotions in verse. He was better at politics.

His very first example of poetry dates to his childhood, written in a copybook when he was about sixteen:

Abraham Lincoln is my nam[e]
And with my pen I wrote the same
I wrote in both hast and speed
And left it here for fools to read[33]

What about the "suicide poem"? Did he really write it?

Probably.

Joshua Speed mentioned to Herndon that Lincoln had written a poem about suicide, and in 2004, a researcher found an anonymous poem in the *Sangamo Journal* for August 25, 1838, titled "The Suicide's Soliloquy," that has the sound of Lincoln's verse. It's embarrassing to read the young Lincoln (if he is the author) urging the "Sweet steel" of his dagger to "Rip up the organs of my breath/And draw my blood in showers!" but it's not inconsistent with the exaggerated, over-the-top style of the

Lyceum address and the Sub-treasury speech that Lincoln would eventually outgrow.[34]

What was his favorite poem?

"Mortality," by William Knox.

> *'Tis the wink of an eye—'tis the draught of a breath—*
> *From the blossom of health to the paleness of death,*
> *From the gilded saloon to the bier and the shroud*
> *Oh, why should the spirit of mortal be proud?*

There are thirteen similar stanzas before this one, all equally cheerful in their assertion that, contrary to Lou Reed, life really is just to die.

Was this Knox his favorite poet?

No, he just liked that one poem.

Was Walt Whitman his favorite poet?

No, although Lincoln had a nodding acquaintance with him.

On his daily rides between the White House and the summer residence at the Soldiers' Home, Lincoln often saw the famous poet on the streets of Washington, and they would exchange nods of recognition. Lincoln may have read *Leaves of Grass* before the war, but the evidence that it was among his favorites is very limited. Lincoln's assassination would move Whitman to write two of his best-known poems, "O Captain! My Captain!" and "When Lilacs Last in the Dooryard Bloom'd."[35]

Then who was his favorite poet?

He liked Robert Burns, Byron, and Shakespeare.

The habit of self-education stayed with Lincoln, but as an adult he just didn't read much for pleasure. His law partner Herndon never saw him read a book from start to finish, but he frequently dipped into the Bible or Shakespeare's works, both of which he could quote readily.[36] His reading tended to be purposeful rather than recreational; in his late forties he decided to learn geometry and studied the first six books of

Euclid until he had mastered the methods of proving theorems and deducing angles.

Was the Confederate anthem "Dixie" really his favorite song?

He thought it was "one of the best tunes I have ever heard" . . .

. . . or at least that's what he said when a band showed up outside the White House to celebrate after the surrender of Lee's army. He told them, "Our adversaries over the way attempted to appropriate it, but I insisted yesterday that we fairly captured it . . . I now request the band to favor me with its performance."[37]

Everybody knows that Lincoln was a great joker. What's the funniest Lincoln joke you know?

This is my least favorite Lincoln question . . .

. . . because audiences expect a funny response, and it's almost impossible to give one. Humor tends to be specific to its time and place, and what seemed funny to the nineteenth century often falls flat in the twenty-first. To make matters worse, Lincoln's best jokes were not stand-alone sound bites. They relied heavily on context. Lincoln's speeches to the Scott Club of Springfield in 1852, for example, are the funniest things he ever wrote. They had the audience shrieking with laughter—I still find it difficult to read them without snorting audibly, disturbing others in the library—but to get to the good parts you have to read several pages of setup, and once you get there the punch lines don't work unless you already know something about Franklin Pierce, Winfield Scott, and Lincoln's relationship with Stephen Douglas.[38]

OK, then what's the least funny Lincoln joke?

That one is easy.

It's a piece called "Bass-Ackwards," which amused Lincoln enough for him to set it down on paper:

> He said he was riding *bass-ackwards* on a *jass-ack*, through a *patton-cotch*, on a pair of *baddle-sags*, stuffed full of *binger-gred*, when the animal *steered* at a *scump*, and the *lirrup-steather* broke, and throwed

> him in the *forner* of the *kence* and broke his *pishing-fole.* He said he would not have minded it much, but he fell right in a great *tow-curd;* in fact, he said it give him a right smart *sick* of *fitness*—he had the *molera-corbus* pretty bad. He said, about *bray dake* he come to himself, ran home, seized up a *stick* of *wood* and split the *axe* to make a light, rushed into the house, and found the *door* sick abed, and his *wife* standing open. But thank goodness she is getting right *hat* and *farty* again.[39]

The original document is in the collection of The Abraham Lincoln Presidential Museum. For many years this piece was known only through a photostatic copy; one Lincoln collector who sought after the original declared that he intended to destroy it if he ever obtained it. One can almost feel sorry that he failed.

Why did he tell funny stories?

To let off steam, for one reason.

"Were it not for this occasional *vent,* I should die," Lincoln once told a Congressman who didn't want to waste time listening to his tales.[40] He also told stories to make points in a way that people could easily understand or to distract his listeners when he didn't want to answer their questions. What he didn't do was to tell stories just for the enjoyment of others. One summer night a drunken major, together with three other officers, blustered his way into the Soldiers' Home and persuaded the servants to fetch the president from his bedroom to deal with some small political matter. Lincoln could barely keep his eyes open, and one of the major's sober companions was mortified when he realized what an imposition they had become. It got worse when the major slapped the president on the knee and asked him to tell a funny story. Lincoln patiently explained that he only told his stories for a purpose, either to avoid long explanations or to take the sting out of having to refuse a request: "Storytelling as an emollient saves me much friction and distress."[41]

How many children did Lincoln have?

Four, all boys.

Robert Todd Lincoln (1843–1926) was the only one who lived to adulthood. He went to Harvard, served briefly during the Civil War, and became a lawyer like his father. He accepted an appointment as secretary of war for presidents Garfield and Arthur and was minister to England for President Benjamin Harrison. He preferred private life and became president and later chairman of the Pullman Palace Car Company. Republicans frequently urged him to run for president, on the strength of his name, but he had no taste for it. He had the misfortune of being nearby (although not an eyewitness) to three presidential assassinations (his father's, Garfield's, and McKinley's).

The other three boys died young: Edward Baker Lincoln (1846–50), William Wallace Lincoln (1850–62), and Thomas "Tad" Lincoln (1853–71).

What kind of father was he?

Extremely permissive, especially for the middle of the nineteenth century.

William Herndon thought that his law partner let his children run wild and hated it when the boys came to the office. Herndon later wrote that if they had defecated in Lincoln's hat (where could that idea have come from?) "and rubbed it on his boots, he would have laughed and thought it smart," which is permissive even for the twenty-first century.[42]

Did he have grandchildren?

None that he lived to see.

Eddie, Willie, and Tad all died young. Robert married Mary Harlan, daughter of an Iowa senator, in 1868, and they had three children. Mary, nicknamed Mamie, married Charles Isham in 1891. Abraham Lincoln II, known as Jack, contracted blood poisoning after surgery and died on March 5, 1890. He was sixteen. Jessie, born in 1875, eloped with a college football player named Warren Beckwith in 1897, the first of her three husbands.

Why isn't Robert Todd Lincoln buried in the Lincoln family tomb?

His wife decided that he should not have to spend eternity as he had lived his life . . .

. . . always in his father's shadow, so she arranged for him to be buried in Arlington National Cemetery. He had earned veteran status by serving briefly on Grant's staff during the Civil War.[43]

Did the president's children have pets?

Yes.

The Lincoln White House was a veritable menagerie. The Lincolns left their dog Fido with friends in Springfield when they moved to Washington but soon replaced it with a little dog named Jip who often sat on the president's lap at lunch. The family cat enjoyed table scraps too. When scolded by Mary for letting it eat from the presidential silverware, Lincoln replied, "If the gold fork was good enough for Buchanan I think it is good enough for Tabby."[44] Tad and Willie had a pair of goats that they hitched to carts or chairs and drove through the hallways. Tad took a special interest one year in the turkey that was being fattened for Christmas, calling it "Jack" and giving it treats. When he learned of Jack's impending doom, he threw a fit that ended only after his father wrote out a presidential pardon for the bird.[45]

Lincoln had always had a soft spot for animals. He used to amuse his fellow circuit-riding lawyers by stopping to rescue a pig stuck in the mud or replace a baby bird that had fallen from the nest. In 1864, when the White House stables caught fire, Lincoln's concern for animals (and perhaps a desire to preserve a living link to the departed Willie) prompted him to risk his life in an unsuccessful effort to save the boys' ponies.

About the turkey pardon—is that where the tradition of the president pardoning a Thanksgiving turkey comes from?

Not directly.

It didn't become a regular practice until the second half of the twentieth century. There's a persistent story that Harry Truman began the modern tradition, but the Truman Library staff has never found any evidence that he did.[46]

Speaking of signing pardons, did Lincoln have good handwriting?

Yes.

One of the small pleasures of studying Abraham Lincoln is how easy it is to read documents that he wrote. That isn't true of many nineteenth-century figures; William Herndon's manuscripts were largely neglected for many years at least in part because of his poor penmanship.

Not everyone who writes about Lincoln knows this. There was a scene in the television version of Gore Vidal's novel *Lincoln* in which the screenwriter had Mary Lincoln pick up one of her husband's speeches, look at it, and complain, "Oh dear, I am afraid that Mr. Lincoln does not write a fair hand." Apparently, as Mark E. Neely Jr., observed, it is possible to compose a major Lincoln screenplay without ever once looking at an actual Lincoln document.[47]

What was his favorite food?

That's a tough question, because Lincoln didn't much care about food.

People who knew him commented on how little interest he took in what he ate. Even his stepmother could not remember him favoring anything in particular. In the White House, Lincoln typically had an "extremely frugal" breakfast of an egg, toast, and coffee; lunch was "a biscuit, a glass of milk in winter, some fruit or grapes in summer," according to John Hay, who said that he "ate less than any man I know."[48] He once commented favorably on a cake that Mary had made, but that was because he was not an idiot.

Was Lincoln a Mason?

No.

He did not belong to the Freemasons, and if he was a member of any other secret society, it's still a secret.[49] Freemasonry was a political issue in Lincoln's lifetime, when many Americans regarded with jealous suspicion any organization, from the Masons to the Catholic church, that might compete for the loyalty of the nation's citizens. Considering that one of the precursors of Lincoln's Whig Party was the Antimasonic political party of the late 1820s, it is not surprising that Lincoln did not join. Masons today acknowledge that Lincoln never belonged to their organization but nonetheless claim him as a sort of posthumous honorary Mason.[50] Members of a fraternal organization called the Knights of Pythias likewise regard Lincoln as their patron, based on a story that he encouraged the group to seek a Congressional charter in 1864, but he never joined that organization either.

Did Lincoln invent something?

Yes.

He designed a system of inflatable chambers for riverboats, to help them float again when they were grounded in shallow water. It was never produced, and it's not clear that it would have worked, since the weight of the machinery to inflate the chambers might have offset any resulting gains in buoyancy, but he did receive patent number 6469 for "Improved Method of Lifting Vessels Over Shoals." No other U.S. president has held a patent.[51]

Did he know that he would be considered by many people to be the greatest president ever?

Probably not, but that's not to say that he was burdened by false modesty.

He was aware of his own intellectual superiority over everyone he met, an awareness that especially rankled smart people like Charles Sumner and Salmon Chase, who were accustomed to deference from uneducated men like Lincoln. His self-confidence contributed to his masterful management ability, since it allowed him to share the credit with his subordinates when things went well and to accept the blame when they didn't. In his letter to General Grant after the capture of Vicksburg, for example, he admitted that he had questioned Grant's strategy and then wrote a sentence that is almost unimaginable coming from the pen of a politician: "I now wish to make the personal acknowledgement that you were right, and I was wrong."[52]

Eight chapters ago, you said that Lincoln wasn't a Christian. Then why did he have "In God We Trust" put on our coins?

That was done by Salmon P. Chase.

Chase, the Secretary of the Treasury, was more conventionally religious than Lincoln. It was Chase who persuaded Lincoln to add a religious invocation to the final Emancipation Proclamation: "And upon this act, sincerely believed to be an act of justice, warranted by the Constitution, upon military necessity, I invoke the considerate judgment of mankind, and the gracious favor of Almighty God." Under the Mint Act of April 22, 1864, the Treasury was authorized to issue a new two-cent coin, on which Chase had inscribed "In God We Trust." Congress specifically authorized the motto for all coins the following year.

Didn't he become more religious when he was president?

Yes.

He keenly felt the burden of leading a nation in wartime. In addition to bearing the responsibility of sending hundreds of thousands of young men to fight and die, Lincoln mourned for personal friends like the young Elmer Ellsworth (the first Union officer killed in the war) and his old Whig comrade Edward Baker, who gave up his Senate seat to lead troops in the field and lost his life at Ball's Bluff in October 1861. These deaths, and especially that of his son Willie, caused him to look hard for a meaning in all the suffering. He seems to have prayed frequently, not so much by reciting memorized pleas to the Almighty as by trying to discern the will of God so that he could act as His instrument. At some point in the war he put on paper a "Meditation on the Divine Will":

> The will of God prevails. In great contests each party claims to act in accordance with the will of God. Both *may* be, and one *must* be wrong. God can not be *for,* and *against* the same thing at the same time. In the present civil war it is quite possible that God's purpose is something different from the purpose of either party . . . He could have either *saved* or *destroyed* the Union without a human contest. Yet the contest began. And having begun He could give the final victory to either side any day. Yet the contest proceeds.[55]

Lincoln was already deeply familiar with the Bible, and could speak in phrases and cadences that resonated with the evangelical Protestants who made up a majority of the American public. When he deployed his rhetorical gifts to express his philosophical understanding of the meaning of the war, the result was the most profound speech ever given by any president, the Second Inaugural Address.[54]

Did he believe in dreams?

Yes, in a precautionary way.

Lincoln did not hire a White House astrologer to help him make decisions of state, but he retained enough of the frontier superstition of his youth that he did sometimes take counsel of his dreams, at least when there was no good reason not to do so. On June 9, 1863, Lincoln sent a telegram to Mary, who was in Philadelphia: "Think you better put 'Tad's' pistol away. I had an ugly dream about him."[55] Tad was a very emotional and poorly disciplined child, so keeping pistols away from him was probably a good idea in any circumstance, but one can imagine Lincoln recalling the almost unbearable pain of Willie's death the year before and deciding to heed his subconscious rather than take a chance.

What about Mary? Didn't she hold a séance in the White House?

Yes, several. Desperate to contact the spirit of Willie . . .

. . . she was easy prey for charlatans who promised that it could be done, including one who called himself "Lord Colchester." Spiritualism was popular in the mid-nineteenth century, and why not? If the telegraph could eliminate distance as a barrier to instant communication, might not there also be a way to overcome the invisible veil separating the living and the dead? A number of séances were held in the White House, some of them attended by Lincoln in an effort to humor his suffering wife.[56]

How did he stand it being married to her?

With the passing of time, the Lincoln marriage continues to grow more and more dysfunctional in the public's mind . . .

. . . although it will be hard to top Dale Carnegie's 1932 comment that "the great tragedy of Lincoln's life was not his assassination, but his marriage." Carnegie saw Mary as "a mean, common, envious, affected, mannerless virago" who "had almost no likable qualities."[57]

Carnegie's conclusion that life with Mary was worse than a bullet in the head may go a bit too far, but it is true that the Lincoln marriage was

Mary Lincoln's interest in spiritualism led a photographer to pretend that he had captured an image of her departed husband laying his hands on her shoulders. (Courtesy of The Lincoln Museum, Fort Wayne, IN, TLM 109)

not without its issues. Lincoln was away riding the circuit much of the time when they lived in Springfield, and Mary was left alone to raise the boys in circumstances considerably more taxing than those of her comfortable slave-served childhood in Kentucky. There's no question that she was under a lot of stress, in Springfield and in Washington, and that Lincoln had to put up with her emotional highs and lows.

I read that she chased him with knives and broke his nose with a stick. Doesn't that go beyond "emotional highs and lows"?

He did show up for work one day in Springfield with a bandage on his nose.

Apparently Mrs. L. had asked him to put more wood on the fire one evening, a simple enough request, which he neglected to do. After two more reminders, each doubtless answered with a patient "Yes, Mother," but no action, Mary finally grabbed a stick of firewood herself and said "I'll make you hear me this time." Perhaps she threw the stick at him to get his attention, and it hit him in the face by accident, or perhaps she really lost her temper and took a two-handed swing at him. We just don't know. In either case, she should not have done it, but he was not blameless either, any more than the time that she yelled at him because while taking the children for a walk in a wagon, he failed to notice that one of them had fallen out.[58]

The problem is that most of what we do know of the Lincoln marriage is based on the gossip of outside observers, and how accurately can a relationship be judged from such sources? It's not hard to find news stories of seemingly perfect couples who turn out to be engaged in all manner of unsavory activities. Many happy marriages may look less than tranquil from the outside. When we do get glimpses into the private world of Abraham and Mary, as in the few surviving letters that they exchanged when he went off to Congress, they reveal nothing extraordinary.[59]

There were certainly times when Mary tried Abraham's patience severely. One of the most embarrassing occurred when the two of them visited the headquarters of the Army of the Potomac near the end of the war. Lincoln went on ahead to begin reviewing the troops of General Ord and was joined by Mrs. Ord, who rode alongside. When Mary arrived and saw another woman near her husband, she went berserk.

A terrible scene followed, in which Mary's behavior shocked everyone present. Lincoln had no choice but to bear it quietly.*

Yet Lincoln did manage to bear it quietly, on that occasion and others. Back in Springfield, Mary once got involved in a dispute with a maid, which escalated when the girl's uncle confronted Mary, who hit him in the face with a broom for his trouble. As a gentleman, he could not strike back at a woman, so he went to find Lincoln to demand an apology, or more, from him. Lincoln's reply was simply to ask if he could not bear with this one example of Mary's temper for friendship's sake, considering that Lincoln himself had "had to bear it without complaint and without a murmur for lo these last fifteen years."[60] The friend agreed to do so, for Lincoln's sake; perhaps we can too.

Everyone knows he was born poor, but didn't Lincoln die rich?

He did all right—his estate was worth $110,294.62 . . .

. . . which was big money in 1865.[61] He was frugal, but he never coveted money, any more than he craved food or drink. As Herndon put it, he had "the avarice of the keep" but "no avarice of the get."[62] After his death, uncashed pay warrants from his presidential salary ($25,000 a year) were found in his desk. Lincoln aspired to, and achieved, a solidly middle-class lifestyle that represented a large economic step up from his origins, but it was never his goal to get rich. Had it been, he could have done much better by sticking with law and speculating in land and stocks, instead of going into politics.

FOR FURTHER READING

Every known Lincoln photograph, and more, can be found in Lloyd Ostendorf, *Lincoln's Photographs: A Complete Album* (1998). *The Lincoln Image* (1984), by Harold Holzer, Gabor Boritt, and Mark E. Neely,

*The code of gentlemanly conduct left no way for Lincoln to restrain his wife in such circumstances. One of his successors in the White House, William McKinley, hosted social events with his wife, who suffered from epilepsy. Since her seizures could not be socially acknowledged, when she was stricken during a reception, President McKinley would calmly continue his conversation with guests while holding a handkerchief over her face until her symptoms subsided.

Jr., analyzes Lincoln in prints and paintings as well as photographs. Karen Winnick, *Mr. Lincoln's Whiskers* (1996), is a beautiful book for children that tells the story of Grace Bedell and Lincoln's beard, with compelling illustrations and reproductions of the letters by Lincoln and Grace.

For Lincoln's health, Joshua Wolf Shenk provides the definitive analysis of his symptoms of depression in *Lincoln's Melancholy: How Depression Challenged a President and Fueled His Greatness* (2005). On Lincoln's friendships, see David Herbert Donald, "*We Are Lincoln Men*": *Abraham Lincoln and His Friends* (2003). David J. Harkness and R. Gerald McMurtry describe *Lincoln's Favorite Poets* (1959). Robert Bray lists every book, of poetry or otherwise, that Lincoln ever read or might have read, in "What Abraham Lincoln Read—An Evaluative and Annotated List," *Journal of the Abraham Lincoln Association* 28, no. 2 (summer 2007), available online. Lincoln's humor is collected in Paul M. Zall, *Abe Lincoln Laughing: Humorous Anecdotes from Original Sources By and About Abraham Lincoln* (1995). Daniel Mark Epstein, *The Lincolns: Portrait of a Marriage* (2008) challenges the traditional view that Mary put Abraham through twenty-two years of domestic purgatory. Lincoln's children are sympathetically chronicled in Ruth Painter Randall, *Lincoln's Sons* (1955); the family's own photographs are beautifully reproduced in Mark E. Neely, Jr., and Harold Holzer, *The Lincoln Family Album* (1990).

On food, Wayne C. Temple has written the definitive "*The Taste Is In My Mouth a Little . . .*": *Lincoln's Victuals and Potables* (1991), which includes the entire text of an 1843 recipe book, but if you actually want to try cooking something Lincolnian, Donna D. McCreary's *Lincoln's Table* (2000) is practical and charming. For Lincoln's religion, see the books cited earlier and also Wayne C. Temple, *Abraham Lincoln: From Skeptic to Prophet* (1995).

{ CHAPTER ELEVEN }

Martyr

I would rather be assassinated on this spot than to surrender it.

—Lincoln, speaking of the Declaration of Independence, 1861[1]

Did Lincoln know John Wilkes Booth?

He knew of him, certainly.

The assassin of President Lincoln was one of the most famous actors in America. As an avid theatergoer, Lincoln could not avoid knowing about him. Further, Lincoln had seen Booth perform in *The Marble Heart* at Ford's Theatre, on November 9, 1863. At the Second Inaugural, on March 4, 1865, Booth and Lincoln switched roles, with Lincoln taking the lead and Booth appearing in the audience.

Did Lincoln have premonitions of death?

Yes.

On the night of April 13, 1865, Lincoln had a recurring dream, which he described to his cabinet the next day. In the dream, he was on a ship heading "with great rapidity towards an indefinite shore."[2] In the past, he said, it had always come the night before a major event, like the victories at Antietam or Gettysburg. This time he thought it would be good news again, perhaps word that Sherman had captured the last major Confederate field army, down in North Carolina. Since the surrender of Lee's army at Appomattox on April 9, Washington had been a scene of celebration, but the war wasn't quite over, and Lincoln was looking forward to hearing that the killing was finally done.

No such news arrived that day, but everyone was still in a good mood. With victory assured and the challenge of reconstructing the divided

In this photograph of the Second Inaugural, John Wilkes Booth listens from the balcony, to the left of the President. (Courtesy of The Lincoln Museum, Fort Wayne, IN, TLM O-108)

Union looming ahead, it seemed like an appropriate moment to take a break and relax, if only for a few hours. A night of comedy at the theater would be just the thing.

How did the assassination happen? Why didn't the Secret Service stop Booth?

In 1865, there was no Secret Service as we know it.

Lincoln preferred to go about his business with no bodyguards or other protection, believing that if someone really wanted to kill him, it could not be prevented. He received numerous death threats in the mail but refused to take them seriously. No other president had been assassinated, and as Secretary of State Seward put it, the whole idea was just too foreign: "Assassination is not an American practice or habit."[3]

Not everyone agreed. Ward Hill Lamon, whom Lincoln had appointed marshal of the District of Columbia, was the closest thing Lincoln had to a security service. He escorted Lincoln when he could and even slept in the hall outside the president's bedroom on occasion, but he could not be everywhere. He tried to persuade Lincoln to take better care of his own safety and warned him that it was an especially bad idea to go to the theater unattended: "When I say unattended, I mean that you went alone with Charles Sumner and a foreign minister, neither of whom could defend himself against an assault from any able-bodied woman in this city."[6] On April 14, 1865, Lamon was in Richmond, Virginia, on a mission for the president.

So there was nobody guarding the president?

On the fatal night at Ford's Theatre, Lincoln was protected by a single Washington policeman . . .

. . . and he wasn't paying attention. The Lincolns and their guests (Major Henry Rathbone and Clara Harris, his stepsister and fiancée) were seated in a private box overlooking the stage from the side. To reach their seats, the Lincolns had entered the theater, gone up to the dress circle level, passed through a doorway into a small corridor, then entered the box itself through a door at the back of the room. Once they were settled in, the policeman assigned to guard them took a seat beside the door from the dress circle to the corridor. Unfortunately, John Parker grew bored with his duties and wandered off to watch the play from a better seat (or, in some accounts, to get a drink at a neighboring saloon). When Booth approached the door Parker was supposed to be guarding, he encountered only an unarmed presidential servant, who took a look at the famous actor's calling card and was happy to let him into the corridor, much as you or I might be eager to do the bidding of a big-time movie star, if one were to ask us for a favor.

Is it true that Booth drilled a hole in the door to the presidential box, so that he could see if anyone was looking before he entered?

It's true there was a hole in the door, but it probably wasn't put there by Booth.

Harry Clay Ford, brother of theater owner John T. Ford, testified after the assassination that he had never seen the hole, but Harry's son claimed for many years after that his father had authorized the drilling of a hole in the door so that the president's guard could check on his charge without having to disturb anyone. Since Lincoln's scheduled attendance was announced only hours before the performance, it was unlikely that Booth would have had much time for drilling or that such an odd act would have gone unnoticed.[5]

Booth doubtless did use the hole, whatever its origins, to see the backs of President Lincoln, in a rocking chair, and Mrs. Lincoln to his right, on a smaller chair. Miss Harris was still farther to the right, in an armchair, with Major Rathbone sitting on a sofa behind her, against the back wall of the box.

Why were Rathbone and Harris invited? Were they special friends of the Lincolns?

No, not particularly.

After four years in Washington, Mary Lincoln had alienated almost everybody of importance in the city. The Lincolns had invited Secretary of War Stanton, General Grant, and half a dozen others, but few people other than Abraham wanted to spend an evening with Mary Lincoln if it could be avoided, so the invitation finally descended on a pleasant couple who were too junior to turn down a presidential invitation. Harris was the daughter of Senator Ira Harris of New York.[6]

The presence of Major Rathbone may have also seemed like a bit of needed security. Stanton, like Lamon, had warned Lincoln not to go to the theater unescorted, but the president, after all, had just ten days earlier strolled through the streets of Richmond, accompanied by little Tad and guarded only by a squad of sailors. If he could walk in safety through the streets of a city filled with people who had been making war against him for four years, surely he could go to the theater in his own capital.

Did Major Rathbone try to stop Booth?

Yes, but too late.

Booth had planned the attack carefully. After entering the corridor leading to the back of the presidential box, he closed the door behind him and blocked it with a wooden bar. He then peeked into the room where Lincoln sat. Finding the two couples fully involved in the play, or (as

Mary later recalled) in pleasant small talk, he quietly slipped in, walked up behind Lincoln, and fired his derringer into the president's head.

Only then did anyone else in the box realize that something was happening. Rathbone leaped up and tried to grab Booth, but the assassin was carrying a large knife with which he inflicted a deep cut on the major's arm. Booth then climbed onto the railing of the box, which put him some twelve feet above the stage. Accustomed to doing his own stunts, he made a theatrical leap to the floor below, but his spur caught on one of the flags decorating the box, tearing the flag and upsetting his balance enough so that he landed awkwardly, possibly fracturing a bone in his left leg.[7] Booth played through the pain, facing the stunned audience and shouting, "*Sic semper tyrannis*" before making his exit stage rear, dashing out to the alley behind the theater where he had a getaway horse waiting, and galloping away.

What does* Sic semper tyrannis *mean?

Thus always to tyrants . . .

. . . which not coincidentally was (and is) the motto of the state of Virginia.

Didn't he say something else?

Possibly.

Booth spoke his line and departed, Mrs. Lincoln screamed, and the audience erupted in confusion. It was a moment that everyone in the room would remember for the rest of his or her life, but as is often the case in times of supreme stress, many different memories emerged.[8] Most accounts of eyewitnesses say that Booth cried out, "*Sic semper tyrannis,*" but several were certain that he yelled, "The South is avenged!" He may have said both.

How did Booth get a horse to wait for him?

Booth had arranged with theater flunky Ned Spangler to have a horse waiting outside . . .

. . . without letting him know of his nefarious purpose. Spangler in turn delegated the lowly responsibility of actually holding the horse to

"Peanut John" Borrows. There was apparently no one lower on the Ford's Theatre food chain, so it was from Peanut John that Booth took the reins and rode away. Even though Spangler had no idea what Booth was up to, he was later accused of conspiring with Booth to murder the president, found guilty of aiding Booth's escape, and sentenced to six years' hard labor.

What happened to Major Rathbone?

He recovered from his wound and married Clara . . .

. . . but their story did not end happily. He eventually went insane, murdered his wife, tried to kill himself, and died in an asylum in Germany.[9]

Could modern medical techniques have saved Lincoln's life after he was shot?

No . . .

. . . but at least they would not have made things worse, as Lincoln's doctors may have done. The first on the scene, Dr. Charles Leale, had some difficulty finding a wound on the body of the president, who remained seated in his rocker, unconscious. An army surgeon, Dr. Charles Taft, soon joined Leale, as did Dr. Albert King. Leale eventually discovered a bullet hole in the back of Lincoln's head, and all three doctors immediately realized that it indicated a fatal wound. After Lincoln was carried across the street to Petersen's boardinghouse, he was attended by more doctors, including the surgeon general and the Lincoln family physician, all of whom had rushed to the scene. They probed the entry wound with surgical tools until they located what they believed to be the bullet, behind the right eye. They continued to keep the wound open and bleeding through the night, as it seemed to ease the president's breathing to do so. He died at 7:22 the next morning.

These facts led Dr. Richard Fraser to write a 1995 article suggesting that it was Lincoln's doctors who actually ended his life, by exploring the wound with unsterile fingers and later by inserting surgical probes deep into the president's brain. There is no question that these procedures do not meet modern medical standards, and Fraser argued persuasively that they did not even meet the most current standards of 1865. However, pointing out what the doctors did wrong does not necessarily mean that there was anything that anyone, then or now, could have done to save Lincoln. Dr. John K. Lattimer, author of *Kennedy and Lincoln: Medical and Ballistic Comparisons of Their Assassinations* (1980), responded with an article denying that Leale could have inserted even the tip of his finger into the entry wound, a conclusion he reached after experimenting by repeatedly shooting .41 caliber derringers into "fresh skulls." The bullets consistently produced tiny holes with sharp edges that would not admit a doctor's finger. More important (and less absurdly ghoulish), Lattimer asserted that it was the damage done by the bullet entering Lincoln's brain that was fatal, not any subsequent probing by the doctors.[10]

Which doctor is right? I am a historian and not a medical professional, but in a lifetime of studying the Civil War era I can recall reading very few accounts of soldiers suffering gunshot wounds to the back of the head and surviving, much less recovering fully. Perhaps Lincoln's doctors should have refrained from inserting probes or otherwise inflicting their primitive medical ideas on the president, but it is to me inconceivable that a different outcome would have followed, no matter what they had done. Abraham Lincoln was doomed the moment John Wilkes Booth pulled the trigger.

Where is the bullet now?

In the National Museum of Health and Medicine in Washington, D.C., along with other relics like bone fragments and the bloodstained shirt cuffs of the doctor who performed the autopsy.

The contents of Lincoln's pockets from that night (two pairs of spectacles, a pocketknife, a watch fob, a handkerchief, a button, and a wallet with some newspaper clippings and a Confederate five-dollar bill) are in the Rare Book Room of the Library of Congress.[11]

Why did Booth shoot Lincoln?

Let's start with reasons that don't explain why Booth shot Lincoln.

He wasn't a frustrated actor, turning to crime in order to find the fame that eluded him on the stage; he was a very successful actor whose performances received generally positive reviews.[12] Nor was he a madman, committing a random act of wanton violence for no apparent reason. He spent months organizing a conspiracy intended to kidnap Lincoln and spirit him away to Richmond, where he could be held hostage for the return of thousands of prisoners of war. When the fall of the Confederate capital made that plan impractical, he turned to murder, but the care with which he planned the operation is evidence that this was no mad crime of passion.

The devil made him do it; an early interpretation of Booth's motive. (Courtesy of The Lincoln Museum, Fort Wayne, IN, TLM 1691)

In fact, Booth knew exactly what he was doing, and why. He was dedicated to white supremacy and to the cause of the Confederacy, but his ego demanded that he serve that cause in some fashion more dramatic than shouldering a musket in Lee's infantry. The kidnapping scheme would have made him the most famous Southern patriot of all and perhaps even have turned the tide of the war. After the fall of Richmond on April 3, 1865, Booth imagined that killing the president would still somehow save the Confederacy from defeat or at least prevent Lincoln from reshaping the South. On April 11, Booth was part of a crowd that gathered outside the White House to hear Lincoln speak of his vision for postwar America. That vision included a society where some limited voting rights could be given to some black Americans, to military veterans for example. When he heard that proposal, Booth responded, "That means n—— citizenship. That is the last speech he will ever make."[13]

Booth saw himself as a hero of liberty who would be remembered forever for slaying an evil tyrant. When he read the first "reviews" of his grand performance, in newspapers smuggled to him as he hid in the woods of rural southern Maryland, he was stunned to learn of the world's general condemnation. Editors who had been criticizing Lincoln in the harshest terms for the past four years were now eulogizing him and turning their hatred upon his assassin. Even Southern papers like the Richmond *Whig* saw nothing good coming out of what Booth had done. Indeed, the murder of Lincoln on Good Friday prompted many clergymen throughout the North to devote their Easter Sunday sermons to comparisons between his fate and that of Jesus Christ.[14]

In response, Booth began to scribble in his diary his own account of what he had done. It was a fantasy version, in which he claimed for example that he had shouted, "*Sic semper!*" before shooting, to refute the charge that he played the coward in attacking a helpless, unaware victim from behind. Further, Booth had already composed and sent to the editor of the *National Intelligencer* a lengthy letter explaining his purposes, which he expected to see published along with reports of his deed. This left no doubt about his ideology: "This country was formed for the white, not for the black man . . . If the South is to be aided it must be done quickly." He closed by comparing himself to Brutus, the assassin of Julius Caesar.[15]

Did Booth act alone?

No.

He had a number of conspirators. On the night of the assassination, one of them, George Atzerodt, was supposed to kill Vice President Andrew Johnson, but he lost his nerve and took no action except to get drunk. Another, former Confederate soldier Lewis Powell, went to the home of Secretary of State William Seward. He pretended to have medicine for the secretary, who was bedridden with a broken jaw from a carriage accident. Forcing his way into the sickroom, he fractured the skull of Frederick Seward (the secretary's son) and then attacked Seward with a knife, which fortunately was deflected by the brace he was wearing for his jaw. An army soldier serving as Seward's nurse, together with another son, managed to drag Powell away. Powell ran from the house, mounted his horse, and escaped.

Still another conspirator, David Herold, met up with Booth after the assassination and joined him in escaping to southern Maryland, where the pair hid out for a week before crossing the Potomac into northern Virginia, where they were finally tracked down by federal cavalry soldiers.

What happened to the doctor who helped Booth? Didn't he get sent to jail and then pardoned?

His name is Mudd . . .

. . . and he was convicted of participating in Booth's conspiracy.* On the night of the assassination (or rather at four o'clock the next morning), Booth and David Herold went to his rural Maryland farm to seek shelter and medical care. Dr. Samuel Mudd's crime was not that of setting Booth's broken leg, as any doctor would do, but of allowing Booth and Herold to spend the night and part of the next day without informing the authorities that the president's assassin was in his house. Mudd's later claim that he did not recognize Booth is hard to reconcile with the fact that the two had met on at least two previous occasions. Even had he not known the identity of the stranger knocking on his door in the middle of the night, surely when he learned of the assassination the next day, he could have put two and two together (had he wanted to) and deduced that the mysterious injured man in his house must be the fugitive everyone was seeking.

Dr. Mudd was sentenced to life imprisonment in a remote island prison in the Dry Tortugas, off the Florida Keys. While there, he bravely treated yellow fever patients and for his efforts was pardoned in 1869 by President Andrew Johnson, but this only ended his punishment and did not exonerate him.

*For the record, the phrase "his name is mud" can be found on p. 122 of a dictionary of slang by "Jon Bee" (John Babcock), printed in 1823; it did not originate with Dr. Mudd.

Since the 1970s, some of his descendants have devoted themselves to getting someone in authority to agree with them that he was innocent of any crime, but with no success. Presidents Carter and Reagan refused to do anything, because Johnson's full pardon of Mudd exhausted the executive's prerogative. There could be no direct appeal of the verdict to the courts because Mudd's guilt was legally moot, both by virtue of the pardon and the fact that he had been in his grave for a century. The Mudd family appealed to the U.S. Army to change the records of the military commission that tried Mudd, under a law allowing veterans to request corrections in their military records. That case wound its way through the military and civil justice systems for more than a decade, with the Mudds winning the occasional procedural point, but it finally died in February 2003, after the D.C. Court of Appeals ruled against the Mudds and their lawyer missed the deadline for filing a petition for a writ of certiorari, a necessary step in asking the U.S. Supreme Court to hear an appeal.

The Supreme Court would probably not have wasted its time on the Mudd family's obsession anyway, especially since William Rehnquist, then chief justice, had written a book on habeas corpus in which he criticized the reopening of the Mudd case as inappropriate.[16] With the courts finally closed to them, and the death of the doctor's grandson Richard Mudd in 2003, the issue might seem to be over, but there are rumors that other family members hope to try the remaining branch of government, by seeking a Congressional resolution regarding Mudd's innocence. Perhaps if they had a hobby . . .

But weren't there also some secret conspirators? Wasn't the secretary of war, Edwin Stanton, really behind the plot?

No.

Although conspiracy theorists have found the idea irresistible, no responsible historian believes that one of Lincoln's cabinet members had him murdered. There is not the slightest evidence to support the idea. But the public loves a sinister conspiracy, and when a chemist named Otto Eisenschiml published *Why Was Lincoln Murdered?* in 1937, he found an audience. As the book's title exemplifies, the author made a practice of asking questions that embody his assumptions. We know why Booth killed Lincoln, but Eisenschiml assumed there must be something else at work, not just a political assassination but a cold-blooded murder by someone on the inside.

Even though there is nothing behind the Eisenschiml thesis, the idea that Stanton (and other unsuspected conspirators) really killed Lincoln gets a new lease on life every few decades. In 1961, *Civil War Times* magazine published an article titled "Was Stanton Behind Lincoln's Murder?"[17] In 1977, a made-for-TV movie called *The Lincoln Conspiracy,* based on a book of the same name by David Balsiger and Charles Sellier, absorbed its allotted fifteen minutes of public attention, even though it was based on "a tissue of preposterous fabrications," in the words of historian Richard Current.[18] In the twenty-first century the publication of similar fantasies, under titles like *Dark Union* and *Abraham Lincoln's Execution,* continues unabated.[19]

Was the Confederate government involved in the plot to kill Lincoln?

Everyone thought so, at first.

Who else would want to kill Lincoln? After Booth's conspirators were apprehended, they were put on trial by a military commission that sought to get to the bottom of the story. A military commission could proceed much faster (and with fewer safeguards for the rights of the accused) than a civil court, and Lincoln had been commander in chief, so it was a panel of military officers that conducted the investigation.

The commission failed to uncover any definitive evidence that Booth was an agent of the Confederate government, and the idea that the killing of the president had any political purpose faded by the late nineteenth century. In that era of national reconciliation, the white majorities in the North and the South were ready to put the war and its causes (especially slavery) behind them. An unspoken agreement arose: the South would forget that it had seceded to preserve slavery, and the North would forget about enforcing the Fourteenth and Fifteenth Amendments, which were supposed to guarantee civil rights and the vote to the former slaves. The war would be depoliticized and remembered only as "the late unpleasantness" fought by brave brothers who happened to have an honest disagreement over federalism and the tariff (but not slavery). Blame for the murder of Lincoln could be pinned entirely on the shoulders of the mad actor, Booth.[20]

A century later, in 1988, the case against the Confederate government was reopened by two retired intelligence officers and a Lincoln assassination expert, with a book called *Come Retribution: The Confederate Secret Service and the Assassination of Lincoln.*[21] They argued that Booth had connections within the rebel government and had met with Confederate agents in Canada as well. Given the increasing barbarism with which both sides were conducting the war by 1864, the authors argued that assassination must have been seen as a legitimate weapon in the South's struggle for national survival. Although they found no documentary "smoking gun" that would firmly implicate Confederate officials in Booth's plan, the circumstantial evidence they presented was enough to reenergize the conspiracy debate and give it a measure of scholarly respectability, which the Eisenschiml "Stanton did it" thesis never achieved. Many historians remain unconvinced that Booth had the formal support of anyone in the Confederate government, but the idea that Booth thought that he was acting in the interests of the Confederacy is now widely accepted.

Was Booth convicted of conspiring with anyone?

No, before he could be captured and tried, he was killed by a soldier named Boston Corbett.

Booth remained on the lam for almost two weeks, hiding out with Confederate sympathizers in southern Maryland and northern Virginia, fuming over the public's misinterpretation of what he thought he had done and dreaming of somehow escaping to Mexico. It was not to be. On the night of April 25, 1865, a cavalry patrol cornered Booth and Davey Herold in a tobacco barn on the property of Richard Garrett. Herold gave himself up, but Booth refused to surrender without a fight. The soldiers set the barn on fire to smoke him out. As Booth moved toward the door, either to surrender or to fight, Sergeant Corbett shot him in the neck. He was pulled out of the building, partially paralyzed and died a few hours later, in the morning of April 26. His last words, as he looked at his motionless hands draped on his chest, were "Useless, useless."

Where is he buried?

In Baltimore's Green Mount Cemetery . . .

. . . in an unmarked spot within the Booth family plot.

Are you sure?

Yes.

The idea that Booth escaped his pursuers and wandered the land anonymously for years has entered folklore, inspired in part by David George, who claimed to be Booth until his death in Enid, Oklahoma, in 1903, and by a book written about him in 1907, called *The Escape and Suicide of John Wilkes Booth.* George's mummified remains (advertised as Booth's) were taken around the country as a sideshow attraction for the next several decades.[22]

As if anticipating such fantasies, in May 1865, federal officials were extremely careful about identifying Booth's body. Besides the broken left leg and a distinctive scar on his neck, he had his initials tattooed on the back of his left hand, all of which served to identify positively the body that was brought back from the Garrett farm. In 1995, a state judge turned down a request to dig up the remains in Green Mount Cemetery and check once more, and in 1996, the decision was upheld on appeal. Sometimes the judges get it right.

What happened to the rest of the conspirators?

Eight were tried by a military commission, and all were found guilty.

Dr. Mudd and two of Booth's cronies, Samuel Arnold and Michael O'Laughlen, were given life in prison for conspiring with Booth. Ned Spangler was acquitted of conspiracy but convicted of aiding Booth's escape and got six years. O'Laughlen died in prison; the other three were pardoned in 1869.

Davey Herold, Lewis Powell (alias Paine), George Atzerodt, and Mary Surratt were sentenced to death. Herold had accompanied Booth to the end, Powell had nearly killed William Seward, and Atzerodt was supposed to have killed the vice president—their sentences were uncontroversial. But Mrs. Surratt, it seemed, had done nothing but run the boardinghouse where some of the conspirators stayed. Judge Advocate General Joseph Holt, who chaired the commission, was convinced of her guilt, but five of the nine commissioners signed a petition asking President Andrew Johnson for clemency. Many people urged the government not to execute her, either because they believed in her innocence or because it so dramatically violated conventional gender roles to hang a woman. The federal government had never executed a woman before; on July 7, 1865, she became the first.

What about her son? Wasn't he involved?

Yes, he was at least as guilty as some of those the commission convicted . . .

. . . having agreed to participate in Booth's kidnapping plot. He was not in Washington at the time of the assassination, however, and fled immediately after to Canada and then to England, Rome, and Egypt, where he was arrested in 1866. He was tried for murder in 1867, but the trial (conducted in a much less heated political atmosphere than the one that convicted his mother) ended in a hung jury, and he went free.

Did anyone else ever try to kill Lincoln?

Yes, on several occasions.

In August 1864, while riding from the White House to the Soldiers' Home late one evening, Lincoln was attacked by an unknown sniper. The sound of the gun scared his horse, which carried him bareheaded the rest of the way to his destination. The next morning, soldiers found the president's stovepipe hat at the scene of the incident—with a bullet hole through it.

In July 1863, while the battle of Gettysburg was raging, Mary Lincoln was nearly killed when the coachman's seat of her carriage came loose, spilling the driver to the ground and leaving her alone in a vehicle pulled by a team of stampeding horses. Jumping out of the moving carriage, rather than waiting for it to overturn or collide with a tree, she suffered a serious cut on her head that became infected. No proof could be found, but suspicion was high that the carriage had been sabotaged and that the intended victim had been her husband.

In February 1861, on his way from Springfield to Washington for his inauguration, Lincoln learned of a plan to assassinate him when he entered Baltimore, a city known for its secessionist sympathies. He took the advice of detective Allan Pinkerton and others to avoid the risk by changing his plans and traveling incognito through the city, wearing a cap instead of his well-known tall hat. For his pains, he was mocked by cartoonists who portrayed him as sneaking into Washington like a thief in the night, disguised in everything from a military cloak to full Scottish regalia, including a kilt. Lincoln would put up with all manner of political criticism, but he would never again let himself be mocked for personal cowardice. He would thereafter be a familiar, accessible figure in Washington, leaving the White House open to all, riding by himself to the Soldiers' Home, and walking alone at night to visit the telegraph office at the War Department. Friends and counselors would advise him to take better care of his personal security, but it was advice that Lincoln consistently resisted, from the day of his first inauguration to his last evening at Ford's Theatre.

FOR FURTHER READING

Until fairly recently, Lincoln assassination writing was dominated by a combination of loopy conspiracy books on one hand, and entertaining but poorly researched potboilers like *The Day Lincoln Was Shot* (1955), by Jim Bishop, on the other. William Hanchett, *The Lincoln Murder Conspiracies* (1983), was the first scholarly attempt to revisit both the assassination and the various conspiracy theories that grew out of it and remains the most sensible guide through the clutter of nonsense that surrounds the subject.

If you are only going to read one book about the assassination, Michael W. Kauffman, *American Brutus: John Wilkes Booth and the Lincoln Conspiracies* (2004), is the best combination of research and readability. George Bryan, *The Great American Myth* (1940), was for many years the best single volume, but much new evidence has emerged since it was written. Edward Steers, Jr., *Blood on the Moon: The Assassination of Abraham Lincoln* (2001), is another strong contender.

John Wilkes Booth explains what he was doing in his own words in John Rhodehamel and Louise Taper, eds., *"Right or Wrong, God Judge Me": The Writings of John Wilkes Booth* (1997). Timothy S. Good, ed., *We Saw Lincoln Shot: One Hundred Eyewitness Accounts* (1995), puts you in the theater. James L. Swanson, *Manhunt: The 12-Day Chase for Lincoln's Killer* (2007), is a cinematic retelling of Booth's flight. James L. Swanson and Daniel M. Weinberg, *Lincoln's Assassins: Their Trial and Execution* (2001), illustrates its subject with rare photographs and artifacts. Elizabeth Leonard, *Lincoln's Avengers: Justice, Revenge and Reunion after the Civil War* (2004), is a scholarly account of how some of the conspirators ended up on the gallows; it makes their trial comprehensible by locating it in the political context of the times. William Harris, *Lincoln's Last Months* (2004), is likewise useful for setting the political and military stage for the assassination.

For Lincoln's funerals, the spectacular reproductions of contemporary photographs in *Twenty Days*, by Dorothy Meserve Kunhardt and Philip B. Kunhardt, Jr. (1965), are worth many thousands of words. Thomas R. Turner, "*Beware the People Weeping*": *Public Opinion and the Assassination of Abraham Lincoln* (1982), analyzes public responses to the tragedy.

Debate over whether the Confederate government was behind the assassination continues. William A. Tidwell, James O. Hall, and David W. Gaddy, *Come Retribution: The Confederate Secret Service and the Assassination of Lincoln* (1988), sets out evidence implying that it was. Some historians, notably Edward Steers, Jr., agree; most do not.

{ CHAPTER TWELVE }

Legacy

What I have done since then is pretty well known.

—Lincoln, from a brief campaign autobiography, 1859[1]

Was Lincoln the greatest president?

Yes, but don't take my word for it.

Since 1948, when Arthur M. Schlesinger, Sr., first asked a group of American historians to rank the presidents, Lincoln has won every time, beating out George Washington or more recently FDR.[2] Even after historians began to splinter into increasingly marginal areas of specialization in the 1970s, they continued to agree on Lincoln. In a 1993 poll that asked professional historians to name three or four history books that they admired, a thousand respondents named hundreds of different titles, with no single book getting more than fifty votes, but when asked for the person in American history they most admired, Lincoln won handily.[3] Polls of the public, like the C-SPAN viewer survey, show that this esteem is not limited to academics.[4] Lincoln is, in the minds of most of those who think about such things, clearly America's greatest president.

Does anyone hate Lincoln?

Not many—but those who do, really do.

The champion Lincoln hater of all time was of course John Wilkes Booth. Booth's reasons for hating (and killing) Lincoln, which he explained in his diary, were doubtless shared by many in the Confederacy, and some in the North, but it was dangerous to express such thoughts in the vengeance-charged atmosphere that followed the assassination. Lincoln's apotheosis from political leader to secular saint made it almost impossible to express public criticism for many years after.

By 1900, national reconciliation had progressed far enough that some unreconstructed Confederates were emboldened to come out of the closet and admit that they still hated Abe. Charles Minor started the ball rolling with *The Real Lincoln*, published in Richmond in 1901. He was followed by Lyon Gardiner Tyler, president of William and Mary College (and fourteenth child of former U.S. president and Confederate Congressman John Tyler), who in 1929 gained national attention for a public feud with *Time* magazine that led him to write *John Tyler and Abraham Lincoln: Who Was the Dwarf? A Reply to a Challenge.*[5] Tyler's Lincoln was an unrefined boor who had set Sherman loose to destroy the glorious Old South, which Tyler imagined as a happy place where contented slaves had learned civilization and Christianity from their benevolent masters.

Tyler made a second career out of criticizing Lincoln in print, but in 1931 he was overtaken in the anti-Lincoln sweepstakes by Edgar Lee Masters, the Midwestern poet best known for his *Spoon River Anthology* (1915). Although Masters shared the same small-town Illinois background as Carl Sandburg, the Lincoln biographies that they produced could not have differed more. In the debunking era that followed World War I, when it turned out that most of the military and political leaders of that conflict had been liars, fools, or both, it became fashionable to assume that the same must be true of all the great figures of history. Masters applied this theory to his biography, *Lincoln the Man* (1931), which portrayed Lincoln as lazy yet tyrannical, ignorant yet cunning, and generally a bad guy in every possible way.

In the 1960s, Lincoln began to draw fire from the left as well as the right. The most vocal and persistent critic of Lincoln as an obstacle to black freedom was Lerone Bennett, whose 1968 *Ebony* magazine article "Was Abe Lincoln a White Supremacist?" revealed that Lincoln shared more of the almost universal racial prejudice of the nineteenth century than was acceptable in the middle of the twentieth. In 2000, Bennett summed up a lifetime of Lincoln criticism in *Forced Into Glory: Abraham Lincoln's White Dream*, a 600-page polemic that accused Lincoln of engaging in political rhetoric whenever he spoke of freedom and telling the truth whenever he downplayed emancipation as a war aim. Most historians had been doing exactly the opposite for 150 years, and Bennett's work was in some ways a useful corrective, but its impact was diminished by its shrill tone.

Making strange bedfellows with Lerone Bennett were a new batch of Lincoln haters who began to publish in the 1990s, led by economist Thomas DiLorenzo.[6] They blamed Lincoln for much of what they disliked in contemporary society, especially the size and power of the federal government. They tended to favor extreme libertarian positions and rarely allowed facts to get in the way of their arguments. In their rhetoric, they echoed arguments used by the original Confederates immediately after the war, who scrambled to disavow the proslavery stances they had taken before and during the fighting, instead recasting the war as a battle over the tariff and states' rights.[7]

What do you think would have happened if Lincoln had not been assassinated?

You probably would not be reading this book . . .

. . . nor would you be able to see Lincoln on Mount Rushmore, or in a grand Memorial at the foot of the Mall in Washington, D.C. Lincoln would surely have done a better job managing Reconstruction than his successor, but it's hard to imagine that he would have gained the same exalted place in our national memory had his life not been cut short so tragically. Contrary to what commentators occasionally write, Lincoln's political popularity was fairly high in 1865 (he had just been reelected and won a war, after all), but his prestige increased enormously with his assassination. Wrestling with Reconstruction, on the other hand, would have required him to spend a lot of the political capital he had amassed.

Would Lincoln have been able to prevent the Radical Republicans from inflicting Reconstruction on the South after the war?

This question embodies the most pernicious myth in American history.

It began with the ex-Confederates who promoted the idea that they had fought for a noble "Lost Cause." It gained professional respectability around 1900 when it appeared in the works of Columbia University professor William A. Dunning and the many students he trained. It grabbed the imagination of white Americans when it appeared on screen in the first blockbuster hit movie, D. W. Griffith's *Birth of a Nation* (1915), praised by President (and historian) Woodrow Wilson as history "written with lightning." It solidified its hold on national memory with the enormous popularity of Margaret Mitchell's novel *Gone With the Wind* (1936), as well as its 1939 film version.

The myth is that Reconstruction was a national tragedy in which vindictive Radical Republicans forced their evil will upon the innocent and helpless South, until finally brave white Southerners "redeemed" their states from the clutches of greedy carpetbaggers, craven scalawags, and their hapless dupes, the former slaves. Lincoln's successor, Andrew Johnson, bravely tried to follow Lincoln's generous and conciliatory policies, but alas, he was impeached for his efforts. If only Lincoln had lived!

In fact, Johnson's policies were nothing like Lincoln's. Lincoln had said of the leaders of the defunct Confederacy that "no one need expect that he would take any part in hanging or killing these men, even the worst of them," but it is inconceivable that he would have granted wholesale pardons to ex-Confederate military and civil officeholders, as Johnson did, allowing them to vote, run for office, and defeat Southern Republicans at the polls.[8] Johnson welcomed the reestablishment of the overwhelmingly Democratic antebellum power structure in the South. At the very least, Lincoln as a Republican would not have made the destruction of his own party in the South a policy goal.

So what would Lincoln have done?

That's a good question, and one that Lincoln himself probably could not have answered in 1865.

He was a pragmatist who made a point of not having fixed policies. During the war, Lincoln viewed the reconstruction of Southern states as a series of unique cases, just as he treated the border states individually at the start of the war.[9] In regard to the reconstruction of Louisiana, Lincoln in his last public speech (April 11, 1865) said of the proposed new state constitution, "It is also unsatisfactory to some that the elective franchise is not given to the colored man. I would myself prefer that it were now conferred on the very intelligent, and on those who serve our cause as soldiers."[10] It seems likely that he would have looked favorably on experiments in black suffrage had any of the reconstructed states been willing to undertake them, if not out of a desire to create a modern multicultural society (which few in the nineteenth century could even imagine), then as a means of strengthening the position of Southern Republicans.

In contrast Andrew Johnson firmly opposed black voting in any form and was overridden by Congress and the states, which ratified the Fourteenth (civil rights) Amendment in 1868 and the Fifteenth (voting rights) Amendment in 1870. It was enforcement of these laws, more than anything else, that constituted the "oppression" of which the white South complained so bitterly in the Reconstruction myth. Had the author of the Emancipation Proclamation lived, it seems likely that he, too, would have "oppressed" the white South by insisting that black Southerners be allowed to participate in the political system.

You think he would have supported black voting? Didn't he once say he was opposed to political rights for blacks?

True, he said that in 1858, in the debates with Stephen Douglas.

The standard pro-Lincoln response to this uncomfortable fact is to claim that his opinions changed over time. The anti-Lincoln answer is to point out that they never went far enough. Instead of these generalizations, consider what Lincoln actually said about political rights. As far back as the Lyceum speech of 1838, he held that it took three things to be a good citizen of a republic: "*general intelligence,* [*sound*] *morality* and, in particular, *a reverence for the constitution and laws.*"[11] In 1858, he had cast doubt on whether black people possessed the "moral or intellectual endowment" of white people.

But a lot had happened since 1858. The 180,000 black men who fought for the Union certainly showed more "reverence for the constitution" than the rebels who tried to overthrow it. The moral fiber of African Americans had been demonstrated for all to see at Fort Wagner, Port Hudson, the Crater, Olustee, and other battlefields. And although no individual could represent an entire race, Lincoln's encounters with the brilliance of Frederick Douglass made it clear to him that "intellectual endowment" was hardly limited to white people. Thus in his last public address, he endorsed suffrage for exactly those African Americans ("the very intelligent, and . . . those who serve our cause as soldiers") who met the qualifications of intelligence, morality, and reverence for the laws that he had long ago specified as necessary for every citizen of a free republic.[12]

Lincoln had first dipped his toe in the pool of full legal and political equality a year earlier, in a letter to the Union governor of Louisiana, who was about to call a convention that would create a new state government. With uncharacteristic timidity, Lincoln wrote: "I barely suggest for your private consideration, whether some of the colored people may not be let in—as, for instance, the very intelligent, and especially those who have fought gallantly in our ranks . . . But this is only a suggestion, not to the public, but to you alone."[13] His last speech showed that he was ready to take the suggestion public. We don't know how much further he would have gone, but he had already gone further than Andrew Johnson, or the Reconstruction mythmakers, would ever have done.

Are there any direct descendants of Abraham Lincoln alive today?

No; the last was his great-grandson Robert Lincoln "Bud" Beckwith, who died in 1985.

Isn't there another descendant, but they paid him to keep it quiet?

Yes, there's someone who's been paid to keep quiet, but he is probably not a missing Linc.

In 1967, when he was sixty-three years old, Robert Lincoln Beckwith married a twenty-seven-year-old college student from Germany named Annemarie Hoffman. Eleven months later she gave birth to a son, Timothy Lincoln Beckwith, but Beckwith (who had undergone a vasectomy some years earlier) denied that the boy was his. Annemarie fled to Europe with her son, and Beckwith divorced her. The question of little Timmy's paternity remained of more than genealogical interest, because a direct descendant of Abraham Lincoln stood to inherit a ten-million-dollar trust fund set up by Robert Todd Lincoln's wife, Mary. If the Lincoln line died out, the fortune would revert to the Red Cross, the First Church of Christ (Scientist), and Iowa Wesleyan University. There was plenty of circumstantial evidence that Timothy Beckwith was not a Lincoln, including his mother's refusal to submit to blood tests and Bud Beckwith's vasectomy, but the institutions waiting for their shares of the Lincoln fortune did not want to take a chance in court. They settled with Timothy Beckwith, paying him a rumored one million dollars to renounce his claim to the Lincoln legacy. He did, and so legally (and probably in fact as well) there are no more Lincolns.[14]

"Other than that, how was the play, Mrs. Lincoln?"

Not nearly as funny as that one-liner.

The play that the Lincolns were attending when the president was assassinated, *Our American Cousin,* is a typical specimen of nineteenth-century comedy, meaning that almost nothing in it seems the least bit funny today. Conversely, the line above still works, based on the fact that even in an age when pundits fret about declining cultural literacy, most Americans still immediately understand the reference.

The same recognition is the basis for a story about the current president, whoever he or she may be when you read this. I've heard it told about every president in my lifetime. It goes like this: The chief executive is so burdened by the cares of office that one night, he slips away from his Secret Service detail and goes for a walk, until he finds himself in front of the Washington Monument. He looks up and says, "George, you were the first president of these great United States! How can I make this country a better place for all?" and a voice replies, "Always tell the truth!" So he tries this, and it works for a while, but the novelty soon wears off and the poll numbers start going down again. So he goes for another walk, this time to the Jefferson Memorial. "Thomas," he says, "you gave us the ideals that define who we are as Americans. What can I do to bring our nation together?" The voice of Jefferson replies, "Always listen to the people." This seems to work for a few weeks, but then the media get tired of it, and his numbers dip again. So he goes on still another walk, to the Lincoln Memorial, and asks, "Abraham? You believed in charity for all, and malice toward none, to build a better future. What can I do to build a better future for the country?" And the voice of Lincoln replied, "Go to the theater . . ."

What was it that Stanton said at the moment Lincoln died?

"Now he belongs to the ages" . . .

. . . is the usual version, but like so much else in the Lincoln story, there's an alternative. Corporal James Tanner, who was present, thought he heard Stanton say, "He belongs to the angels now." If we disregard word order, borrowing the "bag of words" concept from Internet search engines and language theorists, the only difference between the two quotes is "ages" or "angels." Given that Tanner heard it one way, while

John Hay and others heard it another, there's no clear basis on which to decide. Since Stanton himself never corrected the "ages" version, which was eventually inscribed on Lincoln's tomb, we can conclude that whatever he may have said at the moment, he was satisfied to let "Now he belongs to the ages" stand as his epitaph for Lincoln.[15]

Where was Lincoln's funeral?

He had at least twelve, in cities all across the country.

The first was in the White House on April 19, 1865. After his body lay in state in the Capitol, the Lincoln funeral train traveled from Washington, D.C., to Springfield, Illinois, stopping for ceremonies in Baltimore, Harrisburg, Philadelphia, New York City, Albany, Buffalo, Cleveland, Columbus, Indianapolis, Chicago, and Springfield, from April 21 to May 3, 1865. Massive processions took place in the cities where the coffin was unloaded and set up for public viewing. Secretary of War Stanton had to issue a special order to authorities in New York overruling their plan for a "whites only" funeral parade and requiring them to permit African American organizations to participate. Hundreds of thousands viewed the body at these funerals, while hundreds of thousands more lined the tracks just to watch the train pass through their towns.

Where is he buried?

The Lincoln Tomb is in Oak Ridge Cemetery, in Springfield, Illinois.

The body of Willie Lincoln was exhumed and brought back to Springfield on his father's funeral train. Eventually Mrs. Lincoln and Tad were also buried there.

Was Lincoln's corpse ever stolen?

Once, almost.

While the Lincoln Tomb was under construction, his body lay in a temporary vault in Oak Ridge Cemetery. His remains were placed in the tomb after its completion in 1871. Five years later, a gang of criminals hatched a scheme to steal Lincoln's body and hold it for ransom. The police were tipped off and managed to thwart the plot, arresting the would-be thieves after they had removed the casket from the sarcophagus, but before they could open it. To prevent further body snatchings, in 1901 the casket was reburied inside the monument, under several feet of concrete.[16]

Is there a secret message in the hands of the Lincoln Memorial statue?

Yes . . .

. . . Lincoln's hands appear to be forming the signs for the letters *A* and *L* in American Sign Language. Whether that was the artist's intent, however, is not clear.

There is no doubt that sculptor Daniel Chester French (1850–1931) knew about sign language. In 1881, he was commissioned by the National Deaf Mute College (today Gallaudet University) to execute a bust of the late President Garfield. Eight years later, he created a campus memorial to Thomas Hopkins Gallaudet (1787–1851) in which Gallaudet, one of the early proponents of sign language in the United States, is teaching the sign for the letter *A* to his first pupil, Alice Cogswell (1805–30). When French sculpted Lincoln, he modeled the hands from casts of Lincoln's clenched hands made by Leonard Volk in 1860 and casts of his own hands, but he chose to open Lincoln's right hand and separate the first finger from the other three, giving at least the impression of Lincoln's initials in ASL. Was this his way of paying tribute to Lincoln for signing the 1864 legislation that authorized the future Gallaudet University to grant college degrees? French never admitted doing so, and his daughter later wrote that the position of the hands was simply a coincidence. Perhaps it was.[17]

What's the biggest memorial to Lincoln?

It's not the one in Washington . . .

. . . although the seated figure would be about twenty-eight feet tall if he stood up. It's not the one on Mount Rushmore either, which would be close to five hundred feet tall if the entire body were sculpted to the scale of the head. It's the Lincoln Highway, which runs more than 3,300 miles from New York to San Francisco.

In 1913, the same year that Congress authorized construction of the Lincoln Memorial, a group of automobile industry leaders formed the Lincoln Highway Association to sponsor an alternative memorial, in the form of a coast-to-coast highway that would honor the sixteenth president and, incidentally, promote automobile travel.[18] The LHA did not actually build the highway, which was (and still is) a conceptual memorial consisting of existing roads designated "Lincoln Highway" by signs, street names, and map labels. In 1926, a national highway numbering system was introduced, and most of the Lincoln Highway became U.S. 30. In 1928, Boy Scouts installed three thousand small concrete markers along the length of the old Lincoln Highway, dedicating it to Abraham Lincoln. The construction of I-80 made the Lincoln Highway/U.S. 30 obsolete as a long-distance route, but in 1992, a new Lincoln Highway Association was formed to preserve the memories and remnants of the original road.

Who is the best Lincoln impersonator?

Considering that the Association of Lincoln Presenters usually has more than a hundred active members . . .

. . . that's not an easy question. It changes over time, too. One of the premier Lincolns of the mid-twentieth century gained weight as he grew older and discovered that no one wanted to hire a fat Lincoln. The ALP includes all kinds of Lincolns, from tall guys with fake beards who just shake hands at supermarket openings, to thoughtful students of Lincoln like Richard (Fritz) Klein of Springfield who strive to educate the public whenever they put on the stovepipe hat.

What is the Abraham Lincoln Association? Can I join?

It commemorates Lincoln, and anyone can join it.

This wasn't always the case. It was formed as the Lincoln Centennial Association in 1908, in Springfield, Illinois. Springfield that year was also the scene of a violent antiblack riot (which led to the organization of the National Association for the Advancement of Colored People), and the first banquet of the Lincoln Centennial Association in 1909 was an all-white, all-male affair (although ladies could observe from the gallery). In its early years, a highlight of the annual meeting was the moment when those who had known Lincoln personally were asked to stand.

Gradually the association evolved from a purely self-congratulatory body. In 1929, it changed its name to the Abraham Lincoln Association. Under the leadership of Paul Angle, Benjamin Thomas, and Harry Pratt, the association became an active force in Lincoln preservation, research, and publication. It produced the valuable reference work *Lincoln Day-by-Day,* and then in 1953, committed all of its remaining resources to the publication of the *Collected Works of Abraham Lincoln,* edited by Roy P. Basler. The ALA was inactive for years after but recovered by the 1970s. In 1979, the ALA began publishing a scholarly journal that remains the most important in the field of Lincoln studies. It cosponsored the Lincoln Legal Papers project, which uncovered thousands of new Lincoln documents, and it began holding an annual academic symposium on Lincoln's birthday, along with its ceremonial evening banquet.

The ALA's long progress from a local social club to a national scholarly institution was interrupted in 1995 by an internal coup in which its president, Frank Williams (future chief justice of the Rhode Island Supreme Court), was unexpectedly voted out of office by members based in or near Springfield. Subsequent presidents have all been local members, but despite the apparent trend toward parochialism, the ALA continues to thrive.[19]

Are there any Lincoln groups not based in Springfield?

Yes, lots of them.

There's the Lincoln Forum, whose annual meeting in Gettysburg is occasionally broadcast by C-SPAN. The Abraham Lincoln Institute has put on free symposiums in the mid-Atlantic states each year since 1997. There are local organizations like the Lincoln Groups of New York (established in 1978), the District of Columbia (1935), and Boston (1938), the Lincoln Fellowships of Pennsylvania and Wisconsin, the Lincoln Association of Indiana, and the Lincoln Memorial Association in Redlands, California. There's the annual Lincoln Symposium, which rotates through Springfield, Chicago, Fort Wayne, Galesburg, and other sites. In the Deep South there's the Louisiana Lincoln Group in Shreveport. There are even Lincoln Groups in Taiwan and Japan.

All of these organizations feature meetings where members gather to hear about the latest Lincoln scholarship from professors, researchers, and authors. In this regard, the Lincoln era is unusual. Instead of reporting their findings primarily to other historians at dull professional meetings, Lincoln scholars have the opportunity of presenting their research to large, well-informed audiences of interested lay people all over the country, and their readers get to meet them and question them face-to-face. It's the way history ought to work.

What would Lincoln think of all the writers, professors, impersonators, museum guides, souvenir vendors, bicentennial administrators, and others, who make their living from his memory?

He might say the same thing that he said about the Democrats of the 1840s . . .

. . . when he accused them of living off the reputation of the late, great Andrew Jackson. In an 1848 campaign speech, he called them "a horde of hungry ticks . . . stuck to the tail of the Hermitage lion to the end of his life . . . and drawing a loathsome sustenance from it, after he is dead."[20] But I hope he would be kinder to us.

Is it true that Lincoln and Charles Darwin were born on the same day? If so, what does this mean?

Yes, and nothing.

If you assemble a random group of sixty-nine people, the odds are virtually certain (in excess of 99.9 percent) that two of them will share the same birthday. With only twenty-three people, the odds are fifty-fifty that two will share a birthday. If Charles Darwin hadn't been born on Lincoln's birthday, some other famous person would have been.

What's the best book about Lincoln?

Assuming you mean other than this one . . .

. . . there are more than ten thousand titles from which to choose. Many of the outstanding books that deal with a single facet of Lincoln's extraordinary life and times have been listed at the end of each chapter. If you were to read only one book about Lincoln, covering his entire life, the top contenders would have to include these one-volume biographies:

Abraham Lincoln, by Benjamin Thomas (1952). Wonderfully written, but showing its age, as the world of Lincoln research marches on.

The Real Abraham Lincoln, by Reinhard Luthin (1960). The least-known book in this list, more detailed than Thomas and more original than Oates.

With Malice Toward None, by Stephen Oates (1977). Oates portrays Lincoln sympathetically as a twentieth-century liberal. Historian Michael Burlingame, among others, has portrayed Oates as a plagiarist, based on passages in this book that closely resemble those in Benjamin Thomas's book. Read them both and see what you think.

The Abraham Lincoln Encyclopedia, by Mark E. Neely, Jr. (1982). The book you are holding tries to answer questions that people interested in Lincoln tend to ask. Neely's book tries to answer every question about Lincoln, whether anyone is likely ever to ask it or not. A reference work rather than a biography, it remains the most indispensable (least dispensable?) book ever written about Abraham Lincoln.

Lincoln, by David Herbert Donald (1995). More up-to-date than Thomas, more stylish than Luthin, and deeper analytically than Oates, when it was published Donald's book looked like the front-runner out of the gate in the race for best one-volume Lincoln biography. Instead, many readers took issue with Donald's characterization of Lincoln as "passive" and fatalistic. Still, it won a well-deserved Lincoln Prize, and nothing has come along since to top it.

Herndon's Lincoln, by William H. Herndon and Jesse W. Weik (1889), edited by Wilson and Davis (2006). Unlike the other biographies named here, this was written by someone who knew Lincoln well, his longtime law partner Billy Herndon. After Lincoln's death, Herndon wanted to write a "warts and all" biography in reaction to the syrupy hagiography that he saw appearing in the decades after 1865, but he somehow never managed to put the fruits of his prodigious research into book form. The actual writing was done by his collaborator, Jesse Weik, who wrote in the first person as though he were Herndon. Herndon/Weik's no-holds-barred approach alienated contemporary readers, and a subsequent edition removed some material that was too racy for the 1890s. The 2006 edition restores the original material and includes copious reference notes that reveal the sources of Herndon/Weik's stories.

What about the worst Lincoln book?

There have been plenty of bad ones, so let's narrow the field.

We'll exclude the political diatribes that abuse history to promote the ideologies of their authors, like the works of DiLorenzo or Bennett. We can leave out the books of myths written to praise Lincoln (*The Perfect Trib-*

ute) or expose him (C. A. Tripp on Lincoln's sexuality). To narrow the field still further, let's only consider books by people who know how to write; if someone without talent writes a bad book, it's not as though he or she had any choice. This leaves us with two outstanding candidates.

The runner-up is Gore Vidal's *Lincoln: A Novel* (1984), which may be the most widely read Lincoln book of all.[21] It combines the most lurid speculations of Herndon and the reminiscences of many other contemporaries with the author's brilliant and cynical historical imagination to create an image of Lincoln that indelibly fuses historically verifiable fact with artistically invented dialogue and incident. No book has done more to make people aware of the real Lincoln and at the same time to confuse him with an imaginary one, in a work where the threads of history and fiction are inextricably tangled.

Gore Vidal, however, at least did his homework. The same cannot be said for the winner of the Worst Lincoln Book by a Serious Writer, which goes to Jan Morris for *Lincoln: A Foreigner's Quest* (2000). Morris is a gifted writer, as she proved when (under the identity of James Morris) she wrote the brilliant *Pax Britannica* trilogy, a travelogue through space and time that captured the emotional contours of the rise and fall of the British Empire.[22] When she came to America to visit Springfield and offer a new perspective on Lincoln and his times, history readers seemed to be in for a treat. Instead, they got a self-indulgent account of the author's travels through the Midwest, laced with contempt for American culture and unleavened by the slightest familiarity with recent Lincoln scholarship.

The book is filled with factual errors of all kinds. You would think a travel writer could tell the Sierra Nevada (where many of the Donner party perished in 1847) from the Rocky Mountains (where they didn't, contrary to p. 63), or find the Lincoln Home in Springfield, which is not on Seventh and Jackson (contrary to p. 98). Lincoln is liberally misquoted in the book, even though his writings can be found at any library in the country. The author even gets the legends wrong, referring to Lincoln writing his Farewell to Springfield on the back of an envelope. She casually concludes (without citation, as no notes or bibliography are to be found) that Lincoln "had bisexual instincts—and why not?" (p. 45) and credits him with "borrow[ing] the works of Clausewitz from the Congressional Library," which he must have stared at blankly since Clausewitz's masterpiece *Vom Kriege* was not translated into English until

1873.[23] More serious than individually trivial mistakes like these, Morris misunderstands Lincoln's views on slavery throughout and accepts without question the obsolete Dunning School interpretation of Reconstruction (pp. 191–92). By the end of her travels she admits that there might be something to this Lincoln guy after all, but by that time the informed reader is long past caring about her opinion on the subject. No book about Lincoln ever disappointed me more.[24]

Are there any good children's books about Lincoln?

Surprisingly few.

There are some fine books that deal with specific aspects of Lincoln for younger children, like *Mr. Lincoln's Whiskers* (1996), by Karen Winnick, or *Abe Lincoln's Hat* (1994), by Martha Brenner. Russell Freedman, *Lincoln: A Photobiography* (1987), which deserves its Newbery Award, is aimed at the nine-to-twelve set. Beyond these, there are too many books that either fail to make the complex story of war and emancipation comprehensible for a young audience or that sugarcoat it beyond recognition. It's not an easy subject.

Is it true that there are more books about Lincoln than any other historical figure?

Not quite.

In 2002, a search for books about famous people in an online worldwide library catalog found 14,985 entries for Abraham Lincoln. Not bad, but he came in fourth, behind Jesus Christ (80,834), Shakespeare (35,904), and the Virgin Mary (20,948), but well ahead of Buddha, Lenin, and Joan of Arc.[25]

What's the best place to get Lincoln books?

That's easy: the Abraham Lincoln Book Shop in Chicago.

It was founded in 1938 by Ralph Newman, and people like Carl Sandburg and Bruce Catton used to hang out there. The original Civil War Round Table got its start there (there are hundreds of them now around the world), and through its catalogs and Internet presence the ALBS continues to serve as a sort of national salon for Lincoln and Civil War authors and readers. Don't miss it.

All right, enough reading. What about movies and TV? What's the best and worst?

Best Lincoln movie: *Young Mr. Lincoln* (1939), starring Henry Fonda, and *Abe Lincoln in Illinois* (1940), with Raymond Massey, are both classics.

Worst Lincoln Movie: Two made-for-TV movies compete for the prize, and once again Gore Vidal comes in second.

Lincoln (1988), based on his novel, starts with the questionable historicity of its script and the even more questionable casting of Mary Tyler Moore as Mary Todd Lincoln. An excellent performance by Sam Waterston as Lincoln is not enough to redeem it, but it guarantees that it's not as bad as *The Lincoln Conspiracy* (1977), which has Stanton involved in the assassination plot, the wrong man killed at the Garrett farm, and Booth escaping to roam the earth.

Best Lincoln on TV: The best performance is definitely Sam Waterston's (see above), but the best use of Lincoln as a character has to be his appearance in "The Savage Curtain," episode 77 of *Star Trek* (1969).

He arrives floating in outer space and ends up participating in a celebrity death match on a team with Captain Kirk, Mr. Spock, and a Vulcan hero against Genghis Khan and three other bad guys, for the benefit of some alien rock people who want to know whether good is stronger than evil. It is, but Abe gets killed (again). Three out of four stars.

Worst Lincoln on TV: In 1998, a sitcom called *The Secret Diary of Desmond Pfeiffer* aired a few incredibly unpopular episodes.

The premise was that a black British nobleman somehow ended up as Lincoln's butler, creating all kinds of opportunities for comedy against a backdrop of slavery and civil war. If *Hogan's Heroes* could try (albeit unsuccessfully) to make something funny out of life in a Nazi stalag, why not this? Apparently the writers had Mary Lincoln lusting after the butler, Lincoln lusting after young Union soldiers with their washboard abs, and General Grant lusting after anything he could drink. How could it miss? It was canceled so quickly that I have to admit I never saw an episode, yet I still feel confident awarding it the prize for the worst Lincoln ever on TV.

Did scientists raise Lincoln from the dead?

If you believe "America's only reliable newspaper," then yes.

The headline of the *Weekly World News* for October 5, 1993, was: "He's kept alive for 95 seconds! Abraham Lincoln's Corpse Revived." The miracle drug Revivitol, which apparently has not since been approved by the FDA, was used to restore Lincoln's consciousness long enough for him to ask, "Gentlemen, where am I?"

As remarkable as Lincoln's brief resurrection might seem to be, what's more impressive is Lincoln's longevity as a pop culture icon (like Elvis or JFK) who can be instantly identified by readers in a supermarket checkout line glancing at the tabloids.

Speaking of JFK, what about the amazing coincidences between the Lincoln and Kennedy assassinations? What do you make of them?

Not much . . .

. . . because I am too busy trying to find a publisher for my Garfield/McKinley Amazing Coincidences Presidential Assassinations exposé. Garfield has eight letters! McKinley has eight letters! Both were Republicans who favored a high tariff! Both died in September! Both were shot from in front, in the abdomen, with a handgun! Both could have been saved with better medical care! Both were shot in years that started and ended with 1 (Garfield 1881, McKinley 1901)! Now if that is not an amazing set of coincidences that proves beyond reasonable doubt the involvement of the Mafia, the CIA, and the Illuminati in both assassinations, I don't know what is.

The Lincoln/Kennedy coincidence lists have been around ever since 1963. Here's a typical sample:

Abraham Lincoln was elected to Congress in 1846, John F. Kennedy was elected to Congress in 1946.

Abraham Lincoln was elected president in 1860, John F. Kennedy was elected president in 1960.

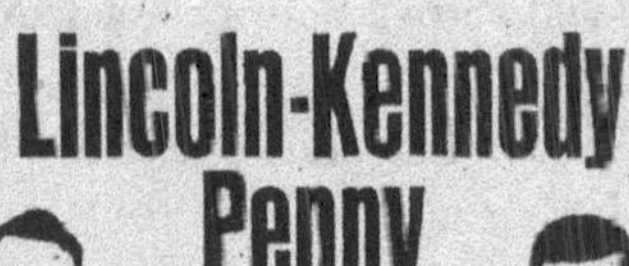

JOHN F
KENNEDY
1917-1963

This uncirculated Lincoln Head penny is stamped with a profile reproduction of John F. Kennedy looking-at-Lincoln. This unusual commemorative piece is truly a collector's item.

ASTONISHING COINCIDENCES

Lincoln was elected in 1860
Kennedy was elected in 1960
There are seven letters in each name
Both Presidents were slain on Friday
Both were slain in presence of their wives
Both were directly concerned with Civil Rights
Both Presidents had legality of elections contested
Kennedy's secretary Lincoln warned him not to go to Dallas
Lincoln's secretary Kennedy warned him not to go to the theater
Both of their successors were named Johnson
Andrew Johnson, Lyndon Johnson
Each name contains 13 letters
Both served in the U.S. Senate
Both were southern Democrats
Lyndon Johnson born 1908
Andrew Johnson born 1808
Booth and Oswald were both southerners favoring unpopular ideas
Oswald shot Kennedy from a warehouse and hid in a theater
Booth shot Lincoln in a theater and hid in a warehouse
Booth and Oswald were murdered before trial could be arranged
Lincoln and Kennedy were carried in death on the same caisson
Booth and Oswald were born one hundred years apart
Lee Harvey Oswald, John Wilkes Booth – each name has 15 letters

Distributed As A Public Service by

THE BURLINGTON STATE BANK

"Sound As A Bell"

Burlington, Indiana

MEMBER FDIC

There are seven letters in each name, but eight in the word "gullible." Coincidence? (Courtesy of The Lincoln Museum, Fort Wayne, IN, TLM 4634)

Given that the assassinations took place ninety-eight years apart and that elections are held in even-numbered years, these facts aren't particularly surprising.

The names Lincoln and Kennedy each contain seven letters. Out of the first forty-two people to occupy the presidency, eight had names with seven letters, eight more had six-letter names, and nine had eight-letter names. The odds of any two randomly chosen presidents having names with the same number of letters is about 16 percent, which falls a little bit short of "amazing."

Both were particularly concerned with civil rights. Lincoln was concerned with slavery, not civil rights. Kennedy's concern for civil rights was growing, but it was not a focus of his administration.

Both wives lost their children while living in the White House. True, although Willie Lincoln was eleven and Patrick Bouvier Kennedy lived only two days.

Both presidents were shot on a Friday. The odds of any two events happening on the same day of the week are 14.3 percent.

Both were shot in the head. OK.

Lincoln's secretary, Kennedy, warned him not to go to the theatre. Lincoln did not have such a secretary. Nicolay, Hay, Stoddard, Neill—yes. Kennedy—no. The nearest Kennedy involved was John A. Kennedy, superintendent of the New York City police. Stanton asked him to send some detectives to Washington, after the assassination.[26]

Kennedy's secretary, Lincoln, warned him not to go to Dallas. Evelyn Lincoln was JFK's personal secretary. She went to Dallas with him. There is no record of her warning her boss about the trip.

Both were assassinated by Southerners. If the assassin could be either a Southerner or Northerner, then the odds of both assassins coming from the same region are 50 percent, exactly the same as the odds of them coming from different regions.

Both were succeeded by Southerners. Ditto.

Both successors were named Johnson. OK, that's a coincidence.

Andrew Johnson, who succeeded Lincoln, was born in 1808.

Lyndon Johnson, who succeeded Kennedy, was born in 1908.

John Wilkes Booth was born in 1839. No, he was born in 1838. Sorry.

Lee Harvey Oswald was born in 1939.

Both assassins were known by their three names. Charles Guiteau and Leon Czolgosz were known by their two names, *and* they're both foreign-sounding! Point for Garfield/McKinley; publishers, take note.

Both names are composed of fifteen letters. Stop it with the numbers, already.

Booth ran from the theater and was caught in a warehouse. Booth was actually caught in a tobacco barn, not a warehouse.

Oswald ran from a warehouse and was caught in a theater.

Booth and Oswald were assassinated before their trials. Booth's shooting was not an assassination. He was armed, not yet in custody, and according to Sergeant Boston Corbett, he appeared ready to shoot. Had Officer J. D. Tippit been able to return fire when Oswald shot him, that would not have been an "assassination" either.

The silliness of the whole exercise is highlighted by the addition of a new "coincidence" to the list, following revelation of details of President Kennedy's private life. Part of it reads:

Days before his assassination, President Lincoln was in Monroe, Maryland.

There isn't any such place. Monroe Run, Maryland, is in the far western part of the state, but Lincoln was in Virginia with the Army of the Potomac and then back in Washington the week before the assassination. As for the counterpart statement, Marilyn Monroe died in 1962.[27]

Are you concerned that by simply repeating stories such as this you will end up perpetuating them?

No. These stories have lives of their own, far above my poor power to add or detract.

Let's say that Lincoln really could be revived. What would he have to say about legalized abortion?

Probably the same thing he would say . . .

. . . if you asked him about using cell phones while driving, or stem cell research, or whether NASCAR is better than open-wheel racing: "Huh?" (although he would express it more elegantly). The technological, social, and political conditions that underlie these issues are so different from those of Lincoln's time that there is no way to know for certain what he would have said about them. We can extrapolate from Lincoln's known views to guess about how he would feel today, but such speculations invariably reveal more about the speculator's political views than Lincoln's, since they always end with Lincoln agreeing with the writer.[28]

One might draw an analogy from the often repeated anecdote that Lincoln, when assured that God was on his side, responded that he thought it more important that he be on God's side.[29] Those who insist that Lincoln would agree with them on various contemporary political issues might likewise do well to check whether they are on Lincoln's side, instead of always proclaiming that he would be on theirs.

What museum has most of Lincoln's things?

None; they are scattered around.

His papers (most of which have been published and are available online) are at the Library of Congress, which also has the contents of his pockets from the night he was shot.[30] The bullet that killed him, along with some bone fragments, is at the National Museum of Health and Medicine in Washington, D.C. Ford's Theatre has the suit he wore that night. The chair in which he was sitting is at the Henry Ford Museum in Dearborn, Michigan, while the cane he carried is at the Abraham Lincoln Museum in Harrogate, Tennessee, on the campus of Lincoln Memorial University. There are remarkable Lincoln objects at museums throughout the country, from the Chicago History Museum, which has the bed in which he died, to the Smithsonian's National Museum of American History (stovepipe hat, size 7⅛). The largest Lincoln museum of all, The Abraham Lincoln Presidential Library and Museum in Springfield, Illinois, is rich in reproductions and re-creations, but when it opened in 2005, critics noted that its exhibit was surprisingly light on actual artifacts.*

I have an artifact of the assassination. It's a copy of the **New York Herald** ***from April 15, 1865. My grandfather passed it on to me, so I know it's old. How much is it worth now?***

It depends on whether it's really an original.

Is the paper yellowing and brittle, or is it still supple and the color of newsprint?

Oh, it's very old-looking and yellowish, and it falls apart if you touch it. So what's it worth?

Unfortunately, nothing.

The original 1865 editions were printed on rag paper and have retained much of their original appearance and flexibility. Paper made from wood pulp replaced rag paper in the second half of the nineteenth century and was used in the 1890s to print souvenir reproductions of the April 15,

*In 2007, the museum acquired the fabulous Lincoln collection of Louise Taper, which included one of three surviving stovepipe hats.

1865 *New York Herald.* Thousands of these cheap copies were saved by patriotic Americans and given to their descendants, who now vainly hope to sell them. If you have an old-looking newspaper front page, it's almost certainly one of those. The same applies to the Gettysburg Address; there are lots of hundred-year-old souvenir copies still hidden in attics across America, waiting to give their owners the delusion of instant wealth.

If you do happen to have an original *Herald*, its value would depend on its condition; contact an appraiser. And if your attic copy of the Gettysburg Address should turn out to be the legendary, long-missing Wills copy, in Lincoln's own hand, then you're set for life.

What if I have an ordinary letter signed by Lincoln? What's that worth?

The volatility of the historical collectibles market . . .

. . . and inflation in general would make any printed answer obsolete before you could read it. To take one example, Lincoln is known to have signed thirteen printed copies of the Thirteenth Amendment. In 1952, one of them was sold at auction for $4,400; in 1979, another sold for $38,500; in 2002, $721,000; and in 2006, $1,868,750.[31] Prices for Lincoln documents increased precipitously starting in the 1980s, when multimillionaire Malcolm Forbes began to collect them. The Forbes collection was sold in 2002, but Lincoln prices have continued to rise. Within the ever-changing market, the value of any Lincoln document will depend on its historical importance, its length, and its authenticity.

How can you tell if a Lincoln document is authentic?

Good question . . .

. . . because crooks have frequently tried to forge them. Some criminals, like Joseph Cosey, developed reputations for their ability to imitate Lincoln's handwriting almost perfectly.[32] The most famous Lincoln-related forgery case involved a series of letters supposedly written by Lincoln and Ann Rutledge that documented their secret love. They were printed in the *Atlantic Monthly* in 1928–29 and fooled Lincoln biographers Carl Sandburg and Ida Tarbell. It turned out that the letters, which belonged to Wilma Frances Minor, were actually written by her mother while channeling the spirits of Abe and Ann.[33]

Which Lincoln museum is the best?

It depends on what you want.

By far the biggest and most impressive is the Abraham Lincoln Presidential Museum in Springfield, but some historians (notably John Y. Simon, who referred to the museum as "Six Flags Over Lincoln") have criticized its Disneyesque use of technology and reproductions at the expense of the presentation of authentic artifacts.[34] Whatever we elitist academics may think of it, visitors to Springfield should definitely see the museum, but they should also take the time to see the real Lincoln sites nearby, especially the Lincoln Home.

Lincoln's New Salem, the Lincoln Boyhood site in Indiana, and the birthplace in Kentucky all feature museums, although the places themselves are the real attractions. Ford's Theatre in Washington, D.C., offers both a fine museum and the transcendent experience of walking through the theater as it appeared in April 1865. The Abraham Lincoln Museum at Lincoln Memorial University, in Harrogate, Tennessee, and the Lincoln College Museum of Lincoln, Illinois (not to be confused with the Lincoln Museum of Hodgenville, Kentucky, an amusingly kitschy wax museum), are also worthwhile.

I know that Lincoln was born near Hodgenville, but wasn't there a Lincoln museum in Fort Wayne, Indiana? Did he live there, too?

No, but he did change trains there once . . .

. . . at 1:00 a.m. on February 23, 1860, traveling from Springfield to New York City to deliver the Cooper Union address. He also passed through on his way home.

It was not these brief visits, however, but the presence of the Lincoln National Life Insurance Company, founded in 1905, that led to the creation of the museum. The company's guiding spirit, Arthur F. Hall, was an admirer of Lincoln who wrote to Robert Todd Lincoln for permission to use the family name. Lincoln agreed and also sent a photograph of his father that the company used on its letterhead for many years. In 1928, Hall hired Louis A. Warren to "do something Lincoln" as a gesture of gratitude to the Lincoln family. Warren began to publish a periodical called *Lincoln Lore* and to collect the documents and artifacts that became the heart of the Lincoln Museum. Over the next seventy years, the collection grew to become a major Lincoln archive, and in 1992, museum director Mark E. Neely, Jr., won the Pulitzer Prize for his book on Lincoln and civil liberties.[35]

In the twenty-first century, the company, now known as Lincoln Financial Group, apparently concluded that it no longer owed anything to its namesake. It began to mock Abraham Lincoln in television commercials by portraying him as a golf caddie for its rich clients, and in 2008 it closed the eighty-year-old Lincoln Museum.

So does that mean Lincoln Financial Field, where the Philadelphia Eagles play, is also named for Lincoln?

Yes, at one remove.

Is it true that Lincoln Logs are also named for Lincoln?

Yes.

They were invented in 1916 by John Lloyd Wright, son of the architect Frank, and were marketed with Abe's picture on the box.

What about the Lincoln Town Car?

Yep.

There is really no limit to the commercial use of Lincoln's name. Sometimes it makes sense, as with a toy that allows children to build a model of his birthplace cabin. In other cases, like the high-end financial services company or the luxury car maker, the connection to Lincoln is through its founder rather than its product. Henry M. Leland's parents didn't allow him to enlist in 1861 at age eighteen, so he spent the Civil War at the Springfield Armory making guns for the Union army. He went on to form a company that built aircraft engines during World War I, and automobiles afterward, until it was bought by Henry Ford in 1921. Leland, who had also worked for Cadillac, continued to work on what he envisioned as a super-Caddy, and his Lincoln division became the luxury branch of Ford Motor Company. Leland apparently did not see the irony in naming a car after his hero that from its inception "was to be no mass model; it was an exclusive luxury item."[36]

What was Lincoln's greatest accomplishment as president, saving the Union or helping to end slavery?

Both, because neither would have meant much without the other.

Here's what Lincoln said in his speech at Peoria in 1854:

> Let us re-adopt the Declaration of Independence, and with it, the practices, and policy, which harmonize with it. Let north and south—let all Americans—let all lovers of liberty everywhere—join in the great and good work. If we do this, we shall not only have saved the Union; but we shall have so saved it, as to make, and to keep it, forever worthy of the saving. We shall have so saved it, that the succeeding millions of free happy people, the world over, shall rise up, and call us blessed, to the latest generations.[37]

Had he wanted only to save the Union, he might have renounced his antislavery views when he became president, and bought permanent Union at the cost of permanent (or at least very long-lasting) slavery. Had he wanted only to end slavery where he could, he might have issued an emancipation proclamation on the first day of his presidency, driving all the remaining slave states into secession and permanently severing the Union (which incidentally would have also prolonged slavery in the South). He did neither, because he believed that the goals of Union and eventual emancipation were both necessary to the success of America's grand experiment in self-government. He achieved them both. That was his greatest accomplishment.

FOR FURTHER READING

To see how Lincoln's image has changed over the past two hundred years, Merrill D. Peterson, *Lincoln in American Memory* (1994), is the place to start. *Abraham Lincoln and the Forge of National Memory* (2000), by sociologist Barry Schwartz, is more academic but also worthwhile. Andrew Ferguson, *Land of Lincoln: Adventures in Abe's America* (2007), looks at how Americans perceive Abe today, with emphasis on fringe groups of Lincoln lovers and haters.

The best way to answer the hypothetical question about how Lincoln would have handled Reconstruction is to read up on both Lincoln and

Reconstruction and decide for yourself. Eric Foner, *Reconstruction: America's Unfinished Revolution 1863–1877* (1988), is the standard modern study, also available in a shortened version (1990) and recapitulated in an accessible illustrated volume, by Foner and Joshua Brown, *Forever Free: The Story of Emancipation and Reconstruction* (2005).

Mark S. Reinhart is the authority on Lincoln movies, and his *Abraham Lincoln on Screen: A Filmography of Dramas and Documentaries, Including Television* (1999) is the definitive reference. For the Lincoln Highway story, read Drake Hokanson, *The Lincoln Highway: Main Street Across America* (1988). If you can find a copy, *Abraham Lincoln: Unforgettable American* (1976), by Mabel Kunkel, is a useful guide to Lincoln monuments and memorials. Stuart Schneider, *Collecting Lincoln* (1997), is an excellent place to start if you want to collect Lincolniana, although the values it lists are no longer current. For up-to-date collecting information, subscribe to *The Rail Splitter,* a quarterly collector's journal published by Jonathan Mann. To keep up with current events in the Lincoln world, check out the most comprehensive Lincoln-related Web site, "Abraham Lincoln Online," at http://showcase.netins.net/web/creative/lincoln.html. For articles, book reviews, and "Lincolniana" news, subscribe to the *Lincoln Herald,* published by Lincoln Memorial University in Harrogate, Tennessee, and the *Journal of the Abraham Lincoln Association.*

SOURCE NOTES

INTRODUCTION

1. Mark E. Neely, Jr., *The Fate of Liberty: Abraham Lincoln and Civil Liberties* (1991), 231.

CHAPTER ONE: THE BOY LINCOLN

1. William H. Herndon and Jesse W. Weik, *Herndon's Lincoln*, ed. Douglas L. Wilson and Rodney O. Davis (1889; new ed. 2006), 15.
2. Blythe et al., *Abraham Lincoln Birthplace Historic Resource Study*, ch. 2; Gloria Peterson, *An Administrative History of the Abraham Lincoln Birthplace National Historic Site* (1968).
3. William H. Herndon to Ward Hill Lamon, March 6, 1870, in Emanuel Hertz, ed., *The Hidden Lincoln: From the Letters and Papers of William H. Herndon* (1938), 73–74; see also Herndon and Weik, *Herndon's Lincoln*, 16.
4. Harry Laughlin, "Model Eugenical Sterilization Law," in *Eugenical Sterilization in the United States* (1922), 446. The issue returned to the public eye briefly in 2002–03, when the governors of Virginia, Oregon, North Carolina, South Carolina, and California issued apologies to the victims of their states' eugenics laws.
5. Paul Verduin, "New Evidence Suggests Lincoln's Mother Born in Richmond County, Virginia," *Northern Neck of Virginia Historical Magazine* 38, no. 1 (December 1988), 4354–89. But the debate continues; see Christopher Callender Child, "The Maternal Ancestry of Abraham Lincoln: The Origin of Nancy (Hanks) Lincoln, a Study in Appalachian Genealogy," *New England Ancestors* 4, no. 1 (winter 2003), 25–29, 55, which acknowledges that "Nancy Hanks's illegitimacy is not an outrageous idea," but concludes that it is not true.
6. Statistics varied by region and over time; premarital pregnancy was more common in the Appalachian backcountry and the Chesapeake than in New England but remained high throughout America at least until the nineteenth century. See D. H. Fischer, *Albion's Seed* (1989), 681; and John D'Emilio and Estelle B. Freedman, *Intimate Matters: A History of Sexuality in America* (2d ed., 1997), 22–23,

73. In place of statistical research, the study of sexual behavior in the colonial era has, like most other fields of historical study, taken a turn for the theoretical. When the prestigious *William & Mary Quarterly* devoted its January 2003 issue to sexuality in early America, the papers it published had much to say about the social construction of sexual identity, but remarkably little about what kinds of sexual behavior were actually common among colonial Americans.

7. Douglas L. Wilson and Rodney O. Davis, eds., *Herndon's Informants: Letters, Interviews and Statements about Abraham Lincoln* (1998), 84.

8. J. G. de Roulhac Hamilton, "The Many-Sired Lincoln," *American Mercury* 5, no. 18 (June 1925), 133.

9. Wilson and Davis, *Herndon's Informants,* 82; Herndon and Weik, *Herndon's Lincoln,* 17. Everyone wants a piece of Lincoln; North Carolina's desperate bid for reflected Lincolnian glory, through the Enloe story, can be found in Jerry Goodnight and Richard Eller, *The Tarheel Lincoln: North Carolina Origins of "Honest" Abe Lincoln* (2003), published by the Tarheel Press of Hickory, N.C.

10. Brian Steel Wills, *The Confederacy's Greatest Cavalryman: Nathan Bedford Forrest* (1998), is the standard modern biography of Forrest, in which the author struggles bravely between his recognition that Forrest did terrible things and his fascination with Forrest's larger-than-life personality.

11. Lincoln to Jesse Lincoln, Springfield, April 1, 1854, in Roy P. Basler, *Collected Works of Abraham Lincoln* (1953), 2:217 (cited hereafter as *CW*).

12. Wilson and Davis, *Herndon's Informants,* 27; R. Gerald McMurtry, "Re-Discovering the Supposed Grave of Lincoln's Brother," *Lincoln Lore,* no. 1619 (January 1973), 1–3.

13. Herndon and Weik, *Herndon's Lincoln,* 16; J[osiah] G. Holland, *The Life of Abraham Lincoln* (1866), 23; George Alfred Townsend, *The Real Life of Abraham Lincoln: A Talk with Mr. Herndon, His Late Law Partner* (1867), 6. Nancy Hanks's early biographers, on the other hand, assumed that their subject was the "angel mother." See Caroline Hanks Hitchcock, *Nancy Hanks: The Story of Abraham Lincoln's Mother* (1899), 105.

14. Wilson and Davis, *Herndon's Informants,* 107.

15. Lincoln to John D. Johnston, Springfield, January 12, 1851, *CW* 2:96–97.

16. Wilson and Davis, *Herndon's Informants,* 136. The idea that Lincoln was working out an Oedipus complex in his presidency, first implied by Edmund Wilson in *Patriotic Gore* (1962), 99–130, enjoyed a brief moment of popularity around 1980. See George B. Forgie, *Patricide in the House Divided: A Psychological Interpretation of Lincoln and His Age* (1979); Dwight G. Anderson, *Abraham Lincoln: The Quest for Immortality* (1982); and (with substantial qualifications) Charles B. Strozier, *Lincoln's Quest for Union: A Psychological Portrait* (1982, rev. ed. 2001).

17. "My Childhood-Home I See Again," 1846, *CW* 1:367.

18. Autobiography for Jesse W. Fell, December 20, 1859, *CW* 3:511.

19. J. J. Wright, quoted in Don E. Fehrenbacher and Virginia Fehrenbacher, eds., *Recollected Words of Abraham Lincoln* (1996), 508.

20. Herndon and Weik, *Herndon's Lincoln,* 15, quoting a letter from John L. Scripps to Herndon, June 24, 1865.
21. The story appears in Herndon and Weik, *Herndon's Lincoln,* 26–27. Herndon did not think much of Thomas Lincoln, whom he never met, which implies that whatever Lincoln said to Herndon about his father must not have been particularly favorable. See also Louise A. Warren, "That Half-Faced Camp," *Lincoln Lore,* no. 557 (December 11, 1939).
22. Autobiography for John L. Scripps, [1860], *CW* 4:61.
23. Scripps autobiography, [1860], *CW* 4:62.
24. Scripps autobiography, [1860], *CW* 4:62. Charles Strozier has analyzed Lincoln's account of using his father's rifle to shoot a turkey in Freudian terms, but most historians believe that in this case, a turkey is just a turkey. Strozier, *Lincoln's Quest for Union,* 29–32.
25. See William Lee Miller, *Lincoln's Virtues: An Ethical Biography* (2002).
26. Scripps autobiography, [1860], *CW* 4:62; Herndon and Weik, *Herndon's Lincoln,* 51.
27. Louis A. Warren, *Lincoln's Parentage and Childhood* (1926), 148.
28. For the Gollaher rescue, see Wilson and Davis, *Herndon's Informants,* 235; for Lincoln's rescue by the future Mrs. Mary Head Berry Mitchell, see "Untold Tale: Lincoln Rescue Unfolds From Antioch Grave," *Oakland* (Calif.) *Tribune,* February 12, 1967.
29. The story comes to us fourthhand, from a conversation Lincoln had with Dr. J. H. Rodman, recounted by Rodman to Charles Friend (a nephew of Dennis Hanks), who wrote about it to William Herndon. Such evidence would not stand up in a court of law, but in the court of history it can only be weighed against the alternatives, and there is no original source for the "paw paw" version at all. Wilson and Davis, *Herndon's Informants,* 676.
30. Brief Autobiography, *CW* 2:459.
31. Wilson and Davis, *Herndon's Informants,* 107.
32. Fell autobiography, December 20, 1859, *CW* 3:511; Scripps autobiography, [1860], *CW* 4:62.
33. Scripps autobiography, [1860], *CW* 4:62.
34. Wilson and Davis, *Herndon's Informants,* 38 (for Hanks's claim), 122 (for its refutation by David Turnham).
35. Speech at Trenton, N.J., February 21, 1861, *CW* 4:236.

CHAPTER TWO: RAILSPLITTER

1. Herndon and Weik, *Herndon's Lincoln,* 62.
2. Mark A. Plummer, *Lincoln's Rail-Splitter: Governor Richard J. Oglesby* (2001), ch. 3, describes how Oglesby, later a general and governor of Illinois, came up with the idea of associating Lincoln with split rails as a piece of political theater.
3. Robert A. Margo, *Wages and Labor Markets in the United States, 1820–1860* (2000), 67, Table 3A.5.

4. F[rancis] B. Carpenter, *Six Months at the White House with Abraham Lincoln: The Story of a Picture* (1866), 98.
5. The evidence for the 1828 antislavery statement is a thirdhand or fourthhand account of a recollection of Allen Gentry. Phillip Paludan, "Lincoln and Negro Slavery: I Haven't Got Time for the Pain," *Journal of the Abraham Lincoln Association* (cited hereafter as *JALA*) 27, no. 2 (summer 2006), 9, describes the "fog between the historical fact and today" regarding this quote as "pretty thick."
6. Second Inaugural Address, March 4, 1865, *CW* 8:333.
7. Anonymous neighbor, quoted in John G. Nicolay and John Hay, *Abraham Lincoln: A History* (1886), 1:42. Offut later left New Salem and became a professional horse whisperer.
8. Jack W. Worth, "*Honest Abe*": *Episodes in the Life of Abraham Lincoln* (1936). The great Lincoln curator James T. Hickey theorized that Lincoln, being as resourceful as he was honest, timed his visit to the Hornbuckle cabin to coincide with the appearance of supper on the table. (Personal communication, Illinois State Historian Thomas F. Schwartz, January 2006.)
9. Rev. Charles Chiniquy, *Fifty Years in the Church of Rome* (1886), 663–64. To be precise, Chiniquy claimed that Lincoln himself had said that Catholics were out to get him and that they were spreading false stories of his Catholic birth and subsequent separation from the church to justify assassinating him. Don and Virginia Fehrenbacher, who evaluated the reliability of hundreds of alleged Lincoln quotes for the invaluable *Recollected Words of Abraham Lincoln* (1996), describe Chiniquy on p. 98 as "perhaps the biggest liar in Lincoln literature."
10. See Edward Steers, "Was Abraham Lincoln a Christian?" *North & South* 2, no. 7 (September 1999), 30–35, disproving various accounts of Lincoln's alleged baptism.
11. Wilson and Davis, *Herndon's Informants,* 360. Mary Lincoln disavowed these comments in 1873, after Herndon gave a public lecture on Lincoln's religion, but Herndon responded with a public letter supporting the accuracy of what he claimed she said. Douglas Wilson has suggested that the phrase "technical Christian" may have been Herndon's. Wilson, "William H. Herndon and Mary Todd Lincoln," *JALA* 22, no. 2 (summer 2001), 18 n. 49.
12. Address Before the Young Men's Lyceum of Springfield, January 27, 1838, *CW* 1:108–15. It was former Confederate vice president Alexander Stephens who first claimed that Lincoln's belief in the Union "rose to the sublimity of a religious mysticism," which Stephens did not mean as a compliment. Stephens, *Constitutional View of the Late War Between the States* (1868), 2:448. Modern historians have more often argued that Lincoln's loyalty to the Union was grounded in logical and legal principles. See, e.g., Drew McCoy, "An 'Old-Fashioned' Nationalism: Lincoln, Jefferson, and the Classical Tradition," *JALA* 23, no. 1 (winter 2002), 55–68.
13. *Hamlet,* Act V, scene ii.

14. Herndon and Weik, *Herndon's Lincoln,* 265–69, summarizes what Herndon learned from his inquiries, including the story of the burned manuscript.
15. Handbill Replying to Charges of Infidelity, July 31, 1846, *CW* 1:382. Lincoln would later use exactly the same rhetorical trick in dealing with the even more politically sensitive issue of racial equality.
16. Gideon Welles, *Diary* (1909), 1:143.
17. Joshua F. Speed, *Reminiscences of Abraham Lincoln* (1884), 32–33.
18. For Lincoln holding the ax, see Carpenter, *Six Months at the White House,* 289.
19. Douglas Wilson, *Honor's Voice: The Transformation of Abraham Lincoln* (1998), devotes the entire first chapter to reconciling the various contradictory eyewitness accounts of this event.
20. Wilson and Davis, *Herndon's Informants,* 74, 141, 366, 451, 482.
21. Wilson and Davis, *Herndon's Informants,* 451–53, mentions town ball and playing fives on nomination day. For billiards, see Tim R. Miller, "Abraham Lincoln and the Art of Billiards," *Lincoln Lore,* no. 1848 (spring 1997), 3–10; and no. 1849 (summer 1997), 4–11. For Doubleday's nonrole in the invention of baseball, see Warren Goldstein, *Playing for Keeps: A History of Early Baseball* (1989), 11.
22. First Debate, Ottawa, Ill., August 21, 1858, *CW* 3:6.
23. Lincoln quoted by Herndon in a letter to Jesse W. Weik, February 7, 1887, in Fehrenbacher and Fehrenbacher, *Recollected Words,* 252.
24. Speed, *Reminiscences of Abraham Lincoln,* 31.
25. Paul M. Zall, *Abe Lincoln Laughing: Humorous Anecdotes from Original Sources by and about Abraham Lincoln* (1982), i–x. This anecdote is actually part of the foreword by Ray Allen Billington, who gives it as an example of a story that cannot be authentically traced to Lincoln, but does "have the ring of a perfect Abraham Lincoln story."
26. Henry Dummer, a Springfield attorney, referred to Lincoln's "insane" love of dirty stories in an interview with William Herndon in 1865 or 1866, but gave no examples. Wilson and Davis, *Herndon's Informants,* 442–43.
27. Garry Wills, *Lincoln at Gettysburg: The Words That Remade America* (1992), 33.
28. Wilson and Davis, *Herndon's Informants,* 104.
29. Herndon and Weik, *Herndon's Lincoln,* 190–91.
30. John Y. Simon, "Abraham Lincoln and Ann Rutledge," *JALA* 11 (1990), 13; Michael Burlingame, *The Inner World of Abraham Lincoln* (1994), xxv. The first full-length study of the Rutledge renaissance was John Evangelist Walsh, *The Shadows Rise: Abraham Lincoln and the Ann Rutledge Legend* (1993).
31. The answer is John Mack Faragher, a historian whose *Sugar Creek: Life on the Illinois Prairie* (1986) remains a classic analysis of life in a Midwestern frontier town, not far from New Salem.
32. The story appears in numerous biographies, based on Speed's own account. See David Herbert Donald, *"We Are Lincoln Men": Abraham Lincoln and His Friends* (2003), 30.

CHAPTER THREE: SPRINGFIELD

1. *CW* 1:78.
2. Owens described her relationship with Lincoln in a series of letters to William Herndon written in 1866, as Mrs. Mary Owens Vineyard. See Wilson and Davis, *Herndon's Informants,* 256, 262.
3. Lincoln to Mrs. Orville H. Browning, April 1, 1838, *CW* 1:117–19.
4. Lincoln to Owens, May 7, 1837, *CW* 1:78. For Lincoln's reaction, see his letter to Mrs. Browning, April 1, 1838, *CW* 1:117–19.
5. Herndon and Weik, *Herndon's Lincoln,* 37. Kate, who married Allen Gentry not long after, always insisted that she had never been in love with Lincoln, which is believable given his lame romantic performance on the riverbank.
6. The recollections of Kate Roby (Mrs. Anna Caroline Roby Gentry) regarding Lincoln are in Wilson and Davis, *Herndon's Informants,* 131–32.
7. Donald, personal communication; Wilson, *Honor's Voice,* 183–84; Strozier, *Lincoln's Quest for Union,* 50–65, esp. n. 74.
8. David Herbert Donald, "*We Are Lincoln Men*": *Abraham Lincoln and His Friends* (2003), 35. Donald was surprised to find this the question he was asked most often on his 1995–96 book tour. Gabor Boritt, Harold Holzer, Catherine Clinton, and other Lincoln scholars have affirmed the popularity of this question at their public appearances.
9. Matthew Pinsker, *Lincoln's Sanctuary: Abraham Lincoln and the Soldiers' Home* (2003), 84–85. Martin P. Johnson argued that all the evidence of the Lincoln-Derickson bed sharing can be traced to a single rumor, in "Did Abraham Lincoln Sleep with His Bodyguard?" *JALA* 27, no. 2 (summer 2006), 42–55.
10. Quoted in Carol Lloyd, "Was Lincoln Gay?," May 3, 1999, http://www.salon.com/books/it/1999/04/30/lincoln/index.html, accessed March 12, 2007.
11. C. A. Tripp, *The Intimate World of Abraham Lincoln* (2005). His original coauthor, Philip Nobile, wrote "Broken Promises, Plagiarism, Misused Evidence and the New Gay Lincoln Book Published by the Free Press," for the History News Network, January 10, 2005, http://hnn.us/articles/9514.html, accessed March 12, 2007.
12. Bruce Burgett, "In the Name of Sex," *William and Mary Quarterly* 60, no. 1 (January 2003), 186, points out that it is problematic to use "our modern terms like homosexual and heterosexual . . . to describe historical agents who may not have understood their sensual practices in those identity terms."
13. Carl Sandburg, *Abraham Lincoln: The Prairie Years* (1926), 1:264; see also Frank Williams, " 'A Matter of Profound Wonder': The Women in Lincoln's Life," in *Judging Lincoln* (2002), 17–33, evaluating the feminine qualities of Lincoln's character.
14. For David Donald, such a guilt-free admission is clear evidence that nothing sexual could have transpired. See Donald, "*We Are Lincoln Men,*" 38.
15. Speech at Chicago, Ill., July 10, 1858, *CW* 2:501.

16. Some people still do this. See James A. Percoco, *Summers with Lincoln* (2008).
17. National Park Service visitors' brochure, Lincoln Boyhood National Memorial (2001).
18. See Martha L. Benner, Cullom Davis, et al., eds., *The Law Practice of Abraham Lincoln: Complete Documentary Edition* (2000).
19. Wilson and Davis, *Herndon's Informants*, 636.
20. Wilson and Davis, *Herndon's Informants*, 707–08. The Shakespeare quote is from *Othello*, Act III, scene iii.
21. Scripps autobiography, [1860], *CW* 4:65.
22. Wilson and Davis, *Herndon's Informants*, 449, from Herndon's interview with Russell Godbey in 1865 or 1866.
23. Lincoln to John M. Brockman, September 25, 1860, *CW* 4:121. Mark Steiner, *An Honest Calling: The Law Practice of Abraham Lincoln* (2006), 29–54, describes Lincoln's legal education and notes that he continued to recommend self-education long after formal law school training had become standard. His own son Robert attended Harvard Law School.
24. Steiner, *An Honest Calling*, 37–40.
25. A romanticized version of the almanac trial appears in the movie *Young Mr. Lincoln*.
26. Herndon and Weik, *Herndon's Lincoln*, 215. Steiner, *An Honest Calling*, 20, notes the heavy reliance on this anecdote by those looking for a moral compass in Lincoln's legal career.
27. *Hurd et al. v. Rock Island Bridge Co.* (N.D. Ill. 1857).
28. *Illinois Central Rail Road v. McLean County* (Ill. S. Ct. 1855). Lincoln offered his services to county officials first, but they did not choose to hire him, to their later regret.
29. By Grant Gilmore, for example, whose *Ages of American Law* (1979) is a concise and classic summary of American legal history.
30. Fragment: Notes for a Law Lecture, [July 1, 1850?], *CW* 2:81.
31. Lincoln actually received $250 from the railroad when he took the case, and $100 on September 23, 1854, but neither side seems to have noticed the discrepancy. Many documents from this case, including the receipt for $250, have been published in facsimile form in Benner et al., *The Law Practice of Abraham Lincoln*.
32. The number fluctuated from eight to seventeen as the legislature changed the boundaries of the district. At its largest, it was bigger than some New England states.
33. Lincoln quoted by Mary Lincoln in her letter to Francis B. Carpenter, November 15, [1865,] in Justin G. Turner and Linda Levitt Turner, *Mary Todd Lincoln: Her Life and Letters* (1972), 285.
34. The most thorough examination of Mrs. Lincoln's mental health is Jason Emerson, *The Madness of Mary Lincoln* (2007), which concludes that she suffered from bipolar disorder (once more commonly called manic depression) with increas-

ingly severe psychotic symptoms. Emerson portrays Robert Lincoln as an anguished son who felt duty-bound to protect his mother from herself, in contrast to earlier historians who excoriated Robert as an ungrateful, cold-blooded snob embarrassed by his mother's eccentric behavior.

35. Wilson and Davis, *Herndon's Informants,* 443, 446.
36. Herndon and Weik, *Herndon's Lincoln,* 137.
37. Lincoln to Joshua F. Speed, Springfield, March 27, 1842, *CW* 1:282.
38. Lincoln to John T. Stuart, Springfield, January 23, 1841, *CW* 1:229–30; Stuart to Daniel Webster, March 5, 1841, in "An Equatorial Change for Lincoln?" *Lincoln Editor: The Quarterly Newsletter of the Papers of Abraham Lincoln* 5, no. 1 (January–March 2005).
39. Herndon and Weik, *Herndon's Lincoln,* 156, 165.
40. The "Rebecca" letter, August 27, 1842, *CW* 1:295.
41. See Douglas Wilson, "Abraham Lincoln versus Peter Cartwright," in *Lincoln Before Washington: New Perspectives on the Illinois Years* (1997), 55–73. Historian Michael Burlingame, in research for a monumental multivolume biography, has identified numerous previously unknown articles as the anonymous work of Lincoln.
42. Herndon and Weik, *Herndon's Lincoln,* 130.

CHAPTER FOUR: POLITICIAN

1. Communication to the People of Sangamo County, March 9, 1832, *CW* 1:8.
2. Scripps autobiography, [1860], *CW* 4:64.
3. Joshua Wolf Shenk, *Lincoln's Melancholy: How Depression Challenged a President and Fueled His Greatness* (2005).
4. Lincoln to Richard Thomas, Springfield, February 14, 1843, *CW* 1:307.
5. William E. Barton, *The Life of Abraham Lincoln* (1925), 232, says Stuart won by fourteen votes; other sources like Reinhard Luthin, *The Real Abraham Lincoln* (1960), 64, and David Herbert Donald, *Lincoln* (1995), 78, say it was thirty-six votes. Fortunately, in 2006, Florida passed a law decreeing that history is "knowable" and should be taught as a set of facts (Florida Education Omnibus Bill, H.B. 7087e3). Professional historians, who have spent their careers wrestling with the ambiguity produced by conflicting evidence and the ever-changing nature of historical interpretation, can take comfort that the solons of the Sunshine State are certain (Florida's own history of ambiguous vote counting notwithstanding) that there is a knowable, factual answer to the question of Stuart's margin of victory.
6. Lincoln to Joshua Speed, March 24, 1843, *CW* 1:319.
7. Speech in U.S. House of Representatives, July 27, 1848, *CW* 1:503–04.
8. "His wife put her foot squarely down on it with a firm and emphatic No. That always ended it with Lincoln." Herndon and Weik, *Herndon's Lincoln,* 192–93.
9. Speech at Peoria, Ill., October 16, 1854, *CW* 2:282.

10. Philip B. Kunhardt, Jr., Philip B. Kunhardt III, and Peter W. Kunhardt, *Lincoln: An Illustrated Biography* (1992), 130.
11. In D. W. Griffith's classic film biography *Abraham Lincoln* (1930), this is exactly how it happens: Abe is sitting in his law office complaining to Billy Herndon about what a failure he is when a knock is heard at the door. It's the nominating committee!
12. Fragment on Stephen A. Douglas, [December 1856?], *CW* 2:383.
13. Communication to the People of Sangamo County, March 9, 1832, *CW* 1:8.
14. Fragment on Stephen A. Douglas, [December 1856?], *CW* 2:383. The Herndon quote is from Herndon and Weik, *Herndon's Lincoln,* 231. As William Lee Miller has noted, no Lincoln biography is complete without it. "When you . . . see on the page the word 'ambition,' you say to yourself, Here comes that engine again, and sure enough, the quotation from Herndon comes chugging along soon thereafter." *Lincoln's Virtues,* 65.
15. Wilson and Davis, *Herndon's Informants,* 63, 631.
16. Address Before the Young Men's Lyceum of Springfield, Illinois, January 27, 1838, *CW* 1:114.
17. Communication to the People of Sangamo County, March 9, 1832, *CW* 1:8.
18. December 15, 1834, *CW* 1:29–30.
19. "There were two things Mr. Lincoln always seemed willing to forget," according to Herndon. The other was his unconsummated duel with Shields. *Herndon's Lincoln,* 146.
20. Herndon and Weik, *Herndon's Lincoln,* 129–30.
21. Lincoln to Joshua F. Speed, Springfield, August 24, 1855, *CW* 2:322–23.
22. Michael F. Holt, *The Rise and Fall of the American Whig Party: Jacksonian Politics and the Onset of the Civil War* (1999).
23. Fell autobiography, December 20, 1859, *CW* 3:512.
24. Allen Guelzo, "Ten 'True Lies' About Abraham Lincoln: Part 1," *For the People* 2, no. 2 (summer 2000), 8; Holzer, personal communication; Dirksen quoted in David Herbert Donald, "Getting Right With Lincoln," in *Lincoln Reconsidered* (1961), 17.
25. Speech at New Haven, Conn., June 6, 1860, *CW* 4:24.
26. Ibid.
27. Fragment on Government, undated, *CW* 2:220.
28. Speech at New Haven, Conn., June 6, 1860, *CW* 4:24.
29. Lincoln to Joshua F. Speed, Springfield, August 24, 1855, *CW* 2:323.

CHAPTER FIVE: SPEAKER

1. Herndon and Weik, *Herndon's Lincoln,* 203.
2. Wilson and Davis, *Herndon's Informants,* 203. See also Louis A. Warren, "Lincoln's Voice," *Lincoln Lore,* no. 340 (October 14, 1935).
3. Garrett Newkirk, "A Boy at Lincoln's Feet: A Reminiscence of a Lincoln-Douglas Debate," *The Outlook,* February 9, 1921, 217. For the impact of the invention of

amplified and recorded sound on political rhetoric, see Allan Metcalf, *Presidential Voices: Speaking Styles from George Washington to George W. Bush* (2004).

4. *CW* 8:433; for context, see Herndon and Weik, *Herndon's Lincoln,* 115–16.
5. Matthew 12:25; Mark 3:25.
6. Quoted in Herndon and Weik, *Herndon's Lincoln,* 242.
7. John Quincy Adams to A. Bronson, July 30, 1838.
8. For this speech, and the process by which Lincoln composed many of his speeches, illustrated by photographs of the original manuscripts, see Douglas L. Wilson, *Lincoln's Sword: The Presidency and the Power of Words* (2006).
9. Speech at Bloomington, Ill., May 29, 1856, *CW* 2:341. Elwell Crissey, *Lincoln's Lost Speech: The Pivot of His Career* (1967), describes the surviving evidence of the speech, imaginatively illustrated by Lloyd Ostendorf.
10. William E. Curtis, "Speculating on Lincoln's 'Fooling the People,' " *Washington Star,* May 8, 1905 (clipping at Lincoln Museum, Fort Wayne, Ind.).
11. Kate Louise Roberts, *Hoyt's New Cyclopedia of Practical Quotations* (1922), 1:182–83, accepts Barnum as the source.
12. Speeches at Clinton, Ill., September 2, 1858, *CW* 3:84.
13. David B. Parker, "A New Look at 'You Can Fool All of the People,' " *For The People* 7, no. 3 (autumn 2005), 1.
14. Elmo Scott Watson, "Did He Really Say It?" undated clipping from *Dearborn Independent* [September 11, 1926], at Lincoln Museum, Fort Wayne, Ind.
15. Carpenter, *Six Months at the White House,* 77. Lincoln was explaining why he was taking so long to issue an emancipation proclamation.
16. See Thomas Schwartz, "Lincoln Never Said That," *For the People* 1, no. 1 (spring 1999); Helen Nicolay, *Personal Traits of Abraham Lincoln* (1912), 380; see also Helen Nicolay, *Lincoln's Secretary: A Biography of John G. Nicolay* (1949), 319–21.
17. R. Gerald McMurtry, " 'Lincoln Never Said That,' " *Lincoln Lore,* no. 1487 (January 1962), 3; Merrill D. Peterson, *Lincoln in American Memory* (1994), 341.
18. Response to a Serenade, July 7, 1863, *CW* 6:319.
19. Farewell Address at Springfield, February 11, 1861, *CW* 4:190–91; includes three versions. See Wilson, *Lincoln's Sword,* ch. 1, for a discussion of Lincoln's revisions of this speech.
20. Speech on the Sub-treasury, December [26], 1839, *CW* 1:178–79.
21. Wilson and Davis, *Herndon's Informants,* 5.
22. "A House Divided": Speech at Springfield, Ill., June 16, 1858, *CW* 2:461.
23. Fell autobiography, December 20, 1859, *CW* 3:512.
24. Speech at Peoria, Ill., October 16, 1854 (hereafter cited as "Peoria speech"), *CW* 2:255.
25. Hammond to Thomas Clarkson, quoted in "Gov. Hammond's Defense of Southern Slavery," *The New Englander* 3, no. 12 (October 1845), 570.
26. Peoria speech, *CW* 2:275. Lincoln was so appalled that a senator would call the Declaration a "self-evident lie" in defense of slavery that he repeated the comment in various public and private settings over the next year. See *CW* 2:283 (speech at

Chicago), 318 (letter to George Robertson), and 368 (speech at Petersburg, Ill.).

27. Peoria speech, *CW* 2:255.
28. Ibid.
29. Ibid., *CW* 2:276.
30. First Debate with Stephen A. Douglas at Ottawa, Ill., *CW* 3:9, 14 (audience responses are set in bold type). Historian David Donald described the debates as a "restless, roaring, brawling exchange in which the audience was vigorously involved." *Lincoln* (1995), 629.
31. Fragment on Stephen A. Douglas, [December 1856?], *CW* 2:383.
32. 60 U.S. 393 (1856). The official name of the case misspells the name "Sanford" as "Sandford."
33. *Dred Scott v. Sandford,* 60 U.S. 393 (1856), 407.
34. Second Debate with Stephen A. Douglas at Freeport, Ill., August 27, 1858, *CW* 3:43.
35. Address at Cooper Institute, February 27, 1860, *CW* 3:538. Lincoln spelled it this way, presumably mocking Douglas's delivery.
36. Lincoln supposedly said after the Freeport debate, "I am after larger game; the battle of 1860 is worth a hundred of this," but there are only secondhand accounts of this. See Herndon and Weik, *Herndon's Lincoln,* 399, and Isaac Arnold, *The Life of Abraham Lincoln* (1884), 151.
37. Zachary Taylor, Millard Fillmore, Franklin Pierce, and James Buchanan.
38. Lincoln to Judd, Springfield, December 9, 1859, *CW* 3:505; Lincoln to Samuel Galloway, Springfield, July 28, 1859, *CW* 3:395; Lincoln to Thomas J. Pickett, Springfield, April 16, 1859, *CW* 3:377; and Lincoln to Trumbull, Springfield, April 29, 1860, *CW* 4:45.

CHAPTER SIX: PRESIDENT

1. *CW* 7:512.
2. Behind James K. Polk and Franklin Pierce. John Tyler and Millard Fillmore had been younger when they took office, but they were not elected.
3. According to the rest of the story, Lincoln shared the joke with Cameron, who was not amused. He confronted Stevens in the House of Representatives and demanded that he retract the comment. Stevens thereupon went to see Lincoln and said, "I told you that I didn't think he would steal a red-hot stove. I now take that back." The whole exchange first appeared in an 1899 biography of Stevens, but unfortunately no contemporary source for it has been found. See Hans Trefousse, *Thaddeus Stevens: Nineteenth-Century Egalitarian* (1997), 106.
4. Douglas wrote a lengthy article for *Harper's* magazine in September 1859 arguing his case for popular sovereignty.
5. South Carolina Unionist James Louis Petigru made this observation in 1860; see William H. Pease and Jane H. Pease, *James Louis Petigru: Southern Conservative, Southern Dissenter* (1995), 156.

6. Herndon and Weik, *Herndon's Lincoln,* 231.
7. Some historians, notably David Donald, accept the story as told. Others question why almost nobody else at the inaugural seemed to notice such a poignant incident. Frank Maloy Anderson, *The Mystery of "A Public Man": A Historical Detective Story* (1948), reprints the text of the "Diary," which originally appeared as a series of magazine articles in 1879. The hat story is on p. 231.
8. For the whole story, see Doris Kearns Goodwin, *Team of Rivals: The Political Genius of Abraham Lincoln* (2005).
9. Michael Burlingame and John R. Turner Ettlinger, eds., *Inside Lincoln's White House: The Complete Civil War Diary of John Hay* (1997), 77. The line is so Lincolnian that it is sometimes misattributed to him.
10. Lincoln to William H. Seward, April 1, 1861, *CW* 4:317. Seward's memo is on pp. 317–18.
11. Seward to Frances Seward, June 5, 1861, in Frederick W. Seward, *Seward at Washington as Senator and Secretary of State* (1891), 590.
12. Attributed to Henry J. Raymond, in Emanuel Hertz, *Lincoln Talks: A Biography in Anecdote* (1939), 226. Raymond was the editor of the *New York Times.* Since Lincoln's brother Thomas died in infancy, he was probably referring to his stepbrother, John D. Johnston.
13. Gideon Welles, *Diary* (1911), 1:202.
14. Nicolay and Hay, *Abraham Lincoln: A History,* 6:271.
15. Hamlin to Lincoln, Bangor, September 25, 1862, in Harold Holzer, *Dear Mr. Lincoln* (1993), 266.
16. This is a minority opinion; most historians side with Don E. Fehrenbacher's view that the absence of credible evidence pointing to Lincoln means that he was not involved. See his article "The Making of a Myth: Lincoln and the Vice-Presidential Nomination in 1864," *Civil War History* 41 (December 1995), 273–90.
17. As an example of the neo-Confederate view, the title of Webb Garrison's *Lincoln's Little War: How His Carefully Crafted Plans Went Astray* (1997) tells all you need to know about how that author saw his subject. Garrison, however, is a veritable Thucydides compared to some of the libertarian pseudo-historians of the early twenty-first century who not only blame Lincoln for starting the war but regard him as the root of all evil since 1861. For a somewhat more scholarly attack on Lincoln's role in the outbreak of the war, see William Marvel's neo-Revisionist *Mr. Lincoln Goes to War* (2006), which blames him for not compromising more and avoiding a war that (in Marvel's view) had more bad results than good ones. Richard Current, *Lincoln and the First Shot* (1963), offers the traditional favorable view of Lincoln's handling of the Sumter crisis.
18. Reply to Baltimore committee, April 22, 1861, *CW* 4:341–42.
19. Article I, section 9.
20. Message to Congress in Special Session, July 4, 1861, *CW* 4:430.
21. See Mark E. Neely, Jr., *The Fate of Liberty: Abraham Lincoln and Civil Liberties* (1991), 113–38.

22. Lincoln to Erastus Corning and Others, [June 12,] 1863, *CW* 6:266.
23. Lincoln to Corning, 1863, *CW* 6:267.
24. See William H. Rehnquist, *All the Laws But One: Civil Liberties in Wartime* (1998), for a sympathetic analysis of Lincoln's actions, set in the context of other wars, written by a chief justice of the U.S. Supreme Court.
25. See Harold M. Hyman, *A More Perfect Union: The Impact of the Civil War and Reconstruction on the Constitution* (1973), 84, erroneously referring to "Lieber Papers no. 2422" in the Huntington Library, San Marino, California. The document is actually No. 2422 in the Ward Hill Lamon Papers, also at the Huntington, and consists of an undated, anonymous memorandum, probably by Lamon, that deals with habeas corpus issues in the Civil War.
26. The standard work on the subject is still Don E. Fehrenbacher, *The Dred Scott Case: Its Significance in American Law and Politics* (1978). Most historians and legal scholars concur with the judgment of *Dred Scott* as the worst Supreme Court decision ever, as noted in Walter Ehrlich, "Scott v. Sandford," in Kermit L. Hall et al., eds., *The Oxford Companion to the Supreme Court of the United States,* 2d ed. (2005), 889. For an intriguing minority view that *Dred Scott* was decided correctly (based on the argument that the Founders intended the Constitution to accommodate the evil of slavery, as the only way to maintain the Union and avoid civil warfare), see Mark A. Graber, *Dred Scott and the Problem of Constitutional Evil* (2006).
27. See Hale to Lincoln, Philadelphia, September 28, 1863, in Harold Holzer, *Dear Mr. Lincoln: Letters to the President* (1993), 57–58, which led to Proclamations of Thanksgiving, October 3, 1863, and October 20, 1864, *CW* 6:497–98 and 8:55–56.
28. Proclamation of Thanksgiving, July 15, 1863, *CW* 6:333–34. Lincoln also closed federal offices on Thursday, November 28, 1861, because local authorities had proclaimed a day of thanksgiving (*CW* 5:32), and called for other days of thanksgiving on April 10, 1862, after Shiloh (*CW* 5:185–86), May 9, 1864, offering premature thanks for the outcome of the battle of the Wilderness (*CW* 7:333), and September 3, 1864, after the capture of Atlanta (*CW* 7:533–34). At the time of his assassination, he was preparing another thanksgiving proclamation for the end of the war (*CW* 8:399–400).
29. William O. Stoddard, *Inside the White House in War Times,* ed. Michael Burlingame (2000 ed.), 5; Elizabeth Grimsley, "Six Months in the White House," *Journal of the Illinois State Historical Society* 19 (1927), 47. Washington, of course, never lived in the White House; John Adams was the first president to occupy the new Executive Mansion.
30. Quoted in the diary of Benjamin French, December 16, 1861. French, the commissioner of public buildings, was enlisted by Mrs. Lincoln to explain to her husband what she had done. His diary was published as Benjamin Brown French, *Witness to the Young Republic: A Yankee's Journal, 1828–1870,* ed. Donald B. Cole and John J. McDonough (1989).

31. Ben: Perley Poore, *Perley's Reminiscences of Sixty Years in the National Metropolis* (1886), 2:115–21, gives a colorful description of the party, including who was there and what they wore.
32. The index of Bruce Tap's detailed study, *Over Lincoln's Shoulder: The Committee on the Conduct of the War* (1998), does not mention Mary Lincoln.
33. The only previous presidents even to come close to doing this were George Washington, who testified before the entire Senate in 1789 on Indian treaties, and Woodrow Wilson, who had members of the Senate Foreign Relations Committee to lunch at the White House, where he gave them testimony regarding the Treaty of Versailles and the League of Nations. See Senate Historical Office, www.senate.gov/artandhistory/history/resources/pdf/PresidentsTestify.pdf (2004), accessed January 21, 2007.
34. See Ruth Painter Randall, *Mary Lincoln: Biography of a Marriage* (1953), 303–04; Poore, *Reminiscences,* 2:143; *New York Tribune,* February 13, 1862.
35. See Mark E. Neely, Jr., "Abraham Lincoln Did NOT Defend His Wife Before the Committee on the Conduct of the War," *Lincoln Lore,* no. 1643 (January 1975).
36. Lincoln, when he was a Congressman, had vigorously opposed the war with Mexico. For the misquote story, see Mary Ann Akers, "Honest, It Wasn't Abe's Comment," *Washington Post,* February 16, 2007, A21. The columnist who started it blamed his copyeditor—nothing is ever anyone's own fault.
37. Elizabeth Smith Brownstein, *Lincoln's Other White House* (2005), 54.
38. A popular story has Lincoln greeting the author of *Uncle Tom's Cabin* with "So you're the little woman who wrote the book that started this great war!" but there's no written evidence that he said this. All that Stowe wrote to her husband was that she "had a real funny interview with the President," promising to tell him the details later. Joan D. Hedrick, *Harriet Beecher Stowe: A Life* (1994), vii, 306.
39. Herndon and Weik, *Herndon's Lincoln,* 309 (quoting Hay), 209 (quoting David Davis). See also p. 312 (quoting Joshua Speed) and p. 196 (Herndon's own comment) for the lack of routine in Lincoln's office.
40. Lincoln quoted in Carpenter, *Six Months at the White House,* 281.
41. Holzer, *Dear Mr. Lincoln,* 6–30.
42. Harold Holzer, ed., *Lincoln's White House Secretary: The Adventurous Life of William O. Stoddard* (2007), 244–45.
43. Hay claimed that Lincoln "gave the whole thing over to me, and signed, without reading them, the letters I wrote in his name." Herndon and Weik, *Herndon's Lincoln,* 309.
44. To John McMahon, August 6, 1864, *CW* 7:483.
45. See, e.g., John Dickerson, "Stranger and Stranger: Why Is George Bush Reading Camus?" *Chicago Sun-Times,* August 20, 2006. Note however that Lincoln was not reading Shakespeare for the first time in 1863.
46. Lincoln to Hackett, August 17, 1863, *CW* 6:392–93; November 2, 1863, *CW* 6:559.
47. Lincoln to Mrs. Lydia Bixby, November 21, 1864, *CW* 8:116–17.

48. See William E. Barton, *A Beautiful Blunder* (1926); and Michael Burlingame, "The Authorship of the Bixby Letter," in Burlingame, ed., *At Lincoln's Side: John Hay's Civil War Correspondence and Selected Writings* (2000), 169–84.
50. Memorandum Concerning His Probable Failure of Re-Election, August 23, 1864, *CW* 7:514.
51. Response to a Serenade, November 10, 1864, *CW* 8:101.

CHAPTER SEVEN: COMMANDER IN CHIEF

1. Burlingame and Ettlinger, *Inside Lincoln's White House*, 191.
2. Speech in the U.S. House of Representatives: The War With Mexico, January 12, 1848, *CW* 1:439.
3. See Luthin, *The Real Abraham Lincoln*, 30.
4. Some people will do anything to sell a book. See Varina Davis, *Jefferson Davis: Ex-President of the Confederate States of America; A Memoir by His Wife* (1890), 1:132–33. Mrs. Davis admitted that her husband could not recall such an encounter, and Nicolay and Hay, *Abraham Lincoln: A History*, 1:96–97, present evidence that Davis was elsewhere when Lincoln's company was enrolled.
5. Isaac Arnold, *The Life of Abraham Lincoln*, 297, has Lincoln telling this story: "McClellan's tardiness reminds me of a man in Illinois, whose attorney was not sufficiently aggressive. The client knew a few law phrases, and finally, after waiting until his patience was exhausted by the non-action of his counsel, he sprang to his feet and exclaimed, 'Why don't you go at him with a *fi. fa.*, *demurrer*, a *capias*, a *surrebutter*, or a *ne exeat*, or something; and not stand there like a *nudum pactum* or a *non est*?' "
6. Louis Warren, "Borrowed Books in the White House," *Lincoln Lore*, no. 129 (September 28, 1931), identifies the book as "Halleck's Science of War." It was checked out from January 8, 1862, to March 24, 1864. General Halleck served as Lincoln's de facto military chief of staff beginning in July 1862.
7. Quoted in Hay's diary; Burlingame and Ettlinger, *Inside Lincoln's White House*, 62.
8. Richard N. Current, *The Lincoln Nobody Knows* (1958), 135. George F. Henderson, *Stonewall Jackson and the American Civil War* (1900), set the tone for early criticism of Lincoln's military record. For the favorable revision of that record after World War I, see Colin R. Ballard, *The Military Genius of Abraham Lincoln* (1926), and Frederick Maurice, *Statesmen and Soldiers of the Civil War: A Study of the Conduct of the War* (1926), reaching its peak with T. Harry Williams, *Lincoln and His Generals* (1952). See Peterson, *Lincoln in American Memory*, 205, 337.
9. Stephen W. Sears, *George B. McClellan: The Young Napoleon* (1988), 103, 132. With the possible exception of Braxton Bragg, no other Civil War general disgusted his biographer as much as McClellan did Sears.
10. January 27, 1862, *CW* 5:111–12. In defense of McClellan, it should be noted that other Union generals also ignored this naive command, which took no account of local conditions and forfeited any element of surprise.

11. Lincoln quoted in Nicolay, *Lincoln's Secretary,* 149. This would remain Lincoln's problem throughout the war. When Navy Secretary Gideon Welles asked him why he didn't replace Meade after Gettysburg, Lincoln said, "What can I do with such generals as we have? Who among them is any better than Meade?" Welles, *Diary,* 1:440.
12. They were Irvin McDowell, Edwin Sumner, Samuel Heintzelman, and Erasmus Keyes. See Stephen R. Taafe, *Commanding the Army of the Potomac* (2006), 10.
13. Williams, *Lincoln and His Generals,* 48.
14. Lincoln to McClellan, October [25], 1862, *CW* 5:474.
15. Herndon and Weik, *Herndon's Lincoln,* 218; Sears, *The Young Napoleon,* 45–47.
16. See Lesley J. Gordon, *General George E. Pickett in Life and Legend* (1998), 153. Among other things, in 1913 Mrs. Pickett published a set of letters, supposedly from her husband, that she had composed herself.
17. Lincoln made the comment to a friend from Illinois, Ozias M. Hatch. Fehrenbacher and Fehrenbacher, *Recollected Words of Abraham Lincoln,* 201.
18. Lincoln quoted by John Hay in Burlingame and Ettlinger, *Inside Lincoln's White House,* 63.
19. See Gerald Prokopowicz, "Military Fantasies," in Gabor Boritt, ed., *The Lincoln Enigma* (2001), 56–71, for a more complete answer to this question. One of Lincoln's fellow state legislators, who later served as paymaster during the war, observed that the volunteer soldiers "generally advocated" the idea of Lincoln taking the field. Wilson and Davis, *Herndon's Informants,* 208.
20. Lincoln to Halleck and Buell, December 31, 1861, *CW* 5:84; Lincoln to Hooker, June 10, 1863, *CW* 6:257; Lincoln to Grant, August 17, 1864, *CW* 7:499.
21. See Pinsker, *Lincoln's Sanctuary,* 140.
22. See Donald, *Lincoln,* 351.
23. McClellan to Ellen Marcy McClellan, July 26, 1861, quoted in Sears, *The Young Napoleon,* 95.
24. Lincoln to Hooker, January 26, 1863, *CW* 6:78–79. In 1861, Leonard Swett alerted Lincoln that some of General John C. Frémont's officers were talking dictatorship for their man as well. Swett to Lincoln, November 9, 1861, *CW* 4:563.
25. The quote is from Alexander McClure, *Lincoln and Men of War Times* (1892), 180. McClure frequently overstated his closeness to Lincoln, and historian Brooks Simpson has shown that his account of the meeting in which Lincoln supposedly made this remark is filled with factual errors. Simpson, "Alexander McClure on Lincoln and Grant: A Questionable Account," *Lincoln Herald* 95 (1993), 83–86. Perhaps because it reflects a larger truth about the relationship that later developed between the president and the general, this dubious quote has continued to appear in books about Lincoln and Grant even after being debunked.
26. Lincoln quoted in Stoddard, *Inside the White House in War Times,* 101. Grant made a similar observation, in *Personal Memoirs of U. S. Grant* (1885; reprint

1982), 525. Grant's reputation as a butcher is belied in part by statistics showing that his forces suffered lighter losses, relatively, than Robert E. Lee's. For favorable interpretations of Grant's military leadership, see J. F. C. Fuller, *The Generalship of Ulysses S. Grant* (1929), and Jean Edward Smith, *Grant* (2001).

27. Waldo F. Glover, *Abraham Lincoln and the Sleeping Sentinel of Vermont* (1936), is the most complete account of the story and how it passed into legend.

28. Thomas P. Lowry, *Don't Shoot That Boy! Abraham Lincoln and Military Justice* (1999), 244.

29. Quoted by Schuyler Colfax, in Allen Thorndike Rice, ed., *Reminiscences of Abraham Lincoln by Distinguished Men of His Time* (1888), 339.

30. Hank H. Cox, *Lincoln and the Sioux Uprising of 1862* (2005), lacks annotations but offers a concise and engaging narrative.

31. David E. Long, "Lincoln, Davis, and the Dahlgren Raid," *North & South* 9, no. 5 (2007), 70–83; see also William A. Tidwell, James O. Hall, and David W. Gaddy, *Come Retribution: The Confederate Secret Service and the Assassination of Lincoln* (1988); and Edwin Steers, Jr., *Blood on the Moon* (2001).

32. Address at Cooper Institute, February 27, 1860, *CW* 3:546–47.

33. According to William Stoddard, he and the president were once accosted by patrolling soldiers for violating the rules against discharging firearms within Washington city limits. *Inside the White House in War Times*, 22.

34. Holzer, *Dear Mr. Lincoln*, 191–93.

35. Lincoln quoted in C. S. Bushnell to Gideon Welles, 1877, in "Negotiations for the Building of the 'Monitor,' " in Robert U. Johnson and Clarence C. Buel, eds., *Battles and Leaders of the Civil War* (1884), 1:748.

36. Assistant Secretary of the Navy Gustavus V. Fox to Admiral Samuel F. Du Pont, February 1861, in Rowena Reed, *Combined Operations in the Civil War* (1978), 285.

37. Peter Messent and Steve Courtney, eds., *The Civil War Letters of Joseph Hopkins Twitchel: A Chaplain's Story* (2006), 165.

38. William C. Davis, *Lincoln's Men: How President Lincoln Became Father to an Army and a Nation* (1999), 223.

CHAPTER EIGHT: GETTYSBURG

1. *CW* 7:17–23.

2. Lincoln to Meade, July 14, 1863, *CW* 6:328.

3. Mary Raymond Shipman Andrews, *The Perfect Tribute* (1906).

4. John Nicolay, "Lincoln's Gettysburg Address," *Century* 47 (February 1894), 601. Images of this article and many other nineteenth-century publications can be viewed at Cornell University's useful "Making of America" Web site, http://cdl.library.cornell.edu/moa/.

5. Lincoln to Stanton, [November 17, 1863,] *CW* 7:16. Lincoln objected to Stanton's original plan to leave Washington at 6 a.m. on the day of the ceremony.

6. Governor Andrew G. Curtin of Pennsylvania glimpsed Lincoln through a doorway at the Wills House, writing on what appeared to be a large yellow envelope; perhaps this contributed to the legend. See Wilson, *Lincoln's Sword,* 217. No one knows exactly which parts of the address were written where. Douglas Wilson made the case that Lincoln conceptualized if not actually composed the entire speech well in advance, while Gabor Boritt in *The Gettysburg Gospel: The Lincoln Speech That Nobody Knows* (2006) emphasized the writing that Lincoln did at the Wills House, suggesting that the address was unfinished when he arrived there.
7. Downloaded from http://norvig.com/Gettysburg/ on January 17, 2007. The site includes a complete PowerPoint presentation of the Gettysburg Address.
8. *The Best of Lord Buckley* (1951), Crestview Records (rereleased on Elektra Records).
9. Rob Kyff, "Efforting to Impact Lincoln's Address," *Hartford Courant,* February 22, 1995.
10. Oliver Jensen, "The Gettysburg Address in Eisenhowerese," in Dwight MacDonald, ed., *Parodies: An Anthology From Chaucer to Beerbohm—and After* (1960), 447–48. Jensen was a cofounder of *American Heritage* magazine.
11. Source unknown, World Wide Web, 2005.
12. Lincoln to Everett, November 20, 1863, *CW* 7:24–25 (including Everett's note to Lincoln of the same day).
13. Clark E. Carr, *Lincoln at Gettysburg* (1906).
14. Chapman, *The Perfect Tribute,* 18–19. The story also has Edward Everett, "the heir of traditions of learning and breeding, of scholarly instincts and resources," on Lincoln's train, apparently not quite scholarly enough to realize that he could get to Gettysburg from Boston via Philadelphia, without a 200-mile detour through Washington. In real life, Everett was in Gettysburg when Lincoln arrived.
15. Lincoln to Everett, November 20, 1863, *CW* 7:24.
16. For newspaper reactions, see Robert S. Harper, *Lincoln and the Press* (1951), 287; Boritt, *The Gettysburg Gospel,* 139; Louis A. Warren, *Lincoln's Gettysburg Declaration: A New Birth of Freedom* (1964), 145–46; and Herbert Mitgang, *Abraham Lincoln: A Press Portrait* (1971), 359–61.
17. Boritt, *The Gettysburg Gospel,* ch. 7, fits the rise of the Gettysburg Address and fall of the Emancipation Proclamation into David Blight's argument (in *Race and Reunion: The Civil War in American Memory,* 2001) that sectional reconciliation was conditioned on an unspoken agreement to forget the issue of slavery that had caused the war.
18. Authorities continue to disagree on the details. Douglas Wilson maintains that the Hay copy was made after the speech (*Lincoln's Sword,* appendix, "Lincoln's Postdelivery Revisions of the Gettysburg Address," 285–93), while Gabor Boritt argues that Lincoln read from the Hay copy and inserted the phrase "under God" on the spot when he gave the speech (Boritt, *The Gettysburg Gospel,* 94, 120, appendix C).

19. Lincoln collector and author Lloyd Ostendorf long claimed to have found the second page of the missing "speaking copy," but had limited success persuading others (including me) of his document's authenticity.
20. Nick Clooney, *Cincinnati Enquirer*, October 24, 2001. See also Louis A. Warren, "Emphasis on the Gettysburg Prepositions," *Lincoln Lore,* no. 781 (March 27, 1944).
21. Garry Wills, *Lincoln at Gettysburg: The Words that Remade America* (1992); Allen C. Guelzo, Review of *Lincoln's Speeches Reconsidered,* by John Channing Briggs, *Indiana Magazine of History* 102, no. 3 (September 2006), 218; *Abraham Lincoln: Redeemer President* (1999), 370–74; and "Apple of Gold in a Picture of Silver: The Constitution and Liberty," in Gabor Boritt, ed., *The Lincoln Enigma* (2001), 86–107.
22. Annual Message to Congress, December 1, 1862, *CW* 5:537.

CHAPTER NINE: EMANCIPATOR

1. John W. Forney, quoting Lincoln, in Carpenter, *Six Months at the White House,* 269.
2. Protest in Illinois Legislature on Slavery, March 3, 1837, *CW* 1:75.
3. Scripps autobiography, [July 1860], *CW* 4:65.
4. Lincoln to A. G. Hodges, April 4, 1864, *CW* 7:281. Lincoln has been accused of opportunism for waiting until 1854 to adopt the antislavery cause. If he really had been an opportunist who didn't care about slavery until then, he must also have had superhuman foresight to go forty years without saying or doing anything that would compromise his antislavery credentials if he did decide one day to take a stand. It seems much more plausible that Lincoln was telling the truth about always being "naturally anti-slavery," but needing the political shock of Kansas-Nebraska to galvanize him into action in 1854.
5. Tony Horwitz, *Confederates in the Attic: Dispatches from the Unfinished Civil War* (1998), 367.
6. Peoria speech, October 16, 1854, *CW* 2:256.
7. Lincoln to Greeley, August 22, 1862, *CW* 5:389.
8. Frederick Douglass, Oration in Memory of Abraham Lincoln, April 14, 1876, in *Autobiographies* (1994), 921. As an abolitionist, Douglass said, Lincoln seemed "cold, tardy, dull and indifferent," but compared to the Northern public as a whole he was "swift, zealous, radical, and determined."
9. Horwitz, *Confederates in the Attic,* 367.
10. The most famous of those workers is Maria Vance, known among Lincoln scholars for a "memoir" attributed to her, based on stories that she may have told around 1900 to Adah Sutton, who wrote them down starting in 1956, supplemented by her own amateur research. See James O. Hall's damning review of Lloyd Ostendorf and Walter Oleksy, eds., *Lincoln's Unknown Private Life: An Oral History by His Black Housekeeper Mariah Vance, 1850–1860* (1995), *JALA* 19, no. 1 (winter 1998), 73–95.

11. See Allen C. Guelzo, "Did the Lincoln Family Employ a Slave in 1849–1850?" *For the People* 3, no. 3 (autumn 2001).
12. Lincoln explained much of this to the audience of his Peoria speech, October 16, 1854, *CW* 2:277. See also Ethan A. Snively, "Slavery in Illinois," *Transactions of the Illinois State Historical Society* (1901).
13. Lincoln mentioned the steamboat incident in letters to Mary Speed, September 27, 1841, *CW* 1:260; and Joshua Speed, August 24, 1855, *CW* 2:320. The Todd Papers at the University of Chicago include materials on the sale of slaves from the Todd estate. For the case of John Shelly, see Herndon and Weik, *Herndon's Lincoln,* 232–33. As president, Lincoln offered to pay a Kentucky judge up to five hundred dollars to free a slave, to end a dispute between the judge and a military officer. Lincoln to George Robertson, November 26, 1862, *CW* 5:512.
14. Fragment on Slavery, [April 1, 1854?], *CW* 2:222–23.
15. First Debate with Stephen A. Douglas, Ottawa, Ill., August 21, 1858, *CW* 3:9.
16. First Debate, August 21, 1858, *CW* 3:16.
17. Scripps autobiography, [June 1860], *CW* 4:62. Lincoln wrote of himself, "He studied and nearly mastered the Six-books of Euclid, since he was a member of Congress." There are thirteen books in Euclid's *Elements,* of which the first six are the most frequently translated.
18. J. G. Randall, *Lincoln the President: Springfield to Gettysburg* (1945), 1:viii; cited in Shenk, *Lincoln's Melancholy,* 5.
19. See generally Peterson, *Lincoln in American Memory.*
20. Lerone Bennett, "Was Abe Lincoln a White Supremacist?" *Ebony* 23 (February 1968), 35–42; Lerone Bennett, *Forced Into Glory: Abraham Lincoln's White Dream* (2000). Ironically, Bennett shares with Gabor Boritt the experience of studying Lincoln's writings before reading the secondary sources; Boritt also developed a new (but very different) interpretation of Lincoln, in *Abraham Lincoln and the Economics of the American Dream* (1978).
21. Bennett, *Forced Into Glory,* 123–37 and throughout.
22. Robert Penn Warren, *The Legacy of the Civil War: Meditations on the Centennial* (1961), 59–66. Note that Warren also chastised Southerners for relying on the war as a crutch to excuse every economic, social, and political failing in their region.
23. Annual Message to Congress, December 1, 1862, *CW* 5:537.
24. Lincoln to James C. Conkling, August 26, 1863, *CW* 6:410 (warning antiwar Northerners); Lincoln to Michael Hahn, March 13, 1864, *CW* 7:243 (proposing limited suffrage); Last Public Address, April 11, 1865, *CW* 8:403.
25. Bennett, *Forced Into Glory,* 64–66. The idea of whiteness as a historical category is in its infancy. Peter Kolchin, "Whiteness Studies: The New History of Race in America," *Journal of American History* 89, no. 1 (2002), 154–73, is a good critical overview of the field in its first years.
26. James Leiker, "The Difficulties of Understanding Abe: Lincoln's Reconciliation of Racial Inequality and Natural Rights," in Brian R. Dirck, ed., *Lincoln Emanci-*

pated: The President and the Politics of Race (2007), 73–98. The Lincoln quote is from the Seventh Debate with Douglas, Alton, Ill., October 15, 1858, *CW* 3:312.

27. Bennett, *Forced Into Glory,* 96–99, assembles a number of references to primary sources, including the *Collected Works,* demonstrating both that Lincoln did use the word and that writers like Carl Sandburg and Paul Angle struggled against admitting the fact.
28. Speech at Hartford, March 5, 1860, *CW* 4:4–5, 10.
29. J. G. Randall and Richard N. Current, *Lincoln the President: Last Full Measure* (1955), 319–20.
30. Lincoln to Orville H. Browning, September 22, 1861, *CW* 4:532.
31. First Inaugural Address—Final Text, March 4, 1861, *CW* 4:270.
32. Lincoln to Greeley, August 22, 1862, *CW* 5:388.
33. Carpenter, *Six Months at the White House,* 22.
34. For example, Michael Vorenberg's otherwise excellent *Final Freedom: The Civil War, the Abolition of Slavery, and the Thirteenth Amendment* (2001), inexplicably begins with the sentence "By itself, the Emancipation Proclamation did not free a single slave" (p. 1), and claims that generations of historians have known this. But one could just as easily say that the Thirteenth Amendment "by itself" didn't free anyone either. They both had to be enforced to take effect; the proclamation just faced more armed resistance.
35. Response to a Serenade, February 1, 1865, *CW* 8:254.
36. Vorenberg, *Final Freedom,* 200.
37. Vorenberg, *Final Freedom,* 222–33. The state of Mississippi did not get around to ratifying the Thirteenth Amendment until 1995.
38. For the gist of Stephens's famous "cornerstone" speech of March 21, 1861, see Thomas Schott, *Alexander H. Stephens of Georgia: A Biography* (1988), 334.
39. Lincoln to Henry J. Raymond, March 9, 1862, *CW* 5:153 (estimating cost). Raymond was the editor of the *New York Times.* Lincoln warned the Kentucky slaveholders on July 12; see Appeal to Border State Representatives to Favor Compensated Emancipation, *CW* 5:318.
40. Slave prices rose significantly in the years just before the Civil War, from an average of $925 in 1850 to over $1,600 by 1860. See William W. Freehling, *The Road to Disunion,* vol. 2, *Secessionists Triumphant: 1854–1861* (2007), 22.
41. Louis Warren, "The Lincoln $64,000 Question," *Lincoln Lore,* no. 1407 (March 26, 1956). Newman and Bennett were unaware that the show was rigged and that word had been passed from the sponsor to the producer that the "Lincoln expert is boring; he wants you to stiff him." Frank J. Williams, "Lincolniana in 1992," *JALA* 14, no. 2 (summer 1993), 96.
42. Jefferson to John Holmes, April 22, 1820, in John P. Foley, ed., *The Jeffersonian Cyclopedia* (1900), 811–12.
43. Eulogy on Henry Clay, July 6, 1852, *CW* 2:132.
44. Address on Colonization to a Deputation of Negroes, August 14, 1862, *CW* 5:371–72.

45. Burlingame and Ettlinger, eds., *Inside Lincoln's White House,* 217.
46. Bennett, *Forced Into Glory,* 66; Michael Lind, *What Lincoln Believed* (2004), 100–15.
47. In 1861, there were 234 African Americans living in Springfield, making up less than 3 percent of the population. Richard E. Hart, "Springfield's African Americans as Part of the Lincoln Community," *JALA* 20, no. 1 (winter 1999), 35.
48. Douglass in Rice, ed., *Reminiscences of Abraham Lincoln,* 193. Historian Phillip Shaw Paludan implied that the question of Lincoln's African contacts, like that of his motives, emotions, and other inner questions, is of little relevance compared to his actions. About the slaves, Lincoln "spent very little time weeping over their plight—all he did was to free them." Paludan, "Lincoln and Negro Slavery: I Haven't Got Time for the Pain," *JALA* 27, no. 2 (summer 2006), 23.
49. To the Editor of the *Sangamo Journal,* New Salem, June 13, 1836, *CW* 1:48.
50. Bennett, *Forced Into Glory,* 88–89, cites contemporary references to the darkness of Lincoln's complexion.
51. Speech at Chicago, July 10, 1858, *CW* 2:501. Stephen Douglas repeatedly quoted this passage in his debates with Lincoln to frighten the voters with Lincoln's egalitarianism.
52. Second Inaugural Address, March 4, 1865, *CW* 8:333.

CHAPTER TEN: LINCOLN THE MAN

1. Fell autobiography, December 20, 1859, *CW* 3:512.
2. Five feet eight and one-quarter inches, to be precise. William F. Fox, *Regimental Losses in the American Civil War* (1889), 62.
3. Gabor Boritt, *How Big Was Lincoln's Toe? or Finding a Footnote* (1989); Louis A. Warren, "A Personal Description of Abraham Lincoln," *Lincoln Lore,* no. 270 (June 11, 1934).
4. Nathaniel Hawthorne, "Chiefly About War Matters," *Atlantic,* July 1862.
5. "Hinchaway Beeswax" to Lincoln, no date, quoted in Carl Sandburg, *Lincoln Collector: The Story of Oliver R. Barrett's Great Private Collection* (1950), 66.
6. Hawthorne, "Chiefly About War Matters," *Atlantic,* July 1862.
7. For evidence supporting the authenticity of the image, see http://www.lincolnportrait.com.
8. Ronald D. Rietveld, "Discovering the Last Lincoln Photograph," in Larry E. Burgess and Richard M. Rollins, eds., *A Day with Mr. Lincoln: Essays Commemorating the Lincoln Exhibition at the Huntington Library* (1994); Stefan Lorant, *Lincoln: A Picture Story of His Life* (1952), 229.
9. See Louis A. Warren, "The First Hesler Portrait," *Lincoln Lore,* no. 116 (June 29, 1931). An alternate version of the story has the photographer mussing Lincoln's hair for him. The Lincoln quote is from his letter to James F. Babcock, September 13, 1860, *CW* 4:114.

10. The text of both letters is in *CW* 4:29–30.
11. Frank Witsil, "Michigan Home to Many Artifacts of Lincoln," *Detroit Free Press*, February 12, 2007.
12. Using an indiscriminate mix of primary and secondary sources of varying reliability (as amateur historians often do), doctors Armond S. Goldman and Frank C. Schmalstieg, Jr., "Abraham Lincoln's Gettysburg Illness," *Journal of Medical Biography* 15 (2007), 104–10, concluded that Lincoln had not been inoculated against smallpox and that presidential physicians downplayed the seriousness of his condition in order to reassure the public.
13. Yoshio Ikeda et al., "Spectrin Mutations Cause Spinocerebellar Ataxia Type 5," *Nature Genetics* 38, no. 2 (February 2006), 184–90; "Descendants of Lincoln Studied for Clues to Disease," *Indianapolis Star*, October 12, 1992.
14. Mark E. Neely, Jr., "Rattling Lincoln's Bones," *Lincoln Lore*, no. 1818 (August 1990), presented the argument against testing. Dr. Philip R. Reilly, a member of the panel, offered reasons for and against in *Abraham Lincoln's DNA and Other Adventures in Genetics* (2000), 1–13.
15. Herndon and Weik, *Herndon's Lincoln*, 351.
16. Lincoln to John T. Stuart, Springfield, January 23, 1841, *CW* 1:229.
17. Wilson and David, *Herndon's Informants*, 25; Shenk, *Lincoln's Melancholy*, 20.
18. Memorandum Concerning Ward H. Lamon and the Antietam Episode, [c. September 12, 1864], *CW* 7:549.
19. Reilly, *Abraham Lincoln's DNA*, 12. Joshua Shenk went so far as to argue that Lincoln's chronic depression was actually an asset that taught him "clarity, discipline, and faith in hard times." *Lincoln's Melancholy*, 126.
20. Lincoln to Fanny McCullough, December 23, 1862, *CW* 6:16–17. Here it is:

> Dear Fanny,
> It is with deep grief that I learn of the death of your kind and brave Father; and, especially, that it is affecting your young heart beyond what is common in such cases. In this sad world of ours, sorrow comes to all; and, to the young, it comes with bitterest agony, because it takes them unawares. The older have learned to ever expect it. I am anxious to afford some alleviation of your present distress. Perfect relief is not possible, except with time. You can not now realize that you will ever feel better. Is not this so? And yet it is a mistake. You are sure to be happy again. To know this, which is certainly true, will make you some less miserable now. I have had experience enough to know what I say; and you need only to believe it, to feel better at once. The memory of your dear Father, instead of an agony, will yet be a sad sweet feeling in your heart, of a purer, and holier sort than you have known before.
>
> Please present my kind regards to your afflicted mother.
>
> Your sincere friend A. LINCOLN.

21. Lincoln to Mary Speed, Louisville, September 27, 1841, *CW* 1:262.
22. Nicolay, *Lincoln's Secretary,* 132–33.
23. Wilson and Davis, *Herndon's Informants,* 631–32.
24. Drew Gilpin Faust, *James Henry Hammond and the Old South: A Design for Mastery* (1982), 376–77.
25. See Norbert Hirschorn et al., "Abraham Lincoln's Blue Pills: Did Our 16th President Suffer from Mercury Poisoning?" *Perspectives in Biology and Medicine* 44, no. 3 (summer 2001), 315–32.
26. Burlingame, *The Inner World of Abraham Lincoln,* 208; the chapter on anger covers pp. 147–235, and includes 369 reference notes.
27. Lincoln quoted by Hay in Burlingame and Ettinger, *Inside Lincoln's White House,* 105. In January 1863, a month after settling a cabinet crisis, Lincoln was visited by two politicians who seemed bent on reigniting the settled issues. "For once in my life I rather gave my temper the rein and I talked to those men pretty Damned plainly," Lincoln recalled later.
28. Wilson and Davis, *Herndon's Informants,* 166.
29. David Donald, ed., *Inside Lincoln's Cabinet: The Civil War Diaries of Salmon P. Chase* (1954), 226.
30. Lincoln to Chase, June 30, 1864, *CW* 7:419. Postmaster General Montgomery Blair later wrote that Chase was "the only human being that I believe Lincoln actually hated." Blair to Samuel J. Tilden, June 5, 1868; quoted in Burlingame, *The Inner World of Abraham Lincoln,* 173.
31. Lincoln to Joseph Gillespie, Springfield, July 13, 1849, *CW* 2:57. Ironically, this warm personal sentiment appears in a purely political letter, written expressly to be shown to a third party to make a point.
32. Herndon and Weik, *Herndon's Lincoln,* 261.
33. Copybook verses, c. 1824–26, *CW* 1:1.
34. Wilson and Davis, *Herndon's Informants,* 337; Richard Lawrence Miller, "Lincoln's Suicide Poem: Has It Been Found?" *For the People* 6, no. 1 (spring 2004), 1, 6. Among historians, Harold Holzer, Douglas Wilson, and Joshua Wolf Shenk think it's Lincoln's; David Herbert Donald isn't convinced. See Shenk, "The Suicide Poem," *New Yorker,* June 14, 2004, 62–65.
35. See Daniel Mark Epstein, *Lincoln and Whitman: Parallel Lives in Civil War Washington* (2004), which makes the most out of the limited connection between the two men.
36. Herndon and Weik, *Herndon's Lincoln,* 200.
37. Response to Serenade, April 10, 1865, *CW* 8:394.
38. To get the flavor of the Scott Club speeches (August 14, 26, *CW* 2:135–57), see Wills, *Lincoln at Gettysburg,* 164–66. Benjamin P. Thomas, *"Lincoln's Humor" and Other Essays* (2002), 3–22, explains why the jokes are hard to retell and gives examples of the purposes for which Lincoln told his stories.
39. *CW* 8:420.
40. Quoted in Carpenter, *Six Months,* 152.

41. Silas W. Burt, "Lincoln on His Own Story-Telling," *Century* 73 (February 1907), 502.
42. Herndon to Jesse Weik, February 18, 1887, quoted in Donald, *Lincoln,* 160; see also Herndon and Weik, *Herndon's Lincoln,* 257–58, for a description of the boys' behavior.
43. Gerald D. Swick and Donna D. McCreary, "His Own Place in the Sun," *Lincoln Lore,* no. 1853 (summer 1998), 3–6.
44. Burlingame, *The Inner World of Abraham Lincoln,* 274.
45. Louis A. Warren, "Christmas at the White House," *Lincoln Lore,* no. 141 (December 22, 1931). This was a parenting motif for Lincoln and his boys. Willie and Tad had a soldier doll, also named Jack, whom they regularly put on trial for desertion, hanged, and buried in the garden. The groundskeeper finally appealed to the president to make them stop, which he did by writing on a card, "The doll, Jack, is pardoned. By order of the President."
46. Cynthia Edwards, "Did Truman Pardon a Turkey?," Truman Presidential Museum & Library Web site, http://www.trumanlibrary.org/trivia/turkey.htm, accessed April 17, 2007. Anthropologist Magnus Fiskesjo analyzes the annual turkey pardon ceremony as a display of arbitrary presidential power (seriously) in *The Thanksgiving Turkey Pardon, the Death of Teddy's Bear, and the Sovereign Exception of Guantánamo* (2003).
47. Mark E. Neely, Jr., "Lincoln Gored by Television," *Lincoln Lore,* no. 1787 (January 1988).
48. Wilson and Davis, *Herndon's Informants,* 108; Herndon and Weik, *Herndon's Lincoln,* 308–09.
49. R. Gerald McMurtry, "Lincoln Was Not a Freemason," *Lincoln Lore,* no. 1594 (January 1971), 1–2.
50. See Larissa P. Watkins, *Our Very Illustrious Brother, Abraham Lincoln* (2007), a bibliography of the Lincolniana collection at the Masonic library in Washington, D.C.
51. See R. Gerald McMurtry, "A. Lincoln Manner of Buoying Vessels," *Lincoln Lore,* no. 1439 (January 1958), 1–3; and no. 1440 (February 1958), 3–4.
52. Lincoln to Grant, July 13, 1863, *CW* 6:326.
53. Meditation on the Divine Will, *CW* 5:403–04. The document is undated. Roy Basler, editor of the *Collected Works,* proposed September 2, 1862, as a possible date, while Nicolay and Hay give September 30, 1862, as their guess. Douglas Wilson makes a persuasive case for an 1864 date in *Lincoln's Sword,* 255–56.
54. See Richard Carwardine, *Lincoln: A Life of Purpose and Power* (2006), for an insightful analysis of Lincoln's use of religious language to secure political support.
55. Lincoln to Mary Lincoln, Washington, June 9, 1863, *CW* 6:256.
56. R. Gerald McMurtry, " 'Lord Colchester'—Spirit Medium," *Lincoln Lore,* no. 1497 (November 1962); "Lincoln's Attendance at Spiritualistic Séances," *Lincoln Lore,* no. 1499 (January 1963) and no. 1550 (February 1963). In December 1864,

someone within the White House borrowed three books on witchcraft from the Library of Congress. Louis A. Warren, "Borrowed Books in the White House," *Lincoln Lore,* no. 129 (September 28, 1931).

57. Dale Carnegie, *Lincoln the Unknown* (1932), 202, 239.
58. Burlingame, *The Inner World of Abraham Lincoln,* 272–73.
59. See "Family Letters: The Letters of Abraham Lincoln, Mary Todd Lincoln, and Robert Todd Lincoln 1848–1865," in David Herbert Donald, *Lincoln at Home: Two Glimpses of Abraham Lincoln's Family Life* (1999), 57–121.
60. Wilson and Davis, *Herndon's Informants,* 714.
61. Harry E. Pratt, *The Personal Finances of Abraham Lincoln* (1943), 141. This did not include the value of real estate Lincoln owned.
62. Herndon and Weik, *Herndon's Lincoln,* 215.

CHAPTER ELEVEN: MARTYR

1. Speech in Independence Hall, Philadelphia, February 22, 1861, *CW* 4:240.
2. Welles, *Diary,* 2:282.
3. Seward to John Bigelow, July 15, 1862, quoted in John Rhodehamel and Louise Taper, eds., "*Right or Wrong, God Judge Me*": *The Writings of John Wilkes Booth* (1997), 1; for death threats, see Holzer, *Dear Mr. Lincoln,* 335–50.
4. Lamon to Lincoln, December 10, 1864, in Lamon, *Recollections of President Lincoln,* 275. Senator Charles Sumner of Massachusetts was tall and well built, but he was a thinker, not a fighter. In a famous 1856 incident, he was severely beaten by Congressman Preston Brooks for giving an antislavery speech and continued to suffer from post-traumatic stress disorder for years afterward. See David Herbert Donald, *Charles Sumner and the Coming of the Civil War* (1960), 336.
5. Frank Ford wrote to the historian at Ford's Theatre on April 13, 1962, that his father Harry used to "blow his top" whenever he heard the story that Booth had drilled the hole in the door. See " 'Ages' vs. 'Angels,' " *American Heritage* 16, no. 6 (October 1965), 93.
6. Donald, *Lincoln,* 594, names Governor Oglesby, General Haynie, Postmaster Howard, Governor Wallace and Mrs. Wallace, and Major Thomas T. Eckert as potential guests who declined to go with the Lincolns. Secretary of State Seward would have been a likely guest, but he was recovering from a carriage accident.
7. When Dr. Mudd examined Booth on the night of the assassination, he found a break in a small bone above the ankle. Two nights later, Booth wrote in his diary, "In jumping broke my leg," but Michael Kauffman has argued that this must have referred to an accident with his horse during the getaway, since witnesses did not see Booth limp when he crossed the stage after shooting the president. See Michael W. Kauffman, *American Brutus: John Wilkes Booth and the Lincoln Conspiracies* (2004), 272–74; Timothy S. Good, ed., *We Saw Lincoln Shot: One Hundred Eyewitness Accounts* (1995), 19–20.

8. You can judge this for yourself by reading the conflicting entries in Good, ed., *We Saw Lincoln Shot: One Hundred Eyewitness Accounts.*
9. *Henry and Clara* (1995), a novel by Thomas Mallon, is a fictionalized account of their lives.
10. Dr. Richard A. R. Fraser, "How Did Lincoln Die?" *American Heritage* 46, no. 1 (February/March 1995), 63–70; Dr. John K. Lattimer and Dr. A. Laidlaw, "Good Samaritan Surgeon Wrongly Accused of Contributing to President Lincoln's Death: An Experimental Study of the President's Fatal Wound," *Journal of the American College of Surgeons* 182, no. 5 (May 1996), 431–48.
11. Mark E. Neely, Jr., "The Contents of Lincoln's Pockets at Ford's Theatre," *Lincoln Lore,* no. 1669 (March 1977). The contents of the pockets were first made public in 1976.
12. Kauffman, *American Brutus,* 125–27.
13. Conspirators David Herold and Lewis Powell heard Booth's reaction. See William Hanchett, *The Lincoln Murder Conspiracies* (1983), 37.
14. For examples, see David B. Chesebrough, "*No Sorrow Like Our Sorrow*": *Northern Protestant Ministers and the Assassination of Lincoln* (1994).
15. Booth to the editors of the *National Intelligencer,* April 14, 1865, in Rhodehamel and Taper, eds., "*Right or Wrong, God Judge Me,*" 147–50. Booth gave the letter to a friend, who never delivered it (pp. 150–53).
16. Many of the issues of the Mudd case involve presidential authority to hold and try individuals who are accused of attacking the government but who are not prisoners of war, issues that were obscure technicalities when the Mudds began their crusade but took on greater relevance after the beginning of the Iraq War in 2003.
17. Robert H. Fowler, "Was Stanton Behind Lincoln's Murder?" *Civil War Times* 3, no. 5 (August 1961), 6–23. Fowler was the editor of the magazine.
18. Current, "Fiction as History: A Review Essay," *Journal of Southern History* 52, no. 1 (February 1986), 77.
19. Leonard F. Guttridge and Ray A. Neff, *Dark Union: The Secret Web of Profiteers, Politicians, and Booth Conspirators that Led to Lincoln's Death* (2003); John Chandler Griffin, *Abraham Lincoln's Execution* (2006). For a detailed critique of the former, see Edward Steers, Jr., and Joan L. Chaconas, "*Dark Union:* Bad History," *North & South* 7, no. 1 (January 2004), 12–30.
20. For the best explanation of reconciliation through forgetfulness, see David Blight's *Race and Reunion: The Civil War in American Memory* (2001).
21. William A. Tidwell, James O. Hall, and David W. Gaddy, *Come Retribution: The Confederate Secret Service and the Assassination of Lincoln* (1988). Tidwell, *April '65: Confederate Covert Action in the American Civil War* (1995), and Edward Steers, Jr., *Blood on the Moon: The Assassination of Abraham Lincoln* (2001), accept this argument.
22. See C. Wyatt Evans, *The Legend of John Wilkes Booth: Myth, Memory, and a Mummy* (2004).

CHAPTER TWELVE: LEGACY

1. Fell autobiography, *CW* 3:512.
2. The top five presidents in various polls over a fifty-year period were as follows.
   Schlesinger, Sr., 1948: Lincoln, Washington, FDR, Wilson, Jefferson.
   Schlesinger, Jr., 1962: Lincoln, Washington, FDR, Wilson, Jefferson.
   Dodder, 1970: Lincoln, FDR, Washington, Jefferson, T. Roosevelt.
   Murray, 1982: Lincoln, FDR, Washington, Jefferson, T. Roosevelt.
   Schlesinger, Jr., 1996: Lincoln, FDR, Washington, Jefferson, Jackson.
3. "A Statistical Summary of Survey Results," *Journal of American History* 81, no. 3 (December 1994), 1206–08, 1210.
4. A C-SPAN viewers' poll in 1999 chose Lincoln, Washington, T. Roosevelt, F. Roosevelt, and Jefferson. A 2007 Gallup poll revealed the distressingly short historical horizon of many Americans, with Reagan, Kennedy, and Clinton finishing second through fourth, ahead of Washington and FDR—but Lincoln was still first.
5. For details, see Dan Monroe, "Lincoln the Dwarf: Lyon Gardiner Tyler's War on the Mythical Lincoln," *JALA* 24, no. 1 (winter 2003), 32–42.
6. DiLorenzo's books include *The Real Lincoln: A New Look at Abraham Lincoln, His Agenda, and an Unnecessary War* (2002), and *Lincoln Unmasked: What You're Not Supposed to Know About Dishonest Abe* (2006).
7. Don E. Fehrenbacher noted that the Confederates who fought Lincoln, the Copperheads who hated where he was taking the country, and the Radicals who wanted him to get there faster were the fountainheads of three types of Lincoln criticism. Gardner, Masters (and DiLorenzo), and Bennett fit within each of those groups, respectively. See "The Anti-Lincoln Tradition," in Fehrenbacher, *Lincoln in Text and Context: Collected Essays* (1987), 197–213.
8. Lincoln quoted in Nicolay and Hay, *Abraham Lincoln: A History* 10:283. Lincoln hoped that Jefferson Davis and other Confederate leaders would flee the country. Instead, most stayed and requested presidential pardons from Andrew Johnson, whose head was thoroughly turned by the spectacle of Southern grandees begging him for clemency.
9. He threatened violence in Maryland, used great restraint in Kentucky, and succeeded in holding both states in the Union.
10. Last Public Address, April 11, 1865, *CW* 8:403.
11. Address Before the Young Men's Lyceum, January 27, 1838, *CW* 1:115.
12. Last Public Address, April 11, 1865, *CW* 8:403.
13. Lincoln to Michael Hahn, March 13, 1864, *CW* 7:243.
14. Michael R. Beschloss, "Last of the Lincolns," *The New Yorker,* February 28, 1994. 54–59.
15. " 'Ages' vs. 'Angels,' " *American Heritage* 16, no. 6 (October 1965), 93; Adam Gopnik, "Angels and Ages: Lincoln's Language and its Legacy," *The New Yorker,* May 28, 2007, 30–37. Gopnik observed that in the absence of compelling evi-

dence, some liberal and conservative writers seem to have staked out positions on the unresolvable question of what Stanton actually said based on their respective preferences for a classical ("ages") or Biblical ("angels") Lincoln.

16. For the full story, see Thomas J. Craughwell, *Stealing Lincoln's Body* (2007).
17. Mrs. Daniel Chester French, *Memories of a Sculptor's Wife* (1928).
18. Christopher A. Thomas, *The Lincoln Memorial and American Life* (2002) details the political struggle among proponents of various memorials to Lincoln.
19. See Thomas F. Schwartz, "Defining the Study of Lincoln: The Contributions of the Abraham Lincoln Association," Abraham Lincoln Association Web site, http://abrahamlincolnassociation.org/history.htm, accessed March 14, 2007.
20. Speech in U.S. House of Representatives on the Presidential Question, July 27, 1848, *CW* 1:508.
21. Peterson, *Lincoln in American Memory*, 393.
22. James Morris, *Heaven's Command: An Imperial Progress* (1973); *Pax Britannica: The Climax of an Empire* (1968); and *Farewell the Trumpets: An Imperial Retreat* (1978).
23. In Gore Vidal's novel, Lincoln learns his Clausewitz from John Hay, who translates for him (p. 248). In real life, Christopher Bassford, *Clausewitz in English: The Reception of Clausewitz in Britain and America, 1815–1945* (1994), 51–55, concludes that there is no firm evidence as to whether Lincoln had even heard of Clausewitz.
24. For a Lincoln-related travelogue that provides much more insight than Morris, with only a fraction of the snobbery, try Andrew Ferguson, *Land of Lincoln: Adventures in Abe's America* (2007).
25. The WorldCat search was reported on the now defunct Stumpers-L listserv, January 28, 2002, at http://listserv.dom.edu/cgibin/wa.exe?A2=ind0201&L=stumpers-l&T=0&P=105600, accessed as cached by Google on July 2, 2006.
26. Kauffman, *American Brutus*, 48.
27. Just to complete the circle, Monroe admired Abraham Lincoln and was a friend of Carl Sandburg. Anthony Summers, *Goddess: The Secret Lives of Marilyn Monroe* (1986), 34, 65.
28. In 2006 *The Colbert Report*, a televised parody of the blowhard partisan political commentary that infests cable news channels, lampooned this tendency by describing itself as "Lincolnish" and confidently boasting that it was "what Lincoln would have watched."
29. See Wolf, *The Almost Chosen People*, 145.
30. The Library of Congress Web site features images of the documents, and includes Lincoln's incoming correspondence; see http://memory.loc.gov/ammem/alhtml/malhome.html. A searchable online version of Basler's edition of the *Collected Works* is at http://www.hti.umich.edu/l/lincoln/.
31. Louis A. Warren, "Distribution of the Barrett Collection," *Lincoln Lore*, no. 1196 (March 10, 1952); Seth Kaller, "Values That Stand the Test of Time," http://www.sethkaller.net/values, accessed July 5, 2007; and Lita Solis-Cohen, "Engrossed

Copy of 13th Amendment Signed by Lincoln Sells for Record Price," *Maine Antique Digest* (May 2006), http://maineantiquedigest.com/articles_archive/articles/may06/f-13thamend0506.htm, accessed July 5, 2007. In 1952, the entire magnificent collection of Oliver R. Barrett sold for $273,632

32. See Charles Hamilton, *Great Forgers and Famous Fakes: The Manuscript Forgers of America and How They Duped the Experts* (1980), and Kenneth Rendell, *Forging History: The Detection of Fake Letters and Documents* (1994), for advice from two prominent autograph dealers on how to spot a fake Lincoln signature.
33. See Don E. Fehrenbacher, "The Minor Affair: An Adventure in Forgery and Detection," in *Lincoln in Text and Context.*
34. For example, the museum includes an elaborate re-creation of the legislative chamber of the Old State Capitol, even though the real Old State Capitol, beautifully restored, is only two blocks away. I believe that Professor Simon overstated his case, but not by a great deal. See Gerald J. Prokopowicz, "Stunning, Appealing, Troubling: The Abraham Lincoln Presidential Library and Museum's Permanent Exhibit," *Ohio Valley History* 6, no. 2 (summer 2006), 34–40.
35. Michael C. Hawfield, *Ninety Years and Growing: The Story of Lincoln National Corporation* (1995), 8, 84–85. Neely's prize-winning book was *The Fate of Liberty: Abraham Lincoln and Civil Liberties.*
36. Mrs. Wilfred C. Leland, *Master of Precision: Henry M. Leland* (1966), 200.
37. Peoria speech, October 16, 1854, *CW* 2:276.

BIBLIOGRAPHY

ONE HUNDRED LINCOLN BOOKS

You can find a list of one hundred essential Lincoln books in *100 Essential Lincoln Books* by Michael Burkhimer, published in 2003. If those don't suit, the Abraham Lincoln Book Shop Web site includes a list of 155 essential Lincoln books. Many more than that were essential to the writing of this one; the hundred listed below were the most useful.

REFERENCES

Basler, Roy P., ed. *The Collected Works of Abraham Lincoln*. 8 vols. New Brunswick, NJ: Rutgers University Press, 1953.

Benner, Martha L., Cullom Davis, et al., eds. *The Law Practice of Abraham Lincoln: Complete Documentary Edition*. DVD, 3 vols. Urbana: University of Illinois Press, 2000.

Miers, Earl Schenck. *Lincoln Day by Day: A Chronology 1809-1865*. 3 vols. Washington, D.C.: Lincoln Sesquicentennial Commission, 1960.

Neely, Mark E., Jr. *The Abraham Lincoln Encyclopedia*. New York: McGraw Hill, 1982.

Ostendorf, Lloyd. *Lincoln's Photographs: A Complete Album*. Dayton, OH: Rockywood Press, 1998.

Reinhart, Mark S. *Abraham Lincoln on Screen: A Filmography of Dramas and Documentaries, Including Television*. Jefferson, NC: McFarland, 1999.

FIRSTHAND ACCOUNTS

Burlingame, Michael, ed. *At Lincoln's Side: John Hay's Civil War Correspondence and Selected Writings*. Carbondale: Southern Illinois University Press, 2000.

Burlingame, Michael, and John R. Turner Ettlinger, eds. *Inside Lincoln's White House: The Complete Civil War Diary of John Hay*. Carbondale: Southern Illinois University Press, 1997.

Carpenter, F[rancis] B. *The Inner Life of Abraham Lincoln: Six Months at the White House.* 1866. Reprinted with introduction by Mark E. Neely, Jr. Lincoln: University of Nebraska Press, 1995.

Chase, Salmon. *Inside Lincoln's Cabinet: The Civil War Diaries of Salmon P. Chase.* Edited by David Herbert Donald. New York: Longmans, Green & Co., 1954.

Fehrenbacher, Don E., and Virginia Fehrenbacher, eds. *Recollected Words of Abraham Lincoln.* Stanford, CA: Stanford University Press, 1996.

Good, Timothy S., ed. *We Saw Lincoln Shot: One Hundred Eyewitness Accounts.* Jackson: University Press of Mississippi, 1995.

Herndon, William H., and Jesse W. Weik. *Herndon's Lincoln.* 1889. Reprint, edited by Douglas L. Wilson and Rodney O. Davis. Urbana: University of Illinois Press, 2006.

Nicolay, John G., and John Hay. *Abraham Lincoln: A History.* 10 vols. New York: Century, 1890.

Rhodehamel, John, and Louise Taper, eds. *"Right or Wrong, God Judge Me": The Writings of John Wilkes Booth.* Urbana: University of Illinois Press, 1997.

Rice, Allen Thorndike, ed. *Reminiscences of Abraham Lincoln by Distinguished Men of His Time.* New York: North American Review, 1888.

Speed, Joshua F. *Reminiscences of Abraham Lincoln and Notes of a Visit to California: Two Lectures.* Louisville: John P. Morton, 1884.

Stoddard, William O. *Inside the White House in War Times: Memoirs and Reports of Lincoln's Secretary.* 1890. Reprint, edited by Michael Burlingame. Lincoln: University of Nebraska Press, 2000.

Turner, Justin G., and Linda Levitt Turner. *Mary Todd Lincoln: Her Life and Letters.* New York: Alfred A. Knopf, 1972.

Welles, Gideon. *Diary of Gideon Welles.* 2 vols. Boston: Houghton Mifflin, 1911.

Wilson, Douglas L., and Rodney O. Davis, eds. *Herndon's Informants: Letters, Interviews and Statements about Abraham Lincoln.* Urbana: University of Illinois Press, 1998.

Zall, Paul M. *Abe Lincoln Laughing: Humorous Anecdotes from Original Sources By and About Abraham Lincoln.* 1982. Reprint, Knoxville: University of Tennessee Press, 1995.

SECONDARY SOURCES

Angle, Paul M. *Here I Have Lived: A History of Lincoln's Springfield, 1821-1865.* 1935. Reprint, New Brunswick, NJ: Rutgers University Press, 1950.

Baker, Jean H. *Mary Todd Lincoln: A Biography.* New York: W.W. Norton, 1987.

Bennett, Lerone. *Forced Into Glory: Abraham Lincoln's White Dream.* Chicago: Johnson, 2000.

Boritt, Gabor S. *Abraham Lincoln and the Economics of the American Dream.* Memphis: Memphis State University Press, 1978.

———. *The Gettysburg Gospel: The Lincoln Speech That Nobody Knows*. New York: Simon & Schuster, 2006.

———, ed. *The Lincoln Enigma: The Changing Faces of an American Icon*. New York: Oxford University Press, 2001.

Burlingame, Michael. *The Inner World of Abraham Lincoln*. Urbana: University of Illinois Press, 1994.

Carwardine, Richard. *Lincoln: A Life of Purpose and Power*. New York: Alfred A. Knopf, 2006.

Current, Richard N. *The Lincoln Nobody Knows*. New York: McGraw Hill, 1958.

Dirck, Brian R., ed. *Lincoln Emancipated: The President and the Politics of Race*. Dekalb: Northern Illinois University Press, 2007.

Donald, David Herbert. *Lincoln*. New York: Simon & Schuster, 1995.

———. *Lincoln at Home: Two Glimpses of Abraham Lincoln's Family Life*. New York: Simon & Schuster, 1999.

———. *Lincoln Reconsidered: Essays on the Civil War Era*. 1956. Rev. ed., New York: Vintage, 2001.

———. *"We are Lincoln Men": Abraham Lincoln and His Friends*. New York: Simon & Schuster, 2003.

Emerson, Jason. *The Madness of Mary Lincoln*. Carbondale: Southern Illinois University Press, 2007.

Fehrenbacher, Don E. *Lincoln in Text and Context: Collected Essays*. Stanford, CA: Stanford University Press, 1987.

———. *Prelude to Greatness: Lincoln in the 1850's*. Stanford, CA: Stanford University Press, 1962.

Fleischner, Jennifer. *Mrs. Lincoln and Mrs. Keckly: The Remarkable Story of the Friendship Between a First Lady and a Former Slave*. New York: Broadway, 2003.

Gienapp, William E. *Abraham Lincoln and Civil War America: A Biography*. New York: Oxford University Press, 2002.

Goodwin, Doris Kearns. *Team of Rivals: The Political Genius of Abraham Lincoln*. New York: Simon & Schuster, 2005.

Greenstone, J. David. *The Lincoln Persuasion: Remaking American Liberalism*. Princeton, NJ: Princeton University Press, 1993.

Guelzo, Allen C. *Abraham Lincoln: Redeemer President*. Grand Rapids, MI: Wm. B. Eerdmans, 1999.

———. *Lincoln's Emancipation Proclamation: The End of Slavery in America*. New York: Simon & Schuster, 2004.

Hanchett, William. *The Lincoln Murder Conspiracies*. Urbana: University of Illinois Press, 1983.

Harris, William C. *Lincoln's Last Months*. Cambridge: Harvard University Press, 2004.

Holzer, Harold, Gabor Boritt, and Mark E. Neely, Jr. *The Lincoln Image: Abraham Lincoln and the Popular Print*. New York: Charles Scribner's Sons, 1984.

Holzer, Harold. *Dear Mr. Lincoln: Letters to the President*. 1993. Reprint, Carbondale: Southern Illinois University Press, 2006.

Hubbard, Charles, ed. *Lincoln Reshapes the Presidency*. Macon, GA: Mercer University Press, 2003.

Jaffa, Harry V. *Crisis of the House Divided: An Interpretation of the Issues in the Lincoln-Douglas Debates*. Chicago: University of Chicago Press, 1959.

Kauffman, Michael W. *American Brutus: John Wilkes Booth and the Lincoln Conspiracies*. New York: Random House, 2004.

Kunhardt, Philip B., Jr., Philip B. Kunhardt III, and Peter W. Kunhardt. *Lincoln: An Illustrated Biography*. New York: Alfred A Knopf, 1992.

Leonard, Elizabeth D. *Lincoln's Avengers: Justice, Revenge, and Reunion after the Civil War*. New York: W. W. Norton, 2004.

Long, David E. *The Jewel of Liberty: Abraham Lincoln's Re-election and the End of Slavery*. 1994. Reprint, New York: Da Capo, 1997.

Lorant, Stefan. *Lincoln: A Picture Story of His Life*. 1952. Rev. ed. New York: HarperCollins, 1976.

Luthin, Reinhard H. *The Real Abraham Lincoln*. Englewood Cliffs, N.J.: Prentice-Hall, 1960.

McMurtry, R. Gerald, and Mark E. Neely, Jr. *The Insanity File: The Case of Mary Todd Lincoln*. Carbondale: Southern Illinois University Press, 1986.

McPherson, James. *Abraham Lincoln and the Second American Revolution*. New York: Oxford University Press, 1991.

Miller, William Lee. *Lincoln's Virtues: An Ethical Biography*. New York: Alfred A. Knopf, 2002.

Monaghan, Jay. *Diplomat in Carpet Slippers: Abraham Lincoln Deals with Foreign Affairs*. Indianapolis: Bobbs Merrill, 1945.

Morel, Lucas E. *Lincoln's Sacred Effort: Defining Religion's Role in American Self-Government*. Lanham, MD: Lexington Books, 2000.

Neely, Mark E., Jr. *The Fate of Liberty: Abraham Lincoln and Civil Liberties*. New York: Oxford University Press, 1991.

——. *The Last Best Hope of Earth: Abraham Lincoln and the Promise of America*. Cambridge: Harvard University Press, 1993.

Neely, Mark E., Jr. and Harold Holzer. *The Lincoln Family Album*. 1990. Reprint, Carbondale: Southern Illinois University Press, 2006.

Oates, Stephen B. *Abraham Lincoln: The Man Behind the Myths*. New York: Harper & Row, 1984.

——. *With Malice Toward None: The Life of Abraham Lincoln*. New York: Harper & Row, 1977.

Paludan, Phillip Shaw. *The Presidency of Abraham Lincoln*. Lawrence: University Press of Kansas, 1994.

Peterson, Merrill D. *Lincoln In American Memory*. New York: Oxford University Press, 1994.

Pinsker, Matthew. *Lincoln's Sanctuary: Abraham Lincoln and the Soldiers' Home.* New York: Oxford University Press, 2003.

Pratt, Harry E. *The Personal Finances of Abraham Lincoln.* Springfield, IL: Abraham Lincoln Association, 1943.

Randall, James G. *Lincoln the President.* 4 vols. Volume 4 with Richard N. Current. New York: Dodd, Mead, & Co., 1946-55.

Randall, Ruth Painter. *Lincoln's Sons.* Boston: Little, Brown & Co., 1955.

Sandburg, Carl. *Abraham Lincoln: The Prairie Years.* 2 vols. New York: Harcourt, Brace & Co., 1926.

———. *Abraham Lincoln: The War Years*, 4 vols. New York: Harcourt, Brace & Co., 1939.

Schwartz, Barry. *Abraham Lincoln and the Forge of National Memory.* Chicago: University of Chicago Press, 2000.

Shenk, Joshua Wolf. *Lincoln's Melancholy: How Depression Challenged a President and Fueled His Greatness.* New York: Houghton Mifflin, 2005.

Simon, Paul. *Lincoln's Preparation for Greatness: The Illinois Legislative Years.* 1965. Reprint, Urbana: University of Illinois Press, 1989.

Slotkin, Richard. *Abe: A Novel of the Young Lincoln.* New York: Henry Holt & Co., 2000.

Steiner, Mark. *An Honest Calling: The Law Practice of Abraham Lincoln.* DeKalb: Northern Illinois University Press, 2006.

Strozier, Charles B. *Lincoln's Quest for Union: A Psychological Portrait.* 1982. Rev. ed., Philadelphia: Paul Dry, 2001.

Thomas, Benjamin P. *Abraham Lincoln: A Biography.* New York: Alfred A. Knopf, 1952.

———. *Lincoln's New Salem.* New York: Alfred A. Knopf, 1954.

Tripp, C. A. *The Intimate World of Abraham Lincoln.* New York: Simon & Schuster, 2005.

Turner, Thomas R. *"Beware the People Weeping": Public Opinion and the Assassination of Abraham Lincoln.* Baton Rouge: Louisiana State University Press, 1982.

Vidal, Gore. *Lincoln: A Novel.* New York: Random House, 1984.

Vorenberg, Michael. *Final Freedom: The Civil War, the Abolition of Slavery, and the Thirteenth Amendment.* New York: Cambridge University Press, 2001.

Warren, Louis A. *Lincoln's Parentage and Childhood.* New York: Century, 1926.

White, Ronald C., Jr. *Lincoln's Greatest Speech: The Second Inaugural.* New York: Simon & Schuster, 2002.

Williams, Frank J. *Judging Lincoln.* Carbondale: Southern Illinois University Press, 2002.

Williams, T. Harry. *Lincoln and His Generals.* New York: Alfred A. Knopf, 1952.

Wills, Garry. *Lincoln at Gettysburg: The Words that Remade America.* New York: Simon & Schuster, 1992.

Wilson, Douglas L. *Honor's Voice: The Transformation of Abraham Lincoln.* New York: Alfred A. Knopf, 1998.

———. *Lincoln Before Washington: New Perspectives on the Illinois Years*. Urbana: Univeristy of Illinois Press, 1997.

———. *Lincoln's Sword: The Presidency and the Power of Words*. New York: Alfred A. Knopf, 2006.

Winger, Stewart. *Lincoln, Religion, and Romantic Cultural Politics*. DeKalb: Northern Illinois University Press, 2003.

Winkle, Kenneth J. *The Young Eagle: The Rise of Abraham Lincoln*. Dallas: Taylor Trade, 2001.

Wolf, William J. *The Almost Chosen People: A Study of the Religion of Abraham Lincoln*. New York: Doubleday, 1959.

INDEX

Page numbers in *italics* refer to illustrations.

Index

Index

ALSO AVAILABLE FROM THE

VINTAGE CIVIL WAR LIBRARY

LINCOLN AND HIS GENERALS

by T. Harry Williams

Since it was first published in 1952, *Lincoln and His Generals* has remained one of the definitive accounts of Lincoln's wartime leadership. In it T. Harry Williams dramatizes Lincoln's long and frustrating search for an effective leader of the Union Army and traces his transformation from a politician with little military knowledge into a master strategist of the Civil War. Explored in depth are Lincoln's often fraught relationships with generals such as McClellan, Pope, Burnside, Hooker, Fremont, and, of course, Ulysses S. Grant. In this superbly written narrative, Williams demonstrates how Lincoln's persistent "meddling" into military affairs was crucial to the Northern war effort and utterly transformed the president's role as commander-in-chief.

History

LINCOLN'S SWORD

The Presidency and the Power of Words

by Douglas L. Wilson

Widely considered in his own time as a genial but provincial lightweight who was out of place in the presidency, Abraham Lincoln astonished his allies and confounded his adversaries by producing a series of speeches and public letters so provocative that they helped revolutionize public opinion on such critical issues as civil liberties, the use of black soldiers, and the emancipation of slaves. This is a brilliant and unprecedented examination of how Lincoln used the power of words to not only build his political career but to keep the country united during the Civil War.

History

LINCOLN RECONSIDERED

Essays on the Civil War Era

by David Herbert Donald

David Herbert Donald, Lincoln biographer and winner of the Pulitzer Prize, has revised and updated his classic and influential book on Lincoln and the era he dominated. When *Lincoln Reconsidered* was first published it ushered in the process of rethinking the Civil War that continues to this day. In the third edition, David provides two important new essays, on Lincoln's patchy education—which we find was more extensive than even the great man realized—and on Lincoln's complex and conflicted relationship to the rule of law. Together with a new preface and a thoroughly updated bibliographical essay, *Lincoln Reconsidered* will continue to be a touchstone of Lincoln scholarship for decades to come.

History

THIS HALLOWED GROUND

A History of the Civil War

by Bruce Catton

The classic one-volume history of the American Civil War simultaneously captures the dramatic scope and intimate experience of that epic struggle, by Pulitzer Prize–winner Bruce Catton. Covering events from the prelude of the conflict to the death of Lincoln, Catton blends a gripping narrative with deep, yet unassuming, scholarship to bring the war alive on the page in an almost novelistic way. It is this gift for narrative that led contemporary critics to compare this book to *War and Peace*, and call it a "modern *Iliad*." Now over fifty years old, *This Hallowed Ground* remains one of the best-loved and admired general Civil War books: a perfect introduction to readers beginning their exploration of the conflict, as well as a thrilling analysis and reimagining of its events for experienced students of the war.

History

THE CIVIL WAR

The Complete Text of the Bestselling Narrative History of the Civil War—Based on the Celebrated PBS Television Series
by Geoffrey Ward with Ric Burns and Ken Burns

When the illustrated edition of *The Civil War* was first published, *The New York Times* hailed it as "a treasure for the eye and mind." Now Geoffrey Ward's magisterial work is available in an edition that interweaves the author's narrative with the voices of the men and women who lived through that trial of our nationhood: not just Abraham Lincoln, Frederick Douglass, and Robert E. Lee, but genteel Southern ladies and escaped slaves, cavalry officers and common foot soldiers who fought in Yankee blue and Rebel gray. *The Civil War* also includes essays by our most distinguished historians of the era: Don E. Fehrenbacher, on the war's origins; Barbara J. Fields, on the freeing of the slaves; Shelby Foote, on the war's soldiers and commanders; and C. Vann Woodward, assessing the America that emerged from the war's ashes.

History